# THE POLITICS OF
# TURMOIL

# THE POLITICS OF TURMOIL

## Essays on Poverty, Race and the Urban Crisis

by Richard A. Cloward
and Frances Fox Piven

Vintage Books
A Division of Random House, New York

FIRST VINTAGE BOOKS EDITION, February 1975

Portions of this book originally appeared in *The Nation* and *The New
Republic*.

Grateful acknowledgment is made to the following for permission to
reprint previously published material:

*The Columbia Forum*: For "The Great Society as Political Strategy,"
by Frances Fox Piven, reprinted from *The Columbia Forum*, Vol.
XIII, No. 2 (Summer 1970). Copyright © 1970 by the Trustees of
Columbia University in the City of New York.

National Committee on Employment of Youth: For "Strategy of
Crisis: A Dialogue" reprinted from the Summer 1966 issue of the
*American Child*.

Rand McNally & Company: For "Federal Intervention in the Cities,"
from Erwin Smigel's *Handbook on the Study of Social Problems*.

*Social Policy:* For "Whom Does the Advocate Planner Serve?" by Frances
Fox Piven, together with responses by others and a rejoinder by Frances
Fox Piven, reprinted from *Social Policy*, May/June, July/August, 1970.

National Association of Social Workers: For "The Case Against Urban
Desegregation," by Frances Fox Piven and Richard Cloward, reprinted
from *Social Work*, Vol. 12, No. 1 (January 1967), pages 12–21; "The
Imperative of Deghettoization: An Answer to Piven and Cloward,"
by Funnyé and Shiffman, reprinted from *Social Work*, Vol. 12, No. 2
(April 1967), pages 5–11; "The Case For Urban Integration," by
Whitney M. Young, Jr. reprinted from *Social Work*, Vol. 12, No. 3,
(July 1967), pages 12–17; "Separatism Versus Integration: A Rejoinder,"
by Frances Fox Piven and Richard Cloward, reprinted from *Social
Work*, Vol. 12, No. 3, (July 1967), pages 110–111.

Transaction, Inc.: For "Militant Civil Servants" reprinted from Volume
7 (November 1969) transaction/SOCIETY.

Library of Congress Cataloging in Publication Data

Cloward, Richard A.
  The politics of turmoil.

  Includes bibliographical references.
  1. United States—Social conditions—1960—  —Addresses, essays, lec-
tures. 2. Poor—United States—Addresses, essays, lectures. 3. United States
—Race question—Addresses, essays, lectures. 4. Cities and towns—United
States—Addresses, essays, lectures. I. Piven, Frances Fox, joint author.
II. Title.
[HN59.C58 1975]     309.1'73'092     74-16446
ISBN 0-394-71383-4

Manufactured in the United States of America

Contents

## PART TWO

## MOBILIZING THE POOR: HOW IT CAN BE DONE

## PART THREE

## BLACKS AND THE CITIES: THE PROSPECTS FOR "BLACK POWER"

## PART FOUR

## THE GREAT SOCIETY: MODERATING
## DISORDER IN THE GHETTOS

During the 1960s blacks emerged as a political force in the United States for the first time. True, "the race problem" had exploded as a major political issue before, an issue so forceful and divisive as to tear the country apart. But in the past it had been an issue only among whites, reflecting the conflicting political and economic stakes of white northerners and white southerners, or white workers and white capitalists, in the caste system. In the 1960s it was blacks who resuscitated the race issue. Poor blacks themselves suddenly became a force to be reckoned with by political leaders at all levels of government.

We ought not to overstate our point. When we say that blacks became a political force in these years, we do not mean that they had sufficient power to shape and benefit from foreign policy or monetary policy, or to garner and profit from huge government contracts and subsidies; power in such decisions has never accrued to the poor in the United States, no matter how large their numbers or how intense their arousal. Nor, when we say that blacks became a political force in the 1960s, do we mean to predict that "black power" will be a lasting feature of American politics. The signs suggest rather that it erupted for a time and is already fading, leaving in its wake the traces of a Great Society, like the traces of a second Reconstruction.

But although the kind of power blacks wielded in the sixties was limited and transitory, we nevertheless believe that the events of that period are important. The most submerged group in the United States rose up and shook American society to its roots. That does not happen often. When it does, much is revealed about the nature of institutions—especially about the nature of political institutions—that would otherwise remain unnoticed. And when such an eruption occurs, even when it fails, something can be learned about what is possible and what is improbable in struggles to transform these institutions.

It is usually the case that new political forces are produced by basic changes in economic and social life. The emergence of black power was no exception. Profound transformations had been taking place in the United States, transformations that had the effect of disrupting accustomed patterns of black life. These transformations would in time loosen blacks from social regulation, giving rise to the widespread disorders—civil-rights demonstrations, the disaffection of black voters, and ghetto protests and riots—that for a time yielded blacks a measure of political influence.

The most fundamental of these changes was the mechanization of southern agriculture. Between 1940 and 1960 some four million blacks who subsisted by sharecropping, tenant farming and day-laboring became economically obsolete. Driven from the land by imminent starvation and evictions, these millions made their way to the cities in what may be the last great migratory wave in American society. And when blacks migrated they concentrated in the core areas of the biggest cities, where established ghettos provided a measure of the familiar in a strange environment and a degree of insulation from harsh rejection by urban whites.

Forced migration itself is catastrophic for the people who undergo it. In this case the catastrophe was worsened by the plight of blacks in the cities. High rates of unemployment and low wages prevailed, especially during the deep recessions of the late fifties and early sixties. Eventually, economic dislocation, migration and continuing high unemployment had the effect that such catastrophes have had on other groups at other times in history: Traditional patterns of social life weakened or shattered—for example, the black family system came increasingly to be headed by women. The traditional consequences of social disintegration also appeared among blacks—for example, crime rates rose. These were all omens of political trouble, but by themselves they were only omens.

That was to change, for the atomized disorders of individuals and families soon congealed into mass disorder. People may suffer silently and indefinitely when they live within a tradition that defines the calamities they experience as inevitable and legitimate.

In large part the sufferings experienced by blacks in the rural South for 300 years must have seemed inevitable, and perhaps even legitimate. But the new calamities in the cities had no such supports in tradition; indeed, tradition of any kind had been virtually destroyed by the uprooting of people and the disintegration of communities. Consequently, blacks in the cities did not long remain passive; they began to react collectively and politically to the dislocations and privations they had experienced.

The first political disturbances began in southern cities in the mid-1950s, and soon took form in a civil-rights movement. Within a few years protests erupted in northern cities as well, and by the mid-1960s the swollen ghettos of the North were in turmoil. As the decade ended, virtually every big city in the United States had been the scene of a major riot.

Meanwhile, as urban blacks grew in numbers and militancy, fierce conflicts were triggered with other groups in a whole range of institutions central to American life, from the local schools to the national Democratic party. In one area after another blacks began to make demands, only to set off resistance by other groups with stakes in what they considered to be *their* schools or *their* neighborhoods or *their* jobs. These conflicts could not easily be ignored by local politicians, but neither could they easily be resolved. On the one hand, blacks were gaining some power, both through their growing voting numbers in the cities and through the unspoken threat of turmoil and riot that backed up each demand. On the other hand, the resistance to mounting black claims came from groups that were established and organized participants in local politics. The resulting stalemate led, in many cities, to virtual paralysis.

Nor could what was happening in the big cities be ignored by national political leaders, for the big cities were the economic and political heart of the nation. The leaders of the national Democratic party who reigned in Washington after 1960 were, of course, especially vulnerable, for they depended on the big cities for votes, which increasingly meant that they depended on the ghettos. The result was an unprecedented effort by government, especially the federal government, to conciliate the black masses.

Much of this effort was symbolic; a new rhetoric flourished in the sixties, a rhetoric which stressed the injustices of racism and poverty and the necessity for a national commitment to overcome them. The gap between rhetoric and action was a wide one, but still there were some tangible gains. Civil-rights legislation and federal enforcement activities weakened historic caste arrangements in the South, primarily by extending the franchise to millions of blacks. For the first time since Reconstruction, state and local authorities in the South now pay at least some deference to black interests. One result is the marked decline in the use of violence and terror to control blacks.

The effort to conciliate blacks took a different form in the cities, where the great majority came to live. The federal government initiated a series of new urban programs, and blacks were the chief constituency. Some of the moneys for these programs were channeled through existing agencies of local government; other moneys went directly to the ghettos, where black-controlled agencies were created. Through these programs, blacks obtained some of the traditional spoils of big city politics—jobs, honorific positions and services. Because of the extreme poverty of many urban blacks, a large portion of the spoils flowed through the public welfare system, leading to a welfare explosion and to the contemporary "relief crisis."

Gains were also scored in urban electoral politics, and the federally sponsored programs in the cities were partly responsible. With blacks massing in the cities, urban electoral succession was probably inevitable. But in many cities, the local party apparatus resisted opening its ranks, and blacks were poorly organized to force their way in. Given time, blacks would have become better organized, and their numbers would have given them the means to overcome that resistance. But the process of succession was accelerated by the federal programs in the cities. Their "participatory" features projected blacks into positions of public leadership and stimulated the organization of black constituencies. One by one, city halls have begun to fall to the newcomers. The control of government in America's major cities represents a vehicle by which blacks may hope to acquire a modest degree of regular and stable political influence.

Many blacks benefited substantially from these changes. They are employed in municipal agencies or attending college, and some have even gone on to executive jobs in industry and to higher public office. But such openings were only accessible to those already poised to enter the middle class. Most lower-class blacks could not benefit from the opportunities for mobility that resulted from these reforms. In other words, those who had rioted in the streets could not take advantage of the reforms precipitated by the rioting.

As a result, lower-class blacks—unlike those who rose into the middle class—have not been absorbed into stable institutional roles. The main concession they won—the greater availability of relief benefits—may have momentarily quieted them, but it did nothing to restore the fabric of occupational, familial and communal life in the ghetto. The atomization of lower-class black life thus persists, as reflected in the strain toward atomized disorders, whether crime, drug addiction or school failure.

The prospects for advances by lower-class blacks in the near future are dimmer still. Changed political conditions, resulting from the turmoil and reforms of the sixties, are limiting the little progress that has been made. In the sixties, National Democratic leaders felt vulnerable to blacks; now they feel vulnerable to their traditional white constituents in the working and middle classes who, provoked in part by black advances, are deserting the Democratic party. That racial resentments and fears have swelled and taken viable political form is due as much, however, to the role played by political leaders as to the spontaneous reactions of working- and middle-class people to the events of the sixties. National Republican leaders have been especially quick to see that racial resentments could be capitalized upon for political gain. The change in climate was as precipitous as it was ominous. In 1965, the President of the United States ended a nationally televised speech with the civil rights-refrain "We shall overcome"; by 1973, another President proclaimed during his inaugural address that Americans ought not ask what government can do for them but what they can do for themselves. In the ensuing assault on blacks, federal programs which mainly aided blacks were slashed and federal procedures for antidiscrimination enforcement were moderated. The antagonistic posture of federal leaders encouraged a similar hostility among state and local leaders. Concerted efforts by states and localities to slash relief costs are one significant result. Nor has the assault run its course.

It is mistaken to hope that the hostile climate and the partial withdrawal of past concessions will provoke a new wave of outrage and disorder in the ghettos. One reason is that the very gains made in the sixties turned many blacks from group struggle to individual advancement. Thousands of veteran activists and hundreds of thousands of younger blacks from whom future activists might have been drawn were absorbed into colleges and universities, into industry and commerce, into the bureaucracies of government and into electoral politics. By this process, actual and potential activists were placated and isolated from the mass of blacks. In an increasingly hostile climate, they are preoccupied with consolidating their gains, not with mobilizing new waves of insurgency.

As for the majority of blacks who were left behind, they are quiescent as well. They have been calmed by the expansion of the relief rolls and left leaderless by the expansion of the black middle class. Perhaps most important, they have been made fearful by a repressive climate. Collective disorders may not always be organized, but neither are they irrational; they are unlikely to occur when people believe there is little to gain and much to lose. Just as the insurgency of the sixties was encouraged by then dominant liberal elites who proclaimed their sympathies to racial progress, so it is now being discouraged by dominant conservative elites who are proclaiming the need for a return to law and order and to the ethic of self-reliance.

Taken together, the events of the 1960s constituted a period of political crisis comparable in many ways to other great periods of political upheaval and electoral realignment in the United States. The political crisis of the 1890s, for example, was precipitated by the dislocations of rapid industrial growth; the political crisis of the 1930s by the dislocations of the Great Depression. The following essays are about different aspects of the political crisis of the 1960s precipitated by the dislocations that followed the great black migration to the cities.

R. A. C.
F. F. P.

New York City
November 1973

PART ONE

The Public
Bureaucracies
and the Control
of the Poor

It was inevitable that the social and political disturbances erupting by the early 1960s would change the way in which different groups thought about American society. The 1960s thus spawned a series of reappraisals; in one sphere after another, the domestic complacency of the 1950s gave way to a new preoccupation with the problems that, it was acknowledged, still plagued the American democracy. Academics and professionals, church leaders and philanthropists, government spokesmen and novelists, the mass media—all began to focus on racism and poverty in America. In this process it was not surprising that the agencies of the welfare state came under scrutiny.

Since the turn of the century, and especially since the New Deal, a multitude of programs had been developed in the United States, many of them initiated and funded by the federal government, which were ostensibly designed to help the poor. These programs have been widely regarded as representing a major change in the philosophy and practice of American capitalism. The basic well-being of people was no longer to be left to the vagaries of "free enterprise"; government now assumed the responsibility of assuring at least a minimum level of subsistence and security for those who could not "hold their own" in the free-enterprise system. Public-welfare agencies were established to provide the poor with income; public-housing authorities provided them with shelter; school systems saw to their education; clinics and hospitals to their health. True, the "welfare state" was still far from perfect; its programs were too limited, failing as they did to cover many people and to address many other kinds of needs. The cure was simply expansion: more programs, more funds, more agencies. This was not easy to achieve, of course, for government social welfare ran against the grain of

3

the American belief in self-reliance, as well as American suspicion of "big government." Each step forward was a battle won. But progress was being made; the welfare state was growing. The most ardent warriors were, of course, those liberal Democrats who thoroughly identified with the New Deal, with the golden age of government responsibility it represented and with the social-welfare bureaucracies it had established.

Increasingly, however, as signs of trouble multiplied in the 1960s, these social-welfare agencies came to be viewed more skeptically, at least by some. Many of the black poor in the cities were not in the economic system, or were only marginally related to it. With the growth of the welfare state, they had come to depend on huge, centralized bureaucracies that presumably provided for their basic needs. But if poverty in America was still so widespread and so deep, especially in the big cities where the welfare agencies were most developed, then the suspicion was inevitable that the agencies did not do what they claimed to do. Something was amiss—but what? The answer given was the classical one of the defenders of the welfare state: The programs were too small, their funds too limited. To a lesser extent some welfare-state advocates preoccupied themselves with what they defined as problems of maladministration in the welfare state, problems that, with intelligence and goodwill, could readily be corrected.

We took a different view. We thought that the nature of the agencies of the welfare state had been misunderstood, that faith in them by the poor, or in the name of the poor, had been misplaced. The inadequacies that were being recognized were not the result of administrative problems or funding problems but reflected problems of power. The so-called failures of these agencies were in a sense deliberate, essential to their survival and growth as political and bureaucratic structures.

The social-welfare bureaucracies were legislated in the name of the poor, but the poor were not their true clientele. The agencies were in fact oriented to other and far more powerful groups that could provide them with the legitimation and political support that public bureaucracies need for survival and expansion. It was these groups that shaped agency policies and practices, and it was to avoid the censure of these groups that the agencies

4

dealt so stringently and harshly with their ostensible clients, the poor.

As for the poor themselves, they could offer the agencies little by way of political support, and so they exerted little influence on agency policies. Moreover, whatever influence the poor might have mustered was diminished by their interaction with the welfare bureaucracies. The agencies dispensed benefits the poor desperately needed, and agency personnel were empowered to give those benefits or to withhold them. This discretion gave the bureaucracies enormous power over the poor, and they regularly used that power to induce submissive behavior. These realities of power and control were only veiled, not altered, by the ideologies of "scientific" helping espoused by the growing class of professional bureaucrats who manned the agencies of the welfare state. We developed this argument in "The Professional Bureaucracies: Benefit Systems as Influence Systems."

In short, the poor-serving agencies were the enemy; they had to be assaulted, not merely expanded, as liberals had argued since the 1930s. In "Poverty, Injustice and the Welfare State," we examined some of the proposals that were being put forward to overcome the vulnerability of the poor in coping with the public bureaucracies—mainly, the introduction of Ombudsmen as well as the providing of advocates for the poor. We concluded that these remedies held little promise. Indeed, we suspected that "advocacy" enjoyed support as a solution to the powerlessness of the poor because it was so easily perverted into a public-relations process on the part of government agencies.

The area of housing and urban redevelopment provided a dramatic case in point. In "Whom Does the Advocate Planner Serve?" Part One, we argued that professional planners acting as advocates were involving local leaders of poor communities in the intricacies of preparing paper plans for their communities that yielded few gains in housing or public facilities. In that process they were also turning these communities away from their only effective leverage in forcing concessions from the housing and planning agencies—namely, their ability to disrupt the regular operations of the agencies and to threaten disorder. This argument evoked a variety of responses, which have been included here in Part Two, together with our rejoinders.

5

# The Professional Bureaucracies: Benefit Systems as Influence Systems

RICHARD A. CLOWARD
AND FRANCES FOX PIVEN

The growth of the bureaucracies of the welfare state has meant the diminished influence of low-income people in public spheres. This has come about in two ways: First, the bureaucracies have intruded upon and altered processes of public decision so that low-income groups have fewer occasions for exercising influence and fewer effective means of doing so; and second, the bureaucracies have come to exert powerful and inhibiting controls on the low-income people who are their clients.

In response to the critics who point to these propensities of the public bureaucracies, several recent federal programs have made special provisions for citizen participation. It is our contention that such measures fail to offset the conditions which permit bureaucratic usurpation of power. Not only is citizen participation by and large a ritual conducted at the discretion of the public agencies, but it tends to become another vehicle for the extension of bureaucratic control.

Political leaders obviously must strive to accommodate groups that will provide them with the votes to win elections. To this extent, the flow of influence is upward. Programs for public benefits, however, are not simple electoral decisions to be made and reconsidered by a new polling of electoral sentiments. They are ensconced in bureaucratic complexes which are the domain of experts and professionals, masters of the special knowledge and techniques considered necessary to run the public agencies and

Copyright by the authors. Originally published in Murray Silberman, ed., *The Role of Government in Promoting Social Change*, New York, Columbia University School of Social Work, November 1965.

administer the public benefits. Whole spheres of decision are made within these agencies, or in deference to their advice. The professional bureaucracies represent a new system of public action, only occasionally subject to electoral control.

The bureaucracies are exposed to direct control by broad constituencies only at periodic formal junctures: elections, budget hearings or public referenda on appropriations. And at those points at which they are vulnerable, public agencies are themselves able to exert powerful counterinfluence in electoral decisions. They bring to bear on their own behalf the weight of their acknowledged (but obscure) expertise and their great organizational capability, as well as a host of supportive liaisons formed with political leaders and other organizations in the public and private sectors.

The low-income clientele whom the bureaucracies are charged to serve, to placate and to contain are a special source of sensitivity to them. Any disruption or assertiveness on the part of clients, to the extent that it is visible, will put in jeopardy the support of groups and organizations that watch over the public agencies. The bureaucracies therefore manipulate the benefits and services on which their clients come to depend in such a way as to control their behavior. In this way, governmental benefit systems have become a powerful source of control over low-income people, used to ensure the conforming client behaviors which the bureaucracies require both for internal stability and in order to maintain electoral support. Through these processes, the bureaucracies come to serve as the filter of power, selectivity accommodating the alert, the organized and the influential, but containing the low-income groups which, by depending on public benefits, fall under bureaucratic control.

Our central proposition is that the public bureaucracies strive chiefly to maintain the conditions necessary for their stability and expansion. They are essentially neutral, aligned with neither class nor party, except as such alignments serve jurisdictional claims or determine the availability of necessary resources. They distribute public benefits in response to organizational requirements, adjusting the distribution to maintain and enlarge the flow of organizational resources. The influence of any group upon them ultimately depends on its role in this process—either contributing resources and supporting jurisdictional claims, or threatening the attainment of these objectives. Public agencies strive to maintain themselves with the least possible internal stress and change and therefore try to use their organizational capacity to limit both the occasion and the extent of their vulnerability to outside groups. Organizational equilibrium and enhancement are, in short, the compelling forces in bureaucratic action.

In this paper we will discuss three sets of tactics by which the bureaucracies pursue these goals: Tactics of organizational consolidation and coalition; tactics of political accommodation; and tactics of low-income-client control.

## TACTICS OF ORGANIZATIONAL CONSOLIDATION AND COALITION

When by legislative mandate we establish an agency and charge it with the distribution of some public benefit, we vest in it powerful resources by which to influence electoral decisions, other organizations and its own clientele. These resources consist of the technical expertise with which the agency is credited, the benefits it is charged with distributing and control of its own elaborate organizational structures and processes. These resources are employed by the public agency to protect and extend its jurisdiction in the following ways.[1]

### THE CONSOLIDATION OF EXPERTISE

Acknowledgment of expertise is a component of the political mandate initially granted to the public agency. It is inherent in political acceptance of technical definitions of problems and solutions, and also in political reliance on complex bureaucratic structures to carry out these solutions.

The expertise that is initially acknowledged to political mandate is itself used by public agencies to extend and consolidate the need for expertise. To acknowledge expertise in a given area is to grant authority. By its nature, expertise is obscure and its appropriate boundaries cannot easily be judged by the nonexpert. It is therefore difficult to contain the propensities of expert-bureaucrats to elaborate still further the specialized knowledge and technique required in the recognition and solution of problems.

There seems to be a tendency, moreover, toward the coalition of expertise, both within and among organizations. Problems are interpreted not only as highly technical but as multifaceted; thus they require the application of a variety of expert skills. Consequently, the public bureaucracies come increasingly to be staffed by coalitions made up of experts from a variety of professions. A nonexpert trying to appraise the claims of the professional bureaucrats has virtually no recourse once the importance of expertise is acknowledged but to turn to other experts. A competitive pluralism among organizations and professions provides some counter to bureaucratic influence, not only by fostering alternative programs but by fostering alternative experts whose opinions may be a basis for evaluating and controlling given programs. Coalitions of experts, by contrast, constitute monopolies on expertise which foreclose alternative appraisals, confronting electoral leaders, the general public, special-interest constituents and competing organizations with a virtually impenetrable professional phalanx.

## THE CONSOLIDATION OF BENEFITS

The professional bureaucracies are vested with control over the distribution of various benefits, presumably to serve some public purpose. Benefits are also inducements or sanctions and therefore are a resource for influence which the agencies control. We have referred to the bureaucratic capacity to distribute benefits which, by serving the purposes of electoral leaders, may procure political support for the bureaucracies. We will subsequently show how the use of benefits as inducements or sanctions also ensures client behaviors which are consonant with the agency's larger political concerns.

In seeking to extend and entrench their jurisdictions, professional bureaucracies reveal a tendency to expand organizational control to a variety of benefits. The emphasis on "multifaceted" problems leads not only to the formation of coalitions of experts under one organizational structure but to the consolidation of a range of benefits within the same structure. The "multiproblem" family is thus said to require a variety of both experts and benefits; thus the web of experts and benefits becomes more intricate with the "saturation" and "comprehensive" approaches to a social problem.

This tendency is everywhere discernible in social-welfare services. The schools include a variety of guidance counselors, psychologists and physicians in their coalition of experts and they dispense the benefits over which these experts have jurisdiction. Public-housing authorities sponsor a host of special programs and services involving many different professionals and many diverse facilities.[2] With each repeated discovery of the persistence of problems in service, the professionals make their bid for more experts and benefits, coopting new and different varieties along the way.

## THE JOINING OF BENEFITS AND EXPERTISE

A third tactic of the professional bureaucracies is to link expertise to benefits so that benefits are conditional on the use of expertise. In this way the importance of benefits tends to accrue to the expertise, and, conversely, the discretion inherent in expertise is employed in the distribution of benefits. We are told that public housing is of little value without social service; that welfare cash assistance must be accompanied by "rehabilitation" programs; that education requires therapeutic and guidance specialists.

The legislation of a benefit ordinarily implies political acknowledgment of a collective problem which the new benefit is intended to ameliorate. Distribution of the benefit is therefore important to the political collectivity. When that distribution is defined as requiring expert skills, expertise gains importance, and experts acquire influence in confrontations with electoral leaders and public groups. And, as will be shown later, a similar use is made of benefits in dealings with clients, for whom benefits are especially critical.

The linkage of expertise and benefits extends the discretion of the professional bureaucracies. Discretion is inherent in expertise; the mystique of esoteric knowledge and technique shields the bureaucratic management of benefits from easy review by political leaders or public groups and from the assertions of client claimants. In this connection, it is interesting to note that those now ensconced in the government bureaucracies—educators, social workers, vocational counselors—are members of the less authoritative and prestigeful professions. Bureaucratic control over benefits and bureaucratic obfuscation of practice lend these professions a complement of authority and prestige. They are thus able to claim critical functions in the public sector in their bid for full professional recognition.

These are some of the tactics by which professional bureaucracies extend and consolidate the resources with which they are initially endowed by public mandate. Concretely these tactics can be recognized in the characteristic efforts of the bureaucracies to "coordinate" different organizational and professional activities, to form "comprehensive" programs and to unify organizational jurisdictions—always under the banner of increased effectiveness and efficiency.

Once they are charged with the distribution of a class of benefits, and once their technical and organizational capabilities are acknowledged, the bureaucracies employ these assets in subsequent confrontations with political leaders, electoral groups and other organizations. Their control of technical and organizational expertise permits public agencies to remove themselves from scrutiny and at the same time to form for public view all-embracing but esoteric legitimations of their operations. Ultimately they succeed in these tactics, of course, only because the functions they perform by distributing benefits have come to be regarded as essential to the society.

## TACTICS OF POLITICAL ACCOMMODATION

For their initial public mandate and for subsequent public allocations, the bureaucracies depend on political decisions. They require the support of political leaders. They also require at least the tacit support of those organized forces in the community that are able to watch over governmental policies and to threaten intervention in political decisions. The agencies must therefore bring their distinctive capabilities to bear in inducing supportive responses and discouraging action which might subvert agency jurisdiction.

## POLITICAL LEADERS

New welfare programs are typically legislated when political leaders are confronted with mounting concern among their electoral constituencies, often in response to some form of social disruption. With newspapers and civic groups in the lead, there is a call for action on some issue which has come to be defined as a public problem. The politician looks for a solution which will placate public concern without jostling any groups on whose support he relies. He tries to find a solution which will appear to be forceful and yet will avoid controversy. The general electorate should feel unduly offended in neither their purses nor their sentiments. Nor should the solution activate and engage any new groups in the fray by threatening their particular interests.

The task in any political proposal is to find that course of public action which minimizes conflict and reflects the broadest possible agreement among those alerted by the issue. Welfare problems bring into public focus the poor, the minorities or the deviants, groups which are not themselves part of the middle-class political consensus and whose cause is as likely to arouse the wrath of some as it is the pity of others. To invent a solution to a welfare problem is not easy. It is vastly facilitated, however, by the professional bureaucracies.

What to the politician is a disturbance in his constituency and a threat to his majority becomes for the professional bureaucrat an opportunity to extend his public mandate, his resources and his jurisdiction. The agencies are ready for liaison with the political leader. They bring to that liaison the capacity to convert political problems into technical problems. Issues which have been framed as "who gets what," are transmuted into issues of method and framed in terms of a technology. That the technology is obscure is largely an advantage; the germinal political issue of "who gets what" is thereby also obscured. Moreover, the authority and prestige of expertise, and the faith in science and progress which it calls forth, are added to the political equation and made still more compelling by the complexity of the proposal. Indeed, the ultimate public action may be a program of research and demonstration to devise or advance the necessary technology.

Once a new program is initiated, the public agencies and their political allies continue in close symbiotic relationship. Politicians rely on professionals for information and recommendations regarding policies which are increasingly esoteric and complex. The bureaucracies, in filling this function, are in turn closely responsive to the concerns of their political patrons.

In this kind of partnership between political leaders and the public agencies, there is clearly gain to be had for both sides. The politicians are able to offer to their constituencies programs which inspire confidence and assuage conflict by their very technicialism. The bureaucracies, for their part, are extended and made more powerful. This, too, is an advantage for politicians, for when public action is contained within bureaucratic spheres, it is less likely to produce politically disruptive change.

## PEER ORGANIZATIONS

Government and private spheres have experienced a parallel growth of large, rationalized organizations. The bureaucracies are vulnerable to these organizational peers which have the resources to maintain a steady watch over the complex activities of public agencies, to decipher the implications of these activities and to threaten to exercise comparable influence in electoral processes.

Large, rationalized organizations are able to keep abreast of the maze of actual and proposed legislation and procedures and exploit many formal and informal occasions for negotiations and bargaining. They have the ability to generate public issues; they have access to the press and the political parties and can call on other organizations with whom they have regular liaisons. In addition, the technical capability of other organizations and their programmatic cooperation are often valuable assets to the public agencies.

Consequently, public agencies strive to form liaisons with organizational peers, public and private, accommodating them in ways designed to ensure their support or at least to avoid attack. A planning commission deals with other municipal agencies and with organizations of realtors and homeowners; a board of education deals with teachers' unions and parents' associations; and social-welfare agencies deal with each other, with professional societies and philanthropic federations.

## TACTICS TO CONTROL CLIENTS

The bureaucracies employ their distinctive capabilities to make certain of client acquiescence in agency actions and to prevent any public display of assertiveness by low-income clients which may reflect on the agency and put in jeopardy the support of other community groups. As a consequence, the political influence of low-income people has been diminished by their involvement as clients of the agencies of the welfare state. Benefits are formed and distributed in ways which inhibit the development of client groups capable of collective action, which in turn limits the capacity of low-income people to exert influence in the electoral system. Ordinarily a group gains influence because it organizes for the collective application of its resources, whether the tactics it employs are negotiation, block voting or disruption. The working classes were organized through the political machines in the residential areas where they lived and through the unions in the factories where they worked. They were able to improve their position in part by political influence through which they secured governmental regulation of economic institutions. Today's poor, by contrast, not only have little leverage as workers in economic spheres but have few organizational resources for influencing government, and they are increasingly cast into a relationship with the institutions of the welfare state which entrenches and reinforces their powerlessness.

### BENEFITS WHICH DISCOURAGE INTERACTION

Public benefits to the contemporary poor inhibit the emergence of collective low-income power in two ways. First, benefits are of a kind which isolates low-income people from major social roles, particularly occupational roles. Second, benefits are designed as individual benefits, and the manner in which they are distributed discourages the aggregation of clients.

*Isolative benefits.* In general, group interests are expressed politically by organizations developed around the major roles which people perform, and principally around economic roles. Regular participation in an institutional role makes possible the tacit organization of people—or rather of their contributions—as a concomitant of role performance. Thus political interest groups are typically associations of tradesmen or professionals or homeowners. Less obviously, civic associations seem to prosper when they are closely linked to economic roles.

Similarly, the power of organized labor depends on the role of workers in economic institutions, and on the factory as a context for building regular and stable union organization. As a consequence, most of the social-welfare innovations of the last few decades have reinforced the occupational role, ensuring economic stability and a higher standard of living for people employed in preferred occupations. The welfare state has come to be the bulwark against downward mobility from the working class for the temporarily unemployed, the survivors of deceased workers and the old. Through organization in occupational roles, workers gained some leverage in private enterprise and came, through the unions, to exert influence in securing various government benefits for the working classes.

The client categories by which public bureaucracies define eligibility for benefits, however, are not coterminous with regular role categories in the social structure. Rather, these categories define people by "nonroles": Clients are school dropouts, broken families or unemployables. Eligibility for benefits is thus established by inability to gain access to or to maintain educational roles, occupational roles, family roles and the like. Consequently, people receiving benefits cannot associate with their status as clients any set of common rights and obligations derived from other major social roles. Nor are people likely to form groups as clients when to do so is to collectively acknowledge and label themselves by the role failure which the client status represents. Finally, and perhaps most important, benefits of this kind, by isolating people from major social roles, also isolate them from major institutional spheres, from the mainstream of social and economic life. Clients do not gain the influence which can be derived from regular participation in major institutions. They remain separated from the leverage inherent in regular role performance and without the opportunity for organizing that leverage which an institutional context provides.

*Individual benefits.* Another important characteristic of benefits to the poor is that they apply to individuals rather than to groups. Nor does the manner in which benefits are distributed tend to aggregate people, a means by which latent incentives for organization might be activated. The right to bargain collectively, for example, was a benefit *to an organization* and therefore an inducement to organize, provided by legislation to those workers who were not yet unionized. No comparable inducement flows out of the benefits provided to the contemporary poor.

At least embryonic organizations must exist before influence can be directed to secure benefits which nurture organizations. The emerging labor movement produced a leadership that was in a position to recognize organizational concerns and to press management and government for the benefits which enhanced the unions as organizations. By contrast, the contemporary poor are disorganized. What influence they have in electoral processes is not exerted for organizing benefits. The working classes were already partially unionized when they pressed for legislation giving them the right to bargain collectively; so were the Negroes of the South when they demanded legislation empowering them to vote. For the most part, today's poor are atomized. Aggregate action, when it occurs, takes form as waves of unrest and disruption—as in the recent uprisings in the North—from which no leadership comes forth. The poor are placated with individual benefits and, by receiving them, remain unorganized.

## TACTICS TO COUNTER COLLECTIVE ACTION

Low-income groups occasionally emerge in the context of public-benefit systems. In some instances benefits simply cannot be managed by individualized distribution (e.g., education and large-scale housing); in other instances bureaucratic action unites people who are already loosely affiliated by imposing on them a common deprivation, uncompensated by benefits (*e.g.,* slum clearance). Such low-income groups are not likely to join the ranks of organized constituents with whom the bureaucracies form accommodating relations. Bureaucratic responsiveness to low-income groups incurs the risk of arousing hostile forces in the community and of eventually undermining electoral support for the bureaucracies. This risk has to do not only with the low-income groups but with the very fact of engaging in reciprocal relations with the poor.[3] Low-income groups can themselves offer the bureaucracies little significant support in a wider community context. Moreover, the bureaucracies have certain capabilities for containing and directing such groups which provide an alternative to accommodation.

Containment and direction are in fact the strategy which the bureaucracies typically employ in response to low-income groups which impinge upon them. For this strategy they are uniquely equipped by their capacity to manipulate information and benefits. First, the bureaucracies can withhold or dispense information about their own procedures which low-income groups require in order to formulate any challenge to bureaucratic action. This is in part a consequence of the highly complex and technical maze of bureaucratic regulation and practice. It also has to do with the fact that most bureaucratic activity is not visible from the vantage point of clients, and even less so from the vantage point of low-income protest groups, which are outside the system entirely. Complexity and obscurity are, as we have noted, an asset in many contests in which bureaucracies strive for influence. Bureaucrats are not likely to take the initiative in so structuring and advertising their actions as to encourage surveillance by anyone, and especially not by low-income groups whose claims will generate controversy or strain their supportive liaisons.

The second major tactic which bureaucracies employ in controlling and directing low-income groups is the manipulation of benefits. When such groups are formed among clients, the bureaucracies are able to offer peripheral benefits as incentives for conformity and to threaten the withdrawal or curtailment of essential benefits as punishment for dissent.

Thus, housing programs seem occasionally to provide a context for the formation of groups among low-income people. In the public-housing program, for example, low-income people were necessarily aggregated in the course of receiving benefits, simply because housing was provided in large projects. The project structure was dictated by other considerations having to do with administrative efficiency and political acceptability (note the recent alarm over the rent-supplement proposal, which might have subsidized low-income tenants to live in middle-class areas). Not long after World War II, and rather early in its bureaucratic life, the New York Public Housing Authority was confronted with militant tenant groups in several of its projects. Not only were these groups taking active positions on public-housing matters but they appeared to have a politically radical character of some notoriety. The Housing Authority reacted by prohibiting the use of project facilities by tenant organizations.

Not only the withdrawal of benefits but also the proffering of benefits can work to weaken low-income groups. This is, of course, a more likely tactic when the bureaucracies confront groups of people who are not yet beneficiaries. When tenants in some of the slum buildings of New York organized "no heat, no hot water" protests, the housing agencies responded by selectively redressing only the most vigorous tenant complaints. With much publicity, the agencies seemed to bring to bear their total armory of legal enforcement and rehabilitation aids, but only on a few star buildings. Tenant leadership was turned aside and the protests were deflated, but the grievances of most slum dwellers remained unanswered.

Public action in urban renewal has occasioned some of the most stubborn and aggressive low-income group protests of recent years. These groups were composed of residents in areas scheduled for renewal. Confronted with the stress of upheaval, the loss of neighborhood and the prospect of greatly increased rentals[4] these people were the hardest hit by the costs of renewal but were not to receive the benefits provided by the new developments. They were people already together in neighborhoods, united by a common deprivation or threat of deprivation to the neighborhood, and in no signficant way appeased by any benefits. The new developments included chiefly high-rental housing; slum clearance was no boon to slum dwellers for whom it meant mainly dislocation.

The adamancy of these local protest groups often threatened to disrupt urban-renewal projects. The agencies countered with programs for "community participation," consisting largely in the careful advertisement of renewal plans to resident groups and the active initiation of local leaders at an early stage in order to "educate" and win them to the plans. Thus programs for directed community participation were developed to offset the spontaneous, but disruptive, participation of local protest groups. At the same time, many of the facts of renewal (*e.g.*, the numbers to be displaced and the relocation alternatives available) continued to be concealed and sometimes appeared to be simply fabricated.

## TACTICS OF POLITICAL SOCIALIZATION

Governmental benefit systems are also structures for political socialization.[5] Low-income people are drawn into these systems as recipients. They are attracted by the promise of benefits, and once in the system they remain tied to it by the benefits they receive. These benefits are typically not vested by law or conferred as a matter of unambiguous right; they are proffered at the discretion of the professional bureaucracy. They can be employed as threats and rewards to influence client attitudes and ensure conforming client behavior. Access to resources which people require—money, housing, education—is made conditional on acceptable behavior, including often acquiescence to professional counseling or therapy. The threatened denial of essential benefits is a powerful sanction to control client behavior.

*Conditional benefits.* All public bureaucracies require some measure of discretion in the distribution of benefits, for no mandates can be so precise and inclusive as to provide firm guidelines for all the varied circumstances presented for decisions. All bureaucracies tend to expand that discretion by elaborating tech-

nical expertise and organizational complexity. When recipients
of a program are primarily low-income people, several circumstances combine to support the further enlargement of bureaucratic discretion.

The initial establishment of a public agency is a consequence
of a collective political decision in which low-income people are
not likely to have been very forceful, and surely not forceful
as organized political actors. The framing of statutes establishing
public benefits for low-income people typically reflects the attitudes of other groups which *are* effective political proponents.
These include the middle-class groups whose attitudes dominate
political consensus, the bureaucracies and the professional associations linked to the bureaucracies. Such proponents prefer to vest
discretion in the public functionaries who deal with the poor
rather than to establish these benefits as a right, to which the
poor are entitled.[6]

The dominant view of the poor among the American middle
class is that they are defective, morally as well as in other ways,
and are likely to take advantage of public beneficence. And
public agency personnel feel themselves constrained by the constant threat of arousing powerful community forces to employ
criteria in defining eligibility for benefits which go beyond objective economic need and take account of widely held invidious
definitions of the poor. The New York City Welfare Department,
for example, enjoins its investigators to discourage malingering,
reminding them in its manual that "the denial or withdrawal of
assistance is as constructive a factor as the granting of assistance,
both to the client and to the community."

The threat of community opposition is real, as attested by the
recurrent attacks upon welfare departments and public-housing
authorities for allegedly fostering immorality and degeneracy
among their clients. Accordingly, the administrators of these
agencies employ the discretion allowed to them in an array
of investigatory and policing practices intended to ensure that
the recipients or potential recipients of benefits will be publicly
regarded as "worthy" of the sums and services dispensed to them.
Public-housing functionaries maintain surveillance over the
morals of their tenants, employing their own police forces and
their own quasi-judicial procedures, made potent by the threat
of eviction and virtually unrestrained by laws or regulations pro-

tecting the rights of tenants. In New York City the project managers have even developed a system of tenant "fines" which are imposed for all manner of behavior which the manager regards as bad tenancy. Similarly, public-welfare departments invest enormous organizational energy in the initial determination of a client's worthiness and eligibility for the dole. Once approved, the recipient is the object of constant surveillance to make sure he continues to meet these conditions. The most striking example of such practice is the "postmidnight raid" to which mothers receiving ADC grants have been subjected in order to catch by surprise a man who may be on the premises.

The ambiguity surrounding the nature of client rights pertains also to procedures for appeal from agency decisions. It is not clear with many benefits whether an aggrieved person has the right to do anything more than complain. By and large, appeals procedures are not defined in legislation. With appeals, as with the initial dispensing of benefits, bureaucratic discretion over low-income clients is supported because it permits practices which accommodate to the invidious attitudes toward the poor held by dominant groups in the community.

The professionals who staff the bureaucracies are a second factor in reinforcing bureaucratic discretion over clients. Professionals generally tend to view the problems of low-income people as resulting from defects in socialization. Remedies for these defects are said to require exposure to professional services, and the discretion inherent in professional services is often employed to make judgments about the dispensing of benefits on which low-income people depend.

The third circumstance which expands bureaucratic discretion in dealing with clients is the general tendency of the bureaucracies to coordinate and consolidate their functions. In an earlier era of private charity, the poor could solicit cash relief or other benefits from one or another private agency, never entirely and finally subject to the judgment of any one. Now they confront one comprehensive welfare bureaucracy from whose decision they have no recourse. Even private agencies have developed mechanisms for maintaining broad supervision of their clientele. The Social Service Exchange, for example, is a device for comprehensive surveillance, designed in part to identify low-income people who shop around for services.

Proposals for bureaucratic reform seem inevitably to involve reorganization to establish more comprehensive jurisdiction over one category of clients or another, and to call for extension of the professionalization of staff and services. Through years of controversy regarding housing-code-enforcement practices in New York City, reformers have repeatedly recommended consolidation of all housing agencies. Whether consolidation will in fact improve the condition of the low-income plaintiff remains questionable. Conflicting and overlapping jurisdictions may be administratively inefficient, but they give the low-income tenant some alternative course of action when, as has frequently been the case, his complaint is not heeded by a given agency. Similarly, the improvement of bureaucratic services means greater professionalization of staff and the extension of professional services and discretion. For example, in reform of criminal practices it is argued that probation officers should be social workers, surveillance should be therapeutic, and therapeutic evaluations should be the basis for criminal sentencing.

That the discretion derived from systems of conditional benefits is a source of enormous power over low-income people is self-evident. For people on public welfare, their very livelihood, however meager, is at stake; for the public-housing tenant it may be his only chance for a decent dwelling; to the family of the child confronted with the possibility of school suspension it is the only chance to give their offspring an education and indeed a future livelihood. There are few institutionalized safeguards against the exercise of discretion by government agencies which distribute conditional benefits to the poor. The laws which establish these benefits are vague, and administrative procedures are complex and ambiguous.

*Political desocialization.* Exposure to bureaucratic discretion leads to political desocialization. First, bureaucratic procedures reflect the premise that the poor have few rights. Recipients of benefits are not apprised of procedures but are continually confronted with apparently arbitrary actions. Bureaucratic procedures are also punitive, reflecting the premise that the poor are unworthy and the constant fear that the client will lapse into sloth and chicanery. Such procedures in fact make people into what they are already said to be, for when their rights are ignored, men do indeed live by their wits, evading what is capri-

cious and arbitrary or lapsing into apathy. Thus the clients of the
welfare state come to live in fear, moving to control their fate
not by political action but by evasion and ultimately by acquiescence. In this way, welfare programs debilitate and demoralize; the attitudes and ways of life into which clients are
forced inhibit their effective participation in even ordinary social
roles and surely inhibit political activism.

Secondly, clients are often socialized to particular forms of
political participation through the exposure to professional services which receiving benefits entails. Professional service is an
opportunity for educating clients in political beliefs and modes
of political participation that are consonant with the views of the
middle-class majority.[7]

For example, public-housing tenants who use recreational
facilities are required to submit to supervision by agents of the
housing authority, and recreation becomes an occasion for political education. In the case described earlier, the New York Public
Housing Authority continued to suffer publicly after eliminating
tenant organizations, not so much for the radicalism of tenants
as for their ostensibly antisocial behavior. The right-wing press
launched periodic exposés of crime, delinquency and abuse of
property in the projects. In time, the Authority developed a
more sophisticated strategy than simple fiat for the containment
of tenants: It undertook to form its own tenant organizations,
linking these to various community services and dominating them
through staff organizers. Tenants were encouraged to participate
in recreational and self-help programs such as project beautifica-
tion, consumer education and household skills,[8] and were steered
away from actions troublesome to the Authority.

Whether the professional bureaucrat is a caseworker, a guidance
counselor, an educator, a recreational expert or a community organizer, and whether the program is a youth employment agency or a "Headstart" operation, the professional is the
agent of socialization, and the program is the vehicle for socialization, as to the legitimacy of existing political arrangements and
the propriety of middle-class political styles. The consequences
of this socialization are clear. Established institutional arrangements are endorsed, their democratic character is asserted and
middle-class styles of formalized participation and negotiation
are inculcated. These beliefs leave no role for the conflict and

protest which often characterized lower-class activism; indeed, they even make conflict and protest immoral. But today's unorganized poor have few of the resources needed for middle-class styles of participation and negotiation. They have little to bargain with and so are partners to no one's negotiations. And by becoming educated in the beliefs and strategies of action appropriate only for groups in higher economic strata, they are rendered ineffective.

To summarize, we see no evidence that government's involvement of the poor will generate a force for social change by nurturing their political capabilities or by activating them with the promise of benefits. Rather, governmental programs for the poor are likely to diminish whatever collective political vitality the poor still exhibit.

Future prospects for social change will be increasingly shaped by the expansionist forces of the public bureaucracies. How low-income people fare through this expansion will depend on the extent and kinds of benefits distributed by the bureaucracies. These benefits have often been formed chiefly in accommodation to the middle-class consensus on which the bureacracies depend for support. At the same time, public benefits have been designed to placate unrest among the poor and to deflect any political articulation of this unrest.

Under these conditions, the best the poor can expect are programs—such as those generated by the Office of Economic Opportunity—that impart to them the skills through which they may be integrated into occupational roles. At worst, they will get more programs such as public assistance which further isolate them—while controlling them—from major social roles in the society. If future programs do successfully impart competitive skills, the bureaucracies, in pursuing their own enhancement, may thereby succeed in raising many low-income people into the middle class. In this way the clients of the bureaucracy can one by one join the middle-class political majority and public benefits can indeed be said to increase their political influence. It will have done so, however, at the price of diminishing the ranks and therefore the influence of those who are still in the lower class. Thus the social change accomplished by bureaucratic expansion will not challenge the middle-class consensus as to appropriate forms of political participation and will not enlarge the capacity of the dispossessed to influence their environment. In particular, it will not enlarge the capacity of the poor to influence the public bureaucracies upon which they depend. This is the path marked out by public-benefit systems which act to reinforce the existing alignment of influence.

## NOTES

[1] We use "jurisdiction" to include the various ways in which an agency's operations are limited by legislative or administrative mandate. There are obviously any number of dimensions according to which jurisdiction can be defined: area, population (or "target group"), duration of operation and a host of criteria limiting the kind of benefits or expertise allowed the agency and the manner or occasion of application.

[2] Most commentators see such expansion as reform. Writing about housing, Wolf Von Eckhardt notes approvingly that "Mrs. Marie C. McGuire, head of the public housing agencies, reports that there are 19,000 community service programs—such as scouting, health care, homemaking, arts and crafts, and literacy training—concentrated in public housing projects throughout the nation. These programs attract 2.6 million people a month . . . they are on the side of good community design, social awareness and social integration" ("The Department of Headaches," *New Republic,* November 6, 1965, p. 20).

[3] See Georg Simmel's essay on "The Poor" (*Social Problems,* Fall 1965, pp. 118–140) for a delineation of the sociological bases for the exclusion of the poor from participation in the administration of public assistance.

[4] For review of problems in relocation see Chester Hartman, "The Housing of Relocated Families," *Journal of the American Institute of Planners,* November 1964, pp. 266–286.

[5] For a general discussion of the political power inherent in public benefits see Charles Reich, "The New Property," *Yale Law Review,* Vol. 73, No. 5, April 1964.

[6] The New York City Public Housing Authority, for example, is not governed by formulated regulations in selecting tenants. Nor have successive reforms impelled by professional and civic organizations moved in this direction. Instead, a maze of criteria establishing prior-

ities and ineligibility has been developed, to be applied largely at the discretion of the agency functionaries.

7 The use of professional service as a means of control is by no means limited to government bureaucracies. The industrial-counseling profession, for example, seems to owe its genesis to the functions it serves for management in allaying worker discontent, a use of counseling first made evident in the Mayo studies.

8 One of the most notorious public-housing projects in the country, the Pruitt-Igoe project in St. Louis, is now undergoing major rehabilitation and reform. In this, the Housing Authority, "aware that fiscal rehabilitation may only provide 'something else to break,' has a series of programs under way to involve the tenant in the process" (James Bailey, "The Case History of a Failure," Architectural Forum, December 1965).

# Poverty, Injustice and the Welfare State

RICHARD A. CLOWARD
AND RICHARD M. ELMAN

### AN OMBUDSMAN FOR THE POOR?

Americans think of justice primarily in connection with agencies of law enforcement, for such agencies have drastic powers, even over life itself. But at a time when the United States Supreme Court is upholding the right to counsel in criminal proceedings of all kinds and otherwise curbing infringements of individual liberties by law-enforcement agencies, it needs to be said that many other government agencies have only slightly less drastic powers, especially over low-income people. It is no small matter that a person may be arbitrarily defined as ineligible for public relief, no small matter that he may be arbitrarily evicted from a public-housing project. There are few institutionalized safeguards against the potentially unjust exercise of power by governmental "poor agencies," and virtually no place where low-income people can turn for assistance in availing themselves of the channels of redress that do exist.

In America, we continue to define poverty as resulting from all manner of personal devils which must be exorcised with commensurate autos-da-fé. Our welfare state is accordingly characterized by a lawlessness, a discrimination by class and race, a disregard for human rights and dignity and a niggardliness that are recurrent, often routine, if not institutionalized. And if our

Originally published in two parts in the *Nation*, February 28 and March 7, 1966. Copyright by the authors.

social-welfare system is regularly unjust, it is because American public opinion about the poor makes it so.

The American poor may not be able to protect themselves from injustice, but affluent groups can. As governmental powers proliferate, middle-class people are also becoming objects of abuses. Accustomed to having their rights respected, they are calling for restraints against government.

Traditionally, representative democracies have relied upon the legislator to mediate between the citizen and the public agency. With the growth of government, however, this arrangement—never very effective—has become mired down in complaints. To cope with the situation, a European legislative innovation, called the Ombudsman, has been proposed for America. Developed in Sweden more than 150 years ago, this innovation has evolved and spread to all other Scandinavian countries and to a number of nations in the British Commonwealth. Last October, the cause of the Ombudsman got a special boost when the British Labour government decided to establish such an office, even preserving the Scandinavian title.[1] On January 1 of this year a somewhat modified version of the Ombudsman was established in Laval, Canada (a suburb of Quebec City); it is the first in North America.

The Ombudsman is a "justice officer," or "citizen's defender." He is usually a highly respected senior member of the judiciary or a renowned professor in law, and is assisted by a small staff of lawyers. Appointed by and responsible to a legislative body —in most countries where the Ombudsman exists, to a parliament—he is charged to investigate all complaints from citizens. In Denmark, for example, the Ombudsman is obliged by statute "to keep himself informed as to whether any person under his jurisdiction [i.e., any civil servant] pursues unlawful ends, makes arbitrary or unreasonable decisions, or otherwise commits mistakes or acts of negligence in the discharge of his duties." If complaints from citizens are declared valid, the offending functionary is asked to provide redress; if invalid, no reprisals can be taken against the complainant.

Typical complaints involve the right of a postman to have in writing the grounds for a disciplinary action against him (the Ombudsman agreed, saying that governmental agencies should routinely inform citizens of the reasons for official decisions); the denial of unemployment benefits to a plumber on what he alleged was inaccurate evidence (the Ombudsman agreed, castigating officialdom for not procuring complete and reliable evidence); a businessman's charge that a national bank required him to conduct all his business with them in writing because he had been abusive to bank employees (the Ombudsman referred the complaining businessman to the ordinary courts which he said had jurisdiction); a charge that the grounds for federal grants for road construction, made selectively to municipalities each year, had not been explained (the Ombudsman ruled for the complaining municipality, saying that criteria of selection should be published).

Judging from a newly published volume of essays about Ombudsmanship around the world,[2] bureaucratic excesses have been effectively curbed by this legislative officer. The success of the Ombudsman is all the more remarkable because his powers are usually limited to investigation and recommendation. The Ombudsman typically publishes recommendations and can thus embarrass the bureaucracies. Representatives of the press are frequently permitted to comb through his correspondence, and his activities ordinarily make news. He is also empowered to make broad recommendations for new legislation intended to remedy sources of injustice by governmental agencies. And because of the esteem in which he is typically held, his recommendations are nearly always heeded. The Ombudsman's chief strength thus derives from intangibles: his personality, his public prestige, the support he cultivates in the press. He cannot, in short, move much beyond public opinion.

Within recent months, a spate of articles have appeared proposing that a parallel complaints office be developed at all levels of American government. Sweden's present Ombudsman, Alfred Bexelius, was interviewed in the *New Yorker*. An article in *Harper's* by Marion K. Sanders suggested that the creation of an Ombudsman might appease Negro demands for citizen review boards to take up complaints of police brutality. In the *New York Times Magazine*, Rep. Henry Reuss of Wisconsin explained his proposal to establish a nonpartisan "Office of Congressional Counsel." Similar bills have been proposed in state legislatures and municipal councils across the country. The general idea has been endorsed by civil-liberties groups for both national and local government.

Proponents of American Ombudsmanship would endow the office with an immense purview. "If there are no avenues for correcting maladministration," Congressman Reuss has pointed out in the *Christian Century*, "programs for the general welfare, such as Social Security, public housing, and veterans' benefits, are full of possibilities for human injustice." Ralph Nader has listed the following abuses with which an Ombudsman proposed for Connecticut might wish to deal:

> . . . preferential treatment and influence peddling, inadequate or unpublished regulations, wrongful detention, state police over-zealousness or laxity, unjust procedures in agency hearings, arbitrary censorship or secrecy, agency reluctance or refusal to give explicit reasons for decisions, patronage excesses, inefficiencies and delays by state personnel, undesirable conditions in prisons and mental institutions, payoffs and kickbacks in state contracts, and discriminatory enforcement or flagrant non-enforcement of state laws.

Given the growing concern here about governmental abuses, it is possible that various adaptations of this mechanism will presently emerge in the United States. The likelihood that they will protect the rights of the poor therefore deserves careful scrutiny.

Debate about an American Ombudsman has thus far focused on questions of governmental organization: Would an American complaints officer weaken rather than strengthen the traditional role of legislators as Ombudsmen en masse; could an institution nurtured in parliamentary systems be successfully adapted to governments marked by separation of powers; would the use of this device not give American courts further grounds for avoiding politically controversial issues in favor of narrowly technical ones?

However, one issue has not been debated. It has been assumed, and not debated, that the Ombudsman's services would be found equally effective by all American citizens. But the poor of our nation still confront special problems of injustice that have been resolved in most other welfare states, and discussions about the Ombudsman have not approached an appreciation of this fact.

In the United States, procedures to review the decisions of public departments have been successful when they found support in public opinion. The Loyalty Review Board, to cite one instance, compiled an extraordinary record, only one of its many recommendations having been spurned by a public department. Years after its abolition, the courts held that it had exceeded its legal authority; but its actions were hardly held to be excessive in the court of public opinion. An Ombudsman for the poor will fail for precisely the reason that the Loyalty Review Board succeeded: His recommendations would run counter to public attitudes toward the rights of the poor.

In countries where the Ombudsman has succeeded, social-welfare principles are generally accepted, even by conservatives. Compared with America, the poor in these countries have a tradition of political organization, often radical in ideology. Through political organizations—such as the British Labour Party—the poor have influenced the shape of social-welfare legislation. By contrast, pressures to reform the welfare apparatus in this country have originated primarily in very limited sectors of the middle-class community, unaided by organized demands from the poor themselves. Deprived of this allied base of power, middle-class reformers have had to compromise the interests of the poor. Knowing of the injustice of social-welfare practices, but fearing that disclosures of any kind might arouse a dormant and hostile public opinion, reformers have worked "behind the scenes" and have not attacked the system forthrightly and publicly. They have found it necessary, in effect, to conspire with administrators (tacitly, at least) to conceal the full facts from the public. This accounts in part for the widespread ignorance that most Americans exhibit about the welfare apparatus and its abuses of the poor.

In America, then, all faces are turned against the welfare apparatus. Given these compelling political facts, one derives no reassurance from the observation that Ombudsmen throughout the world cultivate success by carefully selecting cases "of a decidedly nonpolitical nature." Such judicious screening would, in the United States, eliminate from purview most administrative injustices perpetrated upon the poor. It is important to understand, then, that Ombudsmanship is not a substitute for basic reform, and that only reform will produce justice for the poor. The Ombudsman cannot overturn whole systems of law and administrative practice that are rooted in the culture and politics of a nation. He is not a legislature, or a chief executive, or a court of law. He merely polices functionaries in public agencies according to prevailing values: Ombudsmanship, one observer has noted, "cannot cure all administrative ills. It will work successfully only in a country, province or state that is already reasonably well administered. When an administration is riddled with political patronage or corruption . . . a reform of the whole system is required."

And, one might add, when a social-welfare system is rooted in contempt for its beneficiaries, it is also the system that must be reformed, for the injustices spawned are countless. Taking up these individual cases of injustice, there being literally hundreds of thousands to contemplate, is a task that would shortly overwhelm an American citizen-defender of any kind. It would require, if nothing else, an investigatory apparatus as large as the system being surveyed and policed.

Advocates of an American Ombudsman have not been altogether unmindful of the pressures of public opinion to which the office would be exposed, although it is not opinion about poverty that they have in mind. Rather, they point generally to our loose federalism and diversity of national opinion. The Ombudsman has grown up in countries that are relatively homogeneous, especially in the factor of race. Economically and racially, the United States is among the most heterogeneous countries for which the mechanism has as yet been proposed. Consequently, it has been suggested that early experiments with the office might better be undertaken locally than nationally. There, presumably, one would encounter less diverse population grouping, and the task of cultivating public opinion would be easier.

But group conflicts, along both class and racial lines, are deeper the closer one gets to the local community. In recent years, disputes about integration in education, employment and housing have evoked bitter antagonism at the local level, and local officials have been virtually immobilized because of appar-

ently irreconcilable differences among their constituents. By
and large, federal perspectives on social welfare have been more
liberal; most local practices would be much more punitive were
it not for pressures from federal agencies. At a time when the
Congress has been passing historic civil-rights legislation, state
bodies have been passing residence laws and suitable-home laws,
not to speak of regressive laws in other categories, which partly
reflect growing racial tensions. In New York, mounting pressure
for an unqualified residence law stems from the in-migration
of both Negroes and Puerto Ricans, for the high proportion of
these groups on welfare rolls makes them vulnerable to attack
by conservative political interests. As the Negro continues to
strike at the roots of historic patterns of class and racial dominance, tensions will undoubtedly mount, and further punitive
social-welfare legislation and practices at the local level may
result.

Countries where the Ombudsman has been effective also tend
to have high standards of public service. The success of the
Ombudsman partly depends upon responsible and responsive
government functionaries. America's social-welfare agencies have
slowly been professionalizing, and one might see in these improved standards of personnel training an omen favorable to
an Ombudsman for the poor. There is reason to doubt that
this is so. Professional ideology is rooted in political ideology.
Reflecting the values of their culture, American professional
groups have not argued for the rights of the poor or for the
legitimacy of dependency. Rather they have said that introduc-
ing better-trained personnel into the welfare apparatus will
eliminate moralistic punitive practices and supplant them by
scientific, rehabilitative ones. But whether strategies are puri-
tanical or professional, the poor are still to be lifted from
dependency in spite of themselves. Rehabilitative services should,
of course, be extended to those who can use them, but submit-
ting to such technical services should not be made a condition
for access to economic and other material benefits; and that is
how professionals have always seen it. Public housing, for example, now employs many kinds of professionals. If management
finds the behavior of a tenant objectionable, he may be required
to accept some form of therapy upon pain of eviction. Professionals have thus become new agents in an enveloping fabric of

bureaucratic control of the poor and are, if only unwittingly, part of the problem that needs correcting. When an unwed mother makes application for public housing in New York City for herself and her children, to cite a further example, she is routinely referred to what the Housing Authority calls its "social consultation unit." There professionals employ their higher skills to make a determination of her "suitability"—not her need—for residence in a public project. Thus, the rights of the poor are jeopardized as much by those who find legitimacy for their practices in the sciences as by those who find it in the scriptures.

## CAN THE RIGHTS OF THE POOR BE SECURED?

If the Ombudsman mechanism is not a promising remedy, how then can the rights of the poor be secured? One form of attack upon the social-welfare apparatus should be mounted in the courts. Undue emphasis has been placed upon securing reforms through legislative action, and insufficient attention paid to legal remedies. Two types of legal action are required: one designed to achieve basic changes in the structure of social-welfare law, and the other to insure that laws are faithfully implemented at the administrative level. Crucial precedents are usually more efficiently pursued by organizations which do not offer mass services but specialize in finding test cases. Such organizations can develop specialized legal expertise in a given field and can find the resources to pursue issues doggedly and tenaciously through the labyrinth of appeals, at the end of which a binding precedent may finally be established. We need, in short, an "association for the advancement of social-welfare rights," comparable in purpose and function to the NAACP and the ACLU in their respective fields of interest.

The issues of law that require intensive action are both substantive and procedural. As to the first, no aspect of substantive law in the field of social welfare is so murky as that pertaining to the question of whether various classes of entitlements are matters of legal right or public charity. Ambiguity especially surrounds benefits for the poor; most of the benefits directed toward the regularly employed classes having been less plagued. Here again, "social security" is a case in point. It is virtually unheard-of that recipients require legal assistance in order to obtain this benefit. The clarity with which entitlements are framed and implemented thus reflects the relative political power of the groups which are their object. In the field of public housing, by contrast, ambiguity is striking. Legislation is written in such a way as to deny tenants any of the rights commonly associated with tenancy in private housing. Apartments can be inspected at will by management; leases are month-to-month; eviction can occur without recourse to the courts. Charles Reich, a professor in law, has suggested that social-welfare benefits constitute "new property rights" and should be vigorously pursued in the courts until they are so defined under law.

Ambiguity about "rights" versus "charity" is also reflected in the absence of adequate procedural safeguards. Under the guise of discharging an ethical responsibility to "protect the confidentiality" of information disclosed by clients, welfare departments have resisted the right of clients to be represented by counsel during interviews, investigations and many types of semijudicial proceedings. But perhaps most striking is the fact that it is not clear, with respect to many benefits, whether an aggrieved person has the right to do anything more than complain. Appeals procedures, administrative or otherwise, are not often defined in legislation, and administrators do not usually choose to establish them. If a person has a grievance, it is often not known to whom he should turn or whether he must be heard. Until test cases resolve matters of this kind, rights cannot be effectively asserted.

The second form of attack should be a vigorous campaign of communication. Tyranny is not so likely to take root when men have access to information. The authoritarianism of social-welfare agencies is partly made possible by the pervasive ignorance they engender in their clientele. Where ignorance prevails, myths arise to explain what otherwise seems arbitrary and capricious. It is believed by some on the dole that welfare workers get fifty dollars for each case they can close, for how else is one to understand the hundreds of instances in which recipients are discharged from the rolls for no apparent reason (e.g., "failed to comply with departmental regulations")? Myths serve to order the reality, but they also reinforce ignorance of it. And because recipients do not understand administrative decisions, officials can dismiss complaints out of hand. By converting issues of justice into instances of ignorance, attacks upon the rules are thus deflected and the system remains intact.

One can grant the low education of recipients without supposing that this goes far toward explaining their failure to grasp the workings of the apparatus upon which they depend for survival. Ignorance is a product of the system itself. Our social-welfare state is enormously complex—not because it needs to be, but because it serves our ambivalence toward the poor to make it so. Because, as we have pointed out, statutes are vague and ambiguous as to who can get benefits and strikingly clear as to who cannot, fantastic administrative energy is required to define criteria of eligibility. The resulting proliferation of regulations is incomprehensible even to those who create them. People who need a variety of services (money, housing, health care) must negotiate with an array of autonomous departments, each jealous of its prerogatives, each a complex rules system, each caught up in its own trappings of petty tyranny.

A public department can make itself surveyable to its constituents or can place them under surveillance. Our "social security" agencies assiduously explain themselves, advertising on radio and in newspapers to inform a broad audience of entitlements. They deplore unclaimed benefits and pursue those unschooled in their rights. But the claimants of social security are the once-employed and the propertied; they are, in time, the majority of us, and agencies catering to a majority are not unmindful of its influence. Who advertises for clients for public welfare, for public housing or for any of the "poor agencies"? For every person on the public-welfare rolls, at least one more is eligible but does not apply. Let them find their own way to appropriate agencies and through the maze of procedures that will stand between them and relief. Let them submit without challenge to investigation, for ours is a system obsessed with the fear that benefits will be obtained fraudulently, or by persons of questionable eligibility. No one may certify to his pauperism; it must be proved—repeatedly—and even then the evidence of home visits, interviews, forms and affidavits is not to be trusted. Elaborate patterns of illegal surveillance multiply.

It is not thought that clients require information about the system; rather, the system must know about them.

A massive and aggressive program of public information could go far toward eliminating an ignorance that is both produced by and reinforces these barbaric practices. Such programs are by no means novel or untried. Some three decades ago, Britain's National Council of Social Service, a private organization, established a number of "citizen's advice bureaus" which have been operated with public funds since 1949, and are located in churches, settlements, family agencies, unions and elsewhere, close to those who need them most. The central office generates a constant flow of information to the local bureaus: It summarizes entitlements under new legislation, digests changes in administrative rulings, reports the outcome of appeals on one issue or another and otherwise provides judicious advice and guidance to the users of public services.

American private social-welfare agencies resist making functions of this kind central to their operations. Consonant with America's attitudes toward the poor, private agencies have devoted themselves unceasingly to various forms of moral, cultural and psychiatric uplift. Prior to the Depression, they carried on cash-relief programs, using such funds as could be extracted from the well-to-do. Pressed by heavy demands from their clients, and with relatively little money to disburse, they became experts in making judicious grants, evolving criteria and techniques to distinguish the worthy from the unworthy. They instituted a system of "social-service exchanges" which compiled information on their clientele to insure against the possibility that a few recipients might be pyramiding meager benefits by migrating from agency to agency. When government acted during the depression, many voluntary agencies argued that the new poverty agencies—such as public welfare—should be staffed by experienced social workers who understood how to administer benefits without inducing dependency, that tragic flaw of America's poor.

The mental-hygiene movement also penetrated the field of social work during the depression years, and it was not long before private agencies began to draw from Freudianism their images of man, his needs and his susceptibility to intervention.

And so the private field progressively turned away from environmental assistance and embraced the new personality manipulations. But the economically dispossessed remained stubbornly oblivious to the subtleties of a psychology that stressed man's participation in the creation of his own problems, preferring to believe instead that they were the victims of arbitrary and capricious outer forces beyond human control. With their traditional clientele thus alienated, a good many private agencies announced that they would welcome opportunities to serve people "in need of counseling and guidance, whether financially dependent or not." By the midfifties, many agencies had succeeded in uplifting themselves by attracting a high proportion of middle-class constituents.

Reflecting the culture of which they are instruments, private agencies have thus by and large failed to act as proponents of the rights of the poor. Specializing in "information services" may not lay the best basis from which to assert professional status, but it must be said that the poor need allies against the welfare state a good deal more than they require the therapeutic and other skilled services which are the stuff of professional legitimacy. This is the challenge confronting the private agencies.

Power finally belongs to those who are able to define for others their station in life. If men have been led to believe that they have no rights, being told that they do may matter little, for the belief can overwhelm the telling. In New York State, public-welfare agencies distribute a brochure to every recipient describing, briefly and abstractly, the rights of clients, including the right to take appeals from decisions considered unjust. And the grounds for appeal are abundant.

The third attack, then, must be through the apparatus of appeals. In New York City, which contains more than 500,000 welfare clients, and almost half again as many rejected applicants, how many come to challenge the tens of millions of decisions regarding their various entitlements made in any year? For the whole of the city, in most years, there are about fifteen. Granted that the poor have little education and even less money for legal assistance, this is still unimaginably few.

To what interpretation will such a statistic yield? Only, it would seem, to one showing how the welfare system leads the

poor to participate in their own victimization. Many welfare recipients end by accepting the premises of the system and thus
ascribing legitimacy to its practices. Doubtless, reluctance to appeal also arises from the fear that petty evasions of the rules will
be uncovered during hearings. Nor is this the only instance one
could point to in which men have given allegiance to the rules
by which they are degraded, to the rules which they covertly
violate. The lawless and authoritarian practices of the welfare
apparatus thus produce correlative adaptations among clients. For
when rights are ignored, men come to live by their wits, meeting
caprice with chicanery; or they live witlessly, meeting the arbitrary with acquiescence.

Under such conditions it will take more than information
about rights to make them believable or to lead men to act upon
them. If old patterns of accommodation are to be disrupted,
there must be a demonstration that rights can be successfully
asserted. And that will require advocates willing to pit themselves
against an entrenched system. Where, then, are the poor to find
these advocates?

One answer comes from the Office of Economic Opportunity,
which has been promoting programs of legal services for the
poor. Bar associations have rather vigorously opposed this intrusion by government into their part of the free-enterprise preserve, but that resistance may be overcome, for it is difficult to
find any but the most obviously self-serving arguments to support
it. The plans for "neighborhood law offices" and other legal programs under various auspices are, to be sure, a distinct advance
over the present condition. Until now we have preferred to avoid
the matter by ostentatiously praising the charity and idealism of
those few lawyers in Legal Aid Societies and elsewhere who have
resigned themselves to relative poverty by choosing to serve the
poor. If, through OEO's largess, the number of lawyers entering
the lists against the welfare state can be multiplied five- or tenfold or more, it is certainly all to the good.

The plan to expand legal services, however, has several defects. First, it equates the need for advocacy with the need for
lawyers. But the great bulk of problems that arise in the day-to-
day transactions between recipients and public agencies can be
resolved by persons possessing only a rudimentary knowledge

of the social-welfare establishment, provided that they are willing to be aggressive and tough-minded negotiators. Such pressure is all the more likely to be effective if backstopped by the threat of legal action, should redress not be obtained. The existence of legal power is thus more important than its exercise.

Mobilization for Youth, on New York's Lower East Side, has conducted large-scale advocacy programs through a series of "neighborhood service centers" located in storefronts and staffed by professional social workers and case aides. Lawyers train staff members in the basic laws and rule systems governing public departments. The vast majority of problems brought to the centers are then effectively resolved by these nonlegal advocates, the more difficult cases being referred to MFY's legal unit of five full-time lawyers. With poverty funds, neighborhood service centers patterned after those on the Lower East Side are being established in other cities, although it remains to be seen whether the vigor of advocacy which distinguished MFY's program will be matched elsewhere, for such programs are not popular with the governmental officials who control poverty funds. Aside from this question, the point is that advocacy resources could be greatly expanded if scarce legal resources were conserved for in-service training, appeal procedures, court actions and other matters requiring depth of legal knowledge and experience.

The plan for "neighborhood law offices" also suffers the defect of being an altogether *ad hoc* mechanism. It will thus be dependent for funding on the vagaries of the political process. If the programs generate a great many problems for city government (as they surely will when the job is properly done), pressure may mount to shut off funds. Legal services could also be initiated in stable institutional settings—unions, settlement houses, family-service agencies, inner-city churches. Once again, the question is whether private social agencies will meet the challenge, and the answer is not a hopeful one.

In the end we shall probably require arrangements that do not make access to advocates dependent upon the vagaries of poverty funding or the interests of private organizations. Once again we may need to look to European countries, where legislative measures—such as Britain's Legal Aid and Advice Act of 1949—guarantee the availability of lawyers and provide payment for services for the very poor. Clearly, the country is not yet ready to entertain such measures. But some form of socialized law is necessary if the rights of the poor are finally to be secured.

## NOTES

[1] The British action followed the notorious Crichel Down affair, in which the Ministry of Agriculture and Fisheries tried to rid itself of a particularly irksome farmer by ordering his lands to be confiscated, an action which led to a Question before Parliament.

[2] Donald C. Rowat, *The Ombudsman: Citizen's Defender* (with twenty-nine contributors, including Ombudsmen from thirteen countries), Toronto, Canada: University of Toronto Press, 1965, 361 pp. All quotations, unless otherwise noted, are taken from this volume.

# Whom Does the Advocate Planner Serve? (Part One)

Frances Fox Piven

A new kind of practice, advocacy for the poor, is growing in the professions. The new advocacy has thus far been most vigorous in the legal profession, where the term originates. Traditional legal-defense organizations are bringing test cases that challenge regulations and practices of agencies serving the poor, and new legal agencies offering direct legal services have mushroomed in the slums. Social workers are also stationed in neighborhood storefronts where they act as the advocates of a "walk-in" clientele by badgering public agencies for services. Now planners and architects are offering their services to local groups confronted with neighborhood-development proposals.

To account for this new practice, lawyers would probably trace their inspiration to Jacobus Tenbroeck and Charles Reich, two legal scholars who exposed injustices perpetrated on the poor by agencies of the welfare state. Social workers might see their advocacy as a reaction against a "mental-hygiene movement" which had come to dominate social agencies, orienting practitioners toward a psychiatrically based therapy and a middle-class clientele amenable to such therapy. And planners and architects would probably say that advocacy reflects their growing unease at the devastations visited on the uprooted poor by a decade and a half of urban redevelopment. In other words, each profession sees the emergence of advocacy as the expression of an enlightened professional conscience.

No doubt early volunteer advocates were stirred by the civil-

Reprinted with permission of *Social Policy*, May/June 1970.

rights movement and troubled by the growing concentration of black poverty in the cities. But the efforts of early volunteer advocates were scattershot and ineffective. Nor were their ideas earthshaking. There are always many currents in professional thought.

Now, however, advocacy has become important as a form of professional practice because opportunities for advocate practice have been created by the array of federal programs for the inner city launched during the sixties. Social workers and lawyers were hired by federally funded projects in delinquency, mental health, education and poverty. Now advocate planning also is becoming both feasible and popular with funds provided by the Model Cities program. In our enthusiasm for the idea, we have tended to see professional advocates as free agents because they are independent of local government, and we ignore the federal dollars which support them and the federal interests they serve.

These federal programs were prompted, as was much else that happened in this nation in the last decade, by the massive migration of blacks into cities. However worthy one thinks the social goals attributed to the programs, and whatever their actual social benefits, they also met the political needs of the Democratic administration in adjusting to population changes in the cities. In fact, despite the presumably different social goals, the various programs were remarkably similar. Under the broad umbrella of "community development," each provided a battery of services not unlike those of oldtime political clubs. Each also called for "citizen participation," to be promoted by federal funds under federal guidelines. Whatever the stated goals, these efforts can be understood as a strategy to integrate the new migrants into the political structure of the city by offering them various forms of patronage distributed by local "citizen participants" whom the projects selected and cultivated. To execute the strategy, the projects brought to the ghetto a variety of professionals, many of whom were called "advocates."

There is a minor irony in this, for whatever the variants of the advocacy idea, two elements are essential to it: Professional services must be made available to the poor, and these services should be so structured as to assure that professionals are responsive to the interests of the poor as the poor themselves see them. In other words, it is not so much that professionals have been strangers to the slum; rather, it is that those professionals who work with slum people and slum problems are traditionally under hire by, and therefore responsive to, public and private agencies which represent interests other than those of the poor. There is, of course, a dilemma in the ideal, for if professional services are in the end responsive to whomever finances them, where can the poor find the money to pay their advocates? The dilemma, however, concerns the ideal of advocacy, not the realities of advocate practice on the federal payroll.

To point out that advocacy was promoted by national Democratic political interests is not to deny that the poor have benefited from professional advocacy or, put another way, that the poor have gained from federal efforts to integrate them into local and national politics. Overall, it is difficult to dismiss the results. Social workers who pried loose delayed welfare checks, or harassed housing inspectors into taking action, were in a small way easing oppressive conditions, as were lawyers who prevented an eviction or defended a youngster from police harassment. To argue that these small gains diverted the black poor from making greater demands is to set a dubious possibility against a gain that is real, however limited. Furthermore, small material advances, by raising the expectations of blacks, may actually have spurred them to greater demands. In this sense, the federal strategy for the cities, and especially the poverty program, may have contributed to a growing discontent and turbulence in the ghetto, at least in the short run.

But whatever may be said for the tangible accomplishments of social workers and lawyers stationed in the ghettos, the same cannot be said for planning advocates. Planners offer no concrete service or benefit. Rather, they offer their skill in the planning process. The object, planning advocates would say, is to overcome the vast discrepancy in technical capability between local communities and the city bureaucracy, because it is with the bureaucracy that local groups must contend to protect and improve their neighborhoods.

Implicit in this view is the recognition that planning decisions are decisions about who gets what in the city. That is, to determine what kinds of schools, or hospitals, or housing, or recreational facilities will be built, and where they will be located, is to determine who will benefit from the facilities. And to determine which neighborhoods will be demolished to provide space for new facilities or housing is to determine who will lose out. Planning decisions, in other words, are political decisions.

Implicit in the advocate planner's view also is the notion that the urban poor can influence these decisions once they are given the technical help of a planner—or better still, once they actually learn the technical skills of planning. And this is exactly what many neighborhood groups have been trying to do, sometimes with volunteer planners, more often with the help of eager young professionals hired with Model Cities or poverty-program funds. The results are worth pondering.

One of the earliest and most dedicated of such efforts began in 1959, in a neighborhood called Cooper Square, on the Lower East Side of New York City. Various neighborhood groups had rallied to fight an urban-renewal designation which, familiarly enough, called for demolition of 2150 existing housing units, half of which were renting for under forty dollars a month. They secured the services of Walter Thabit, a dedicated New York planner, who set to work in consultation with neighborhood representatives on an "Alternate Plan for Cooper Square." By 1961 the Alternate Plan was presented to the public with much fanfare, and the chairman of the city's Planning Commission pronounced it commendable. Then, from 1961 until 1963, the Cooper Square Committee and its advocate planner negotiated with city officials. In 1963 the city prepared once more to move on its own renewal plan. Again the neighborhood rallied, with mass meetings of site tenants. The city withdrew, and new conferences were scheduled to discuss the Alternate Plan. In 1966, however, a new mayor announced indefinite postponement. Then, in January 1968, Walter Thabit was asked to prepare a new, smaller plan, and in 1969 new meetings were conducted between city officials and the Cooper Square Committee.

Early in 1970 the Board of Estimate approved "an early action plan." After ten years of arduous effort on the part of an extraordinary neighborhood group, a small portion of the Alternate Plan had been given formal sanction even though that portion was still far from implementation. The chief accomplishment was that the neighborhood had stopped the early threat of renewal. As Walter Thabit said sourly when it was all over, "Protest without planning could have done as much."

Most advocacy efforts are not yet old enough to provide such overwhelming discouragement. But the signs so far are bleak. In one city after another, local groups in Model Cities neighborhoods are involved in the technical dazzlements of planning, some to prepare plans, others to compete with counterplans. But there is little being built in these neighborhoods. Nor are locally prepared plans likely to change the pattern. A plan, of itself, is not force; it is not capable of releasing the necessary federal subsidies or of overcoming the inertia of the city agencies. Quite the contrary, for those people who might otherwise have become a force by the trouble they made are now too busy. As one advocate planner for a Harlem neighborhood that is still without construction funds proudly said, "They are learning how to plan."

What all of this suggests is that involving local groups in elaborate planning procedures is to guide them into a narrowly circumscribed form of political action, and precisely that form for which they are least equipped. What is laid out for the poor when their advocate arrives is a strategy of political participation which, to be effective, requires powerful group support, stable organization, professional staff, and money—precisely those resources which the poor do not have. Technical skill is only one small aspect of the power discrepancy between the poor and the city bureaucracies.

Not only are low-income groups handicapped when politics becomes planning but they are diverted from the types of political action by which the poor are most likely to be effective. For all the talk of their powerlessness, the masses of newly urbanized black poor did prompt some federal action long before advocates came to their aid. The threat of their growing and volatile numbers in the voting booth and in the streets exacted some responses from national and local political leaders: the curtailment of slum clearance; the expansion and liberalization of some existing services, such as public welfare; and the new federal programs for the ghetto. But the planning advocates who came with the new programs have not added to the political force of the ghetto. Quite the contrary, for the advocates are coaxing ghetto leaders off the streets, where they might make trouble. The absorbing and elaborate planning procedures which follow are ineffective in compelling concessions, but may be very effective indeed in dampening any impulse toward disruptive action which has always been the main political recourse of the very poor.

To be sure, a few neighborhood leaders do gain something from these planning activities. The lucky members of the local "planning committee" become involved in overwhelming and prestigious rites and mysteries, which often absorb them even while action for their neighborhood is going forward without them. In effect, those few selected leaders are drawn away from their base in the community into a lengthy educational program, the end product of which, if all goes well, may be a neighborhood plan. Once produced, that plan is easily stalled by the city, negotiated beyond recognition or accepted only to be undermined in implementation. In the meantime, the local "planning process" has diverted and confused, and perhaps divided, the community, and surely has not advanced it toward effective political mobilization.

Although the language is new, this kind of advocacy follows a long tradition of neighborhood councils in the slums, through which local residents were encouraged to "participate" in the elaborate rituals of parliamentary procedure as if that were the path of political influence for the very poor. In the past such participation absorbed slum leadership and rendered it ineffective. That may well be the chief result of current planning advocacy. It deflects conflict by preoccupying newcomers to city politics with procedures that pose little threat to entrenched interests. It is a strategy which thus promotes political stability in the city. But if the force of the poor depends on the threat of instability, planning advocacy does little to promote equity.

### Sumner M. Rosen Comments:

Frances Piven's critique of advocacy planning is consistent with her distrust of politically integrating techniques as co-optative as well as her preference for direct group action as a

*At the time of this debate, Sumner M. Rosen was an economist at the Institute of Public Administration, specializing in problems of manpower and social policy.*

route to political effectiveness. She grudgingly concedes that some efforts—by lawyers, social workers, etc.—have gained limited benefits for individual clients, but nothing more. She ignores the recent extension of legal advocacy to the level of class actions, directly challenging fundamental patterns of injustice and discrimination in the law. This new level of action is the further development of a practice of social intervention which logically began with the individual client and moved beyond the individual to the group or class as experience taught the advocates the necessary political lessons. The advocates' maturity and growing effectiveness are attested to by recent efforts in California to kill the OEO-funded system of legal services to the poor. In short, the Establishment has been hurt, and the judicial system moved, by advocacy.

More important is the question of where, in Piven's scheme of things, substantive issues ought to be discussed and programmatic choices clarified. Health advocacy is fairly new. Its practitioners believe that community-based groups need to know the implications of the choices to be made in the use of resources, as between, for example, new hospital facilities, more ambulatory-care facilities, more group-practice centers, more public-health expenditures, etc. The answers are not self-evident, but each plausible pattern of response, besides exerting important influence on the quality, cost and accessibility of health care, will benefit one group of providers, increase the influence and power of one point of view, advance or retard the achievement of a decent, humane and effective health-care system. Community groups need to participate in these decisions, to understand the stakes and to decide what is in their own best interest. Good advocacy will help them to the necessary understanding.

New York's Health Policy Advisory Center exemplifies this approach. Health-PAC's experience to date indicates that this infusion of expertise is not politically debilitating; on the contrary, by demythologizing the planning process it serves to energize local groups by showing them the direct connection between the planning process and the quality of their own lives. It also connects local insurgency with other levels of decision-making and overall resource allocation. Neither Health-PAC nor ARCH (Architects Renewal Committee for Harlem) was founded with federal funds, nor does Health-PAC receive any today. No one who has followed health-planning controversies in New York City in recent years can seriously question either Health-PAC's independence or its ability to increase the pressure of the community on the political establishment without reducing the level of militance. Sophistication is no enemy of effective political action, provided always that the experts are kept "on tap, not on top."

Piven apparently believes that programs which governments adopt in response to political needs are thereby tarnished and rendered suspect. But any political system survives because those who run it understand and respond to the expression of needs, whether these take organized or disorganized form, whether they are made manifest through normal channels or through the mobilization of people in the street. There is a difference between response and co-optation.

The political task of the insurgent, and the advocate who seeks to serve insurgency, is to preserve the independence and freedom of action of those who are demanding change. The secret of success is not perpetual militance but earning and keeping the support of one's primary constituency. Integrating new groups into the social and political structure is not inherently bad; what matters is the terms on which such integration occurs. Groups that acquire more power, and thus can more effectively serve the needs of their members, gain from the process of political integration. To bring new groups into the "mainstream" does not automatically mean that the older mainstream elements will control, dominate or manipulate them. Good advocacy will help people to move with maximum effectiveness and minimum loss of freedom of action, option or ally. An alternative plan may, in the short run, move leaders off the streets, as Piven says (does she want them always there?); the real issue is what they bring with them when they return to the streets.

To learn the methods by which the established planning forces use technique and "objectivity" as smoke screens is important in the struggle to move the issue to the political plane, where—as Piven correctly says—it belongs. But how will the militants bring their constituents to wage an effective long-run struggle unless they can show what the stakes are, who and where the real allies and opponents are, what steps are involved in an effective struggle? And how will they go outside the base of their own direct support, when it is too narrow to win un-aided, to get the allies they need over the long haul, unless the decisions at issue are politically linked to the interests and welfare of those who may not appear to be directly involved?

Uninstructed militance can be self-defeating. At the 1969 Health Forum, Piven's and my own favorite example of orga-nized militance, the National Welfare Rights Organization, seized the microphone at the closing session to demand that every welfare family be provided *access to a family doctor!* At this level of sophistication, the Establishment need have no fears. Such slogans leave wholly untouched all of the basic problems of the American health system, particularly its domination by the organized free-standing practitioners. In this as in many other cases, a little advocacy would have gone a long way.

### Frances Fox Piven Replies:

I am puzzled by Sumner Rosen's response. He fails to deal with the main issue I raised: Do the poor benefit from planning advocacy?

Let me first clear away a few of Rosen's assertions which an-swer points I did not make. Since I regard political integration as inevitable, I do not worry whether to be for it or against it. I also regard integration as necessarily co-optative, as I un-derstand the meaning of that word. The questions I addressed follow from my assumption that the process of integration is natural to government: First, what kind of force will precipitate governmental efforts to integrate the poor, and do planning ad-vocates escalate or curb that force? Second, what are the terms of integration—that is, do the poor get anything from the pro-cess—and do planning advocates help them get more?

Rosen does not discuss planning advocacy (except to assert, incorrectly, that ARCH did not receive federal funds). Instead he discusses legal advocates, whom I also commented upon favorably, though with a less sweeping enthusiasm. The poor got those legal advocates through OEO, a government program launched in response to the increasing volatility of urban blacks at the ballot box and in the streets. In other words, it was the turbulence of the poor, not their sophistication about legal in-

equities, that produced the legal gains—the integrative concessions—that Rosen and I agree upon. It is precisely because such
concessions make some difference in the life conditions of the
poor that I am for "direct group action as a route to political
effectiveness."

As for Health-PAC, it is a group I admire. It generates a
steady stream of information and critical analysis of health systems, and sometimes manages to draw some public attention to
health issues. But that said, why is Health-PAC being raised up
as an example to defend advocate planners?

Health-PAC's kind of radical analysis of public programs is
all to the good (and writing analyses is usually all we can think
to do). But that is not to say that information and analysis will
turn the world around; it is not the correctness of the slogans
which makes the Establishment tremble. When the National
Welfare Rights Organization seizes the mike, their militancy
over health issues may be more important than whether they
demand "More Ambulatory Care Facilities" or "A Family Doctor for Every Welfare Family." The slogan will not determine
government's health-care responses any more than NWRO's
"demands" for a $5500 guaranteed income determined govern-
ment's welfare responses. It was not NWRO's "demands" which
led to rising welfare expenditures and proposals for welfare reform. But trouble in the cities did, and the turmoil NWRO
created in welfare centers compounded that trouble.

No one would quarrel with Rosen's ideal that "community
groups need to participate in these decisions, to understand the
stakes and to decide what is in their own best interest." But
ideals aside, the reality is that the poor get responses from government mainly through disruption, and the question to ask
about any radical analysis we contribute is whether it stimulates
action or mutes it. If instead of agitating in welfare centers
NWRO groups had devoted the last few years to studying guaranteed-income plans to decide "their own best interest," they
still would not have gotten a guaranteed income, or the welfare
dollars they did get.

But it is into such intellectual exercises that advocate planners are leading community groups who are aroused by bad
housing or the threat of redevelopment, and the planners generally lack even the virtue of a radical outlook. Study and analy-

sis, of course, are only the first step, a step to be followed by endless meetings and lengthy negotiations with innumerable bureaucrats. Years later, there may be a plan, but, as sad experience shows, one that will probably never be implemented. Meanwhile, no housing is built and no mass-transit facilities are added, and with leaders absorbed in bureaucratic minuets there may be no force left in the community to press for them. That is my argument, and Sumner Rosen did not answer it.

# Whom Does the Advocate Planner Serve? (Part Two)
## Additional Commentaries

### But Which Advocate Planner?

SHERRY R. ARNSTEIN

Frances Piven argues that advocacy planning is a disservice to the poor because it diverts them from street protests. It negates the need for political mobilization of the ghetto, she says, and therefore the poor people's plans can easily be ignored, circumvented or rejected by the powerholders.

I share her jaundiced view of *this model* of advocacy planning, which was conceived and originally promoted by well-meaning, socially oriented city planners and architects. I do not share her view of other, more recent models that have emerged as a result of significant input from ghetto leaders and social planners.

Under the original formulation of advocacy, the planners could indeed be playing into the hands of politicians by "coaxing ghetto leaders off the streets." Under the more recent and multidisciplinary models, political mobilization of the poor is viewed as a *sine qua non* for successful negotiation of the ghetto-developed plan.

With the broader conceptualizations of advocacy, communities are obtaining technical assistance from teams of specialists, including social planners, physical planners, lawyers and com-

*At the time of this debate, Sherry R. Arnstein was a planner and an Associate of OSTI, a national research-and-consulting firm.*

Reprinted with permission of *Social Policy*, July/August 1970.

munity organizers, or from one or more generalists with a mix of such technical skills.

These technicians are hired by a community group to work on a three-pronged approach to community development. Simultaneously they help the group (1) to become increasingly more representative and accountable to the neighborhood, (2) to conceptualize what programmatic approaches will benefit the community and to define which trade-offs can be supported at the negotiating stage, and (3) to design the political strategies needed to achieve the group's priorities.

The newer model views the planning process *per se* as only one prong. To teach the have-nots to become physical and/or social planners is not an objective of this process. Rather, the model aims at aiding the poor to reach increased levels of sophistication about what makes the city system (and subsystems) tick, to learn who and where the powerholders are and which levers to press to effect action, and to incorporate such sophistication into concrete programmatic approaches.

In short, the community group develops the capability to design political socioeconomic plans that effectively dent the status quo instead of unwittingly supporting palliative approaches which actually maintain it. In this way the planning process becomes a tactic by which the poor can anticipate the traditional Mickey Mouse games that debase them and prepare a sufficient store of chips to play the game and come out ahead.

Such an advocacy-planning model does not preclude street strategies. On the contrary, it incorporates them into a community group's spectrum of possible actions and reactions to be drawn upon when appropriate. It recognizes that the issue is not whether the poor need sticks or pencils to achieve social equity. The fact is that they need both: sticks to gain and hold the attention of the powerholders, and pencils to articulate their priorities and aspirations.

## *Advocacy Planning Polarizes the Issues*

PAUL AND LINDA DAVIDOFF

Advocacy in planning consists in developing and presenting plans that advance the interests of a particular group or
class, rather than that of "the public interest" or the "general
good," however defined. We have argued that all planning is
advocate planning, whether it recognizes itself as such or not;
and we feel that the growing movement for advocacy planning
on behalf of the poor is a step forward in broadening the process of planning to include formerly unrepresented groups. To
the extent that planning is carried on, it should be carried on
in behalf of the poor as well as of the rich.

Writing from the perspective of an ideological advocate planner, Frances Piven contributes the worthwhile warning that participation in the planning process may deflect potentially more
important or more effective political activity. Piven's view of
political activity for the poor and nonwhite seems, however, to
lack a sense of the process by which low-income and nonwhite
communities reach decisions about appropriate courses of group
action.

Assuming that we agree that it is sound practice for those
seeking social change to plan the acts required to produce the
desired objectives, then planners are required. The planners may
exclude, include, or be limited to professional planners. If the
planners for minority groups are middle-class white professionals, like Piven and ourselves, then manipulation of the clients
by those professionals and imposition of the professionals' ideas
upon the clients will always be a potential danger.

Neither of these outcomes need raise problems if we accept
the elitist notion that the professional knows best about what
the client should do. If we reject the elitist notion of social
change, as we do, then a planning process prior to action calls
for participation by the group for whose benefit the action is
planned, and poor people and blacks must therefore be "plan-

*At the time of this debate, Paul and Linda Davidoff were Director and Research
Associate, respectively, of Suburban Action, a nonprofit institute for community
research and action, located in White Plains, New York.*

ners"; that is, they must have some set of concepts to guide them in making decisions about developing their political power.

In another sense, too, the poor must be planners and must have the assistance of planners. Piven stresses the importance of street demonstrations and "making trouble" as appropriate forms of political expression for the poor. But what are the demonstrations about? A demonstration is an exercise in creating public pressure (power) to implement a series of demands for change in a situation which the demonstrators find intolerable. The formulation and presentation of these demands— as well as the massing of force to support them—are at the heart of mass action for social change. This is where advocacy can be of assistance: to help people draw up their demands on a given part of the power structure. The welfare-rights movement, in which Piven has played a key role, provides many examples of the close relationship between the development of demands (rescind certain welfare-budget cutbacks, drop work requirements, provide a decent guaranteed minimum income) and the creation of mass demonstrations to back up these demands.

Bringing poor people into the process of preparing and presenting demands is not, as Piven unfortunately seems to imply, involving them in something that is beyond their intellectual capacity. It is part of building a movement whose leaders are capable both of seeing what is wrong with their society and of organizing to do something to change it.

The difficulty Piven perceives—the waste of the limited resources of the poor and nonwhite on the nonproductive procedures of plan development—should not really be directed against advocacy. It would be far closer to the mark to attack such programs as Model Cities, which create elaborate procedural requirements for citizen participation in plan preparation, but which have never received enough money in appropriations to permit execution of plans created under these requirements. So long as Congress fails to provide the needed funds, Model Cities' failure to bring about significant social change will not be caused by the action or inaction of advocate planners.

Piven sees the process of creating an Alternate Plan for Cooper Square as a waste of energy. What she fails to consider is that the members of the Cooper Square Committee, as a result of their ten-year battle, gained considerable political maturity and sophistication in the ways of New York City politics. Piven asserts that protest was successful in halting the original bulldozer plan and, therefore, that the Alternate Plan was unnecessary. This is too glib. It is possible that citizen protest without the benefit of advocate planning could stop the threat of the neighborhood's destruction; but what program of affirmative action for decent housing would have taken its place?

The Thabit Alternate Plan has played an important role in the Cooper Square area and in other areas of the nation. It signifies an approach to city rebuilding based on resource allocation to classes of the population having the greatest economic need, as opposed to perpetuation of traditional renewal policies favoring the rich at the expense of the poor and the nonwhite.

Still another ground for holding Piven's thesis incorrect is that she has narrowly defined advocacy planning as wholly client-oriented. In a number of situations, a clientless advocacy has developed. We are now engaged in such an advocacy-planning program dedicated to changing public policy about urban development so as to take account of the tremendous land and employment opportunities available in the suburbs. In this activity, we have no client but work with the support of foundations.

Frances Piven has herself been an active clientless advocate planner. Along with Richard Cloward, she has presented plans for the way the poor and the nonwhite should act in order to get a fair share of the nation's resources.

Clientless advocacy, ideological advocacy, radical advocacy may work to assist the poor and the black, or they may fail. But the key point is that the professional planner engaged in advocacy tends to polarize issues about urban-development policies. He thus moves planning decisions from nonpolitical into political forums, where power of many varieties may be exercised and where the power of the poor to promote greater equity may operate along lines that Piven herself may find effective.

## The Advocate Planner: From "Hired Gun" to Political Partisan

CHESTER W. HARTMAN

Frances Piven has some incisive and valid things to say about social policy, emphasizing the underlying politics of the nascent advocacy-planning movement and the critical test of who gets what. It seems to me, however, that she is describing only one kind of advocacy planning and that her observations ought to be considered not as a put-down of advocacy planners generally but as a corrective, at a time when the movement is still in its formative stage, to what clearly can be reactionary results from their work.

Certainly, if "plans" are the end product of the work of advocacy planners, low-income communities will benefit little and the "planning process" can divert real energies for social change. Seen merely as an attempt to firm up the negotiating position of the poor, advocacy planning may serve only to stabilize the system and emasculate any real movement for change.

Advocacy planning for the poor, if it is to have any real meaning, must be planning for power, planning for political and social change. It must serve to organize the community, help the community perceive and understand the workings of the system by which it is oppressed, and direct political energies toward the realization of long-range, as well as tangible short-range, goals. And these goals must be substantive—a larger share of the pie, different kinds and sizes of pies, the acquisition of real political power. My four years of experience working with Urban Planning Aid (at this point, probably the largest advocacy-planning group in the country) lead me to a somewhat different set of conclusions from that of Piven about the potentials and problems of this kind of work.

*At the time of this debate, Chester W. Hartman was an assistant professor of city planning at Harvard University and served on the board of directors of Urban Planning Aid, Inc. In refusing to renew his contract for the year following this debate, Harvard alleged that his "method of teaching conveys a sense of political strategy more than the substance of city planning." His teaching also often led to opposition to the university's policies and expansion in the community.*

In the first place, I have seen numerous instances where the presence of advocacy-planning assistance itself served as a critical catalyst to community organization. The Cooper Square area of New York, which contains a fairly high proportion of middle- and lower-middle-class families and is fairly sophisticated politically, is not typical of the areas in which we have done our work. In really low-income areas with a rather low level of political organization, the very existence of one's own "hired guns" can serve as an important catalyst. The fact that someone is taking notice of the community's problems, that the neighborhood has its own professionals to counter the establishment's professionals, frequently dispels the prevailing hopelessness, and the advocate professionals become the node around which local organization begins to build.

The critical point of any advocacy work is the building of political organization: where the local group, once organized, moves around the advocacy effort, or (in the Cooper Square type of situation) what a group does with an organization that is already formed. Here the advocate planner can play a very useful role, but there exists at present considerable ambivalence among advocate planners themselves about what their role should be. The "pure" model stresses the "hired gun" notion: we are here to do the community's bidding, to see that it gets what it wants. Since the communities that need advocates are usually those which the present system most neglects, and since advocate planners tend to be concerned with issues of social justice, a rough "fit" does prevail. Advocate planners have been terribly concerned not to be or appear manipulative, not to impose their values and political goals on the community. Because of the inherent similarity between the goals of advocate planners and advocate plannees, overt conflict rarely occurs. When it does (e.g., the case of a low-income white community which wants to use planning tools to prevent entry of nonwhites), the planners can always withdraw on principled grounds. However, many of us are beginning to reject the "hired gun" model, although it has taken a good deal of experience, similar to that which Piven describes in Cooper Square, to lead us to a new concept of our role.

That new role is one in which politics and organization are primary. Advocate planners should have a clear political analysis of the way the system works as a whole and the way in which individual elements of the system relevant to their field operate: the housing market, urban renewal, the highway program, etc. If it is accepted that advocate planners can and should have a political analysis that infuses and guides their work, the real question becomes how to make this operational. It is foolish to think that most low-income communities are going to share the same wavelength, and nothing could be more destructive than to apply rigid political tests as a precondition for working in a given community. The process would seem to be one in which the advocacy group deals with the immediate issues that threaten and oppress the community and, in the process of working around these issues, develops an understanding of and organization around a deeper analysis of the nature of the community's problems and the kinds of solutions that are called for.

To give a concrete example. The advocate planner is asked by a tenants' organization to assist in exposing the inadequacies of a much-heralded, large-scale rehabilitation program. Good professional staff work by architects, engineers, lawyers and accountants produces irrefutable documentation of shoddy workmanship, high profits, excessive rents, failure of supervision by FHA and local officials, inadequate relocation assistance and a host of other defects.

Such a report can lead to different conclusions and levels of analysis. It can be used to create a scandal, a horror story of corruption, and can lead to immediate patching up of the poor results of this one project. Or it can be used to educate the community and the public about the workings of the system; that the system of profit-motivated developers, surrounded by government aids but few government controls, without any meaningful participation of the community itself in this rebuilding process, will inevitably lead to the results described. If the advocate planner's understanding of the situation leads him to analyze the system as a whole, it is his responsibility to frame his findings in broader systematic terms and to attempt to persuade the community that this analysis is correct. The action implications are, of course, quite different, depending on the analysis.

That analysis should also lead to a consistent program of

action which can provide guidance as to whether the planning group works with certain communities or not. For example, the group convinced of the destructive impact of the interstate-highway program and its failure to meet metropolitan transportation needs is working with a community threatened by the program in an effort to stop construction of a new highway. Clearly, it should not work at the same time with a community group which wants assistance in changing to a depressed route a planned elevated segment of the highway. It may be possible to persuade the second community to join the fight against the overall construction program, but both the analysis underlying the work of the planning group and the need to build strong community organization dictate a consistent policy.

With regard to the second critical issue of community political organization, the style of advocacy planning which Piven so rightly criticizes is that of professional-speaking-to-professional. The community goes through all the standard procedures and attempts to persuade the powers-that-be of the superiority of its plan, using all the accepted tools and terminology. It would seem clear from both our sets of experiences that unless the community develops political muscle which can cover the entire spectrum, from sophisticated conventional organizations to disruption and rebellion, there is no certainty that its plans will be implemented. The process of developing a plan of action must be a process of political organizing. It may be that the rehabilitation report described above could produce some improvements without concomitant political organization among the tenants, because of the outrageous nature of the case and the clear documentation provided by the investigation. But the improvements would be minimal and short-lived in the absence of underlying organization. If that entire system is to be changed into one which is controlled by the community to insure maximum economic benefits from the millions of dollars expended on the project, to produce low rents and a high quality of work and to create a system by which the community controls its own housing stock, such change can come about only through political action.

Above all, the advocate planner should employ his professional skills as a node around which political organizing can take place. His job is to persuade those for whom he works that the necessary course of political action derives from a radical analysis of the reasons why the system has not produced adequate.

## Rejoinder: Disruption Is Still the Decisive Way

FRANCES FOX PIVEN

If anyone who plans for social change is a "planner," as Paul and Linda Davidoff argue, then, of course, we are all planners, albeit with little effect. And if to be an advocate is simply to be *for* something, then we are all advocate planners, also with little effect. Having named everyone "advocate planner," however, we still have to decide just what we can do specifically that might get something for the poor.

Our role, the Davidoffs say, is to aid the poor in drawing up their demands. The difficulty is that people with very limited power do not name their own terms in political dealings. At times of mass disturbance, such as we witnessed in the cities during the 1960s, the poor may be able to exert pressure, because street protests, riots or erratic voting behavior threaten civic order and political stability. To restore order, government agencies and business leaders may grant concessions. But just what will be conceded is determined by what it takes to quiet the disturbances, and not by any list of demands to be presented and negotiated by the "leaders" (or planners) who come forward at the critical times.

To be sure, the leaders will get something. They will be invited into negotiating sessions, honored with a bit of recognition and patronage—enough to make them eschew future disturbances for fear of losing their new position and payroll. The poverty agencies are populated with former activists whose militancy now seems confined to squabbling over the division of funds.

Can we, as Chester Hartman and Sherry Arnstein say, overcome this historical pattern of disturbance and limited concessions by adopting a model of the advocate as a political tutor of the poor? Such a planner should, Arnstein says, educate the poor, enable them to "learn who and where the powerholders are and which levers to press to effect action, and to incorporate

such sophistication into concrete programmatic approaches."
Hartman adds that the planner should "persuade those for
whom he works that the necessary course of political action
derives from a radical analysis of the reasons that the system has
not produced adequately."

The advocate, in other words, will no longer teach the community how to plan; now he will teach the poor how to use
the political process, presumably so they will have influence.
But regular political processes do not work for the poor. If they
did, the poor would no longer be poor.

Just what political routes will the planner lay out for the
poor community? Will he educate them in the use of their vote?
Or teach them to lobby? Or to negotiate with bureaucrats? For
radicals, if such we are, we make a curious, if tacit, assumption:
that if only the poor learned how and *tried,* they could exert
substantial influence by conventional means—by lobbying, voting, planning, or whatever—as groups elsewhere in the society
do. It is only a matter of *educating* them as to the paths of
influence. But the poor are a small minority in the voting booth,
and in any case most policy decisions are not made in the voting booth; they are scarcely equipped to contend with the powerful interests that regularly lobby in legislative halls and
bureaucratic offices; and that is why their plans can be ignored
or washed out with delay or absurd tokenism.

Radicals also place great value on organization. If only the
poor organized, then they would be able to press those power
levers. And advocates can provide the expertise and education
to help the organizing process along.

It should be clear by now that educational efforts do not
build organizations, among the poor or anyone else. The poor
remain unorganized, not for lack of information or exhortation
but because there is little to be gained by their joining together.
When businessmen or professionals get together, their aggregate
resources—economic, social and political—make their organization influential, so it can obtain the governmental concessions
which make continued membership worthwhile. The poor have
no resources to aggregate, so whatever groups they may form
are too weak to produce the payoffs that attract and hold members. Without a poverty program or Model Cities program to
provide incentives, stable organizations of the poor do not form

—which is only to say that, like other groups in the society, the poor participate when it is worth their while.

Nor will educational efforts by advocate planners, or black militants, or whoever, keep the small organizations that do come into being on a radical course. Doctrine goes only so far. Organizations, whether of welfare mothers or city planners, have to worry over the payroll and the rent, and, rhetoric aside, whoever meets the payroll calls the tune—and over time fixes the agenda and the priorities.

In a way, such debates as this are idle. Whatever the models we put forward describing what advocate planners should or should not do, there is a more substantial reality than that which we create with our exhortations. Hartman, Arnstein, and the Davidoffs all agree in criticizing the advocate planning done under the federal urban programs, especially Model Cities. They have something very different in mind. But Model Cities, and not what we have in mind, is the reality.

The irony is that the poor get the payroll and the rent money for their organizations, in the first place, not because they have community organizations, but through mass disturbances. Mass disturbances sometimes produce more important concessions as well: a $10-billion welfare budget, for example. That is not much, perhaps, but it is more than the poor have gotten until now, and it is much more than they are likely to get again soon, especially if they rely on their new community groups and professional advocates, and on the paths of conventional organization and influence.

# PART TWO

Mobilizing the Poor:
How It Can
Be Done

Black protest in the 1960s welled up over grievances in many and disparate areas, such as civil rights, housing, employment, education and public welfare. And the protests took irregular forms, such as marches and demonstrations, sit-ins and mob-ins, traffic tie-ups and rent strikes.

Many erstwhile sympathizers with the grievances of the black and the poor found these forms of political action disconcerting, to say the least. Established liberals began to worry publically that such obstreperous and flamboyant tactics would antagonize those well-meaning people who could otherwise be induced to support efforts at reform. Poor people, these sympathetic critics argued, surely had justifiable grievances, but they ought to act on them as all good citizens do—by pressing for redress in a reasoned way, through regular bureaucratic and political channels.

If liberal sympathizers were disconcerted by unrest among the black poor, younger activists were excited by it. To them, unrest signaled new opportunities for building political organizations. Disciplined organization, they believed, would be far more effective in securing fundamental reforms than the relatively inchoate disturbances (such as riots) then beginning to spread in the ghettos. The credo of the time among organizers of the poor was simple to state and not very different from the credo of earlier American radicals: The poor had to be enlisted into stable mass-based organizations, thus yielding them the capacity to exert influence through conventional channels of the political system.

Both the liberal critics and the radical activists were, we thought, making an astonishingly similar assumption. Both believed that the political system was open, accessible, permeable:

Any group that wanted to exert influence could exert influence, if it organized. It was an extremely doubtful assumption.

In an article written in 1963 entitled "Low-Income People and the Political Process" we made our first effort to refute these arguments. Poor people, we said, were without the resources to use regular political channels effectively; they had neither money, nor status, nor any of the attributes generally considered resources for influence, and a variety of studies of the community power structure tended to confirm our view. Poor people were also without large-scale organizations to represent their interests. The lack of resources that made them politically ineffectual as individuals also made whatever organizations they formed ineffectual—unable to win concessions. And organizations which cannot win concessions cannot win many members. We concluded that the disruptive protests then taking place were in fact the only political option available to the black and the poor.

But spontaneous protests provided little guidance for organizers and activists. How should they relate themselves to mass unrest? If low-income people could not use regular political strategies, then what kinds of political strategies could be used to force concessions from the society, and why would they be effective? A new theory of political action seemed to be required. The theory had to begin with the recognition that the political system was closed to those at the bottom, and that reliance on regular political participation, through regular political channels, was therefore self-defeating. Second, the theory had to identify methods for mobilizing political action by the poor that did not depend on the vain hope of developing sustained mass participation in a formal organizational framework.

In subsequent articles we spelled out a series of disruptive political strategies available to the poor. Civic lessons aside, other groups use disruptive strategies regularly and effectively, as when workers strike, or producers threaten shortages. A group engages in disruption when it withdraws or threatens to withdraw its contribution to the functioning of an organization or an institution. Poor people, of course, are not particularly important as workers or producers. Their chief contribution to most institutions is their acquiescence to institutional norms, and that is what they could withdraw; they could defy the rules governing their behavior on which major institutions depend. The slum-housing system, for example, depends on poor people acquiescing to property norms; massive defiance of the injunction to pay the rent would bankrupt that system. The relief system depends on poor people acquiescing to the norm defining the dole as shameful; massive defiance of the prohibition against going on relief would cause chaos in relief offices and would bankrupt localities.

Such institutional disruptions would, in turn, have widespread political repercussions, activating significant electoral groups—some hostile, some sympathetic, but all aroused. And, while a small and impotent poor peoples' lobby can be ignored with impunity by political leaders, institutional breakdowns which arouse large and variegated segments of the electorate cannot be ignored. To avoid the worsening polarization of electoral groups and to restore a degree of institutional stability, political leaders would either have to promulgate concessions or institute repressive measures. This capacity to create political crises through disrupting institutions is, we thought, the chief resource for political influence possessed by the poor. For organizers, then, the critical questions should be: How can mass unrest be mobilized into major institutional disruptions? And what are the electoral conditions under which concessions, rather than repression, can be expected?

An initial effort to apply this theory was set out in 1966 in an article entitled "A Strategy To End Poverty." What we proposed was a plan to mobilize a disruptive assault on the public-welfare system by overloading the rolls, and we predicted the likely consequences of such an assault. Tens of thousands of reprints of this article were subsequently requested by activists across the country, and the plan was widely debated. One of those debates is recorded in "Strategy of Crisis: A Dialogue." The participants included George A. Wiley* who went on to form and lead the National Welfare Rights Organization.

Once formed, the welfare-rights movement burgeoned, a phenomenon we described one year later in "Birth of a Movement." Women and children on the Aid to Families with Dependent Children (AFDC) rolls were the first to be orga-

---

* George A. Wiley died tragically in a boating accident on August 8, 1973.

nized. Because we thought the movement would be better able to resist repression if it enlisted working-class support, we proposed in 1968 that low-paid male workers be organized to obtain wage supplements from welfare departments under "home relief" or "general assistance" categories. This particular strategy, outlined in "Workers and Welfare: The Poor Against Themselves," was never implemented, mainly because the leaders of the welfare-rights groups across the country had come by this time to be preoccupied with problems of organizational maintenance.

We made two other efforts to apply the evolving theory of disruption. In "Rent Strike: Disrupting the Slum System," we examined the failure of the 1963–64 efforts in New York City to build a stable citywide tenant organization through a rent strike. We explained how a disruptive rent strike might have been mobilized instead, and why electoral conditions were then favorable for securing slum-housing reforms by disruptive tactics. Finally, we reanalyzed the history of the southern phase of the civil-rights movement, which led to the major reforms contained in the Civil Rights Act of 1964 and the Voting Rights Act of 1965. The movement succeeded, we thought, precisely because it had not tried to develop mass-based permanent organizations among the southern black poor, but had rather mobilized a succession of confrontations, defying and disrupting historic caste arrangements and creating extreme polarization within the national Democratic party. That polarization, in turn, ultimately made political concessions to the movement necessary in order to rebuild the Democratic coalition. Our analysis of these events is contained in "Dissensus Politics." We hoped these articles would stimulate a reexamination of the lore of organizing.

# Low-Income People and the Political Process

FRANCES FOX PIVEN

In recent months, as protests by low-income blacks have escalated, a certain brand of righteous criticism has also escalated that claims to sympathize with the grievances of the poor, but not with their disruptive tactics. What poor blacks ought to do, according to this critique, is to seek redress like proper Americans, informing themselves about the institutional practices which are the source of their grievances, negotiating with institutional managers for change and backing up these negotiations with informed and disciplined pressure at the polls. In sum, the critique assumes that the resources required to engage in regular modes of political influence are freely available to all people—to the poor as well as to the rich, to blacks as well as to whites. We think this argument wrong. The disruptive tactics being used by blacks today are in fact their only resource for political influence. The analysis which follows is intended to show why.

## THE DISTRIBUTION OF POLITICAL RESOURCES

We mean by "political power" the ability to control actions of the body politic (i.e., actions of the community expressed through its political institutions). We mean by "political resources" the attributes by which individuals or groups gain power, or exert

Prepared for a training program sponsored by the community organization staff at Mobilization for Youth, 1963. Not previously published.

influence, in these community actions. Such attributes may pertain to individuals or to organizations, and may reside in objective conditions of political action or in subjective states of the political actors.

Considered abstractly, apart from any given political system, political resources include anything that can be used by the political actor to induce others in the collectivity to make choices in a preferred direction: the offering or withdrawal of material goods, social prestige, normative authority, knowledge, personal persuasiveness or coercive force.[1] And, considered abstractly, apart from any given political system, the entrepreneurial use of any of these attributes tends naturally to a pyramiding of resources. We take for granted that people can increase their wealth by employing it. Similarly, prestige, knowledge, authority or persuasiveness can often be capitalized upon to bring more of these or other assets, which in turn constitute resources for additional influence. One would expect, therefore, that just as the rich get richer, so do the powerful become more powerful, and, of course, so can the rich become more powerful.

However, the institutionalized arrangements by which political activity is carried on modify the use and effectiveness of various resources and in addition generate resources distinctive to political institutions. Thus, democratic political institutions are marked by electoral arrangements for succession to positions of collective authority, and by the wide and equal distribution of the vote as a resource for controlling the use of that authority. In democratic principle the vote permits each and every citizen to exercise his due influence on decisions of the collectivity, either through direct referendum or by selecting the officials who make decisions. Each and every citizen is also, however, subject to a variety of inducements in the use of his vote. The full range of resources by which men and women can sway each other in their choices are therefore also political resources, tempering the egalitarian distribution of the vote.

To illustrate we need only point to some structural features of a formally democratic polity. The authority to make given kinds of decisions for the collectivity is fixed in designated positions in government. Since the occupants of these positions are—more and less directly—subject to removal by the electorate, they are influenced in their decisions by the preferences, expressed or anticipated, of electoral groups. These officials are, however, also subject to influence by other groups on grounds which make other resources effective.

First, resources for influence are in a general way interchangeable. Electorate control of officials depends on the singular effectiveness of the inducement of continued political power, but officials, as men, are obviously subject to other inducements. (Only when these are clearly inappropriate to official roles do we speak of corruption.) And even insofar as they seek power, officials depend on the votes of men and women who can, in turn, be influenced by a variety of inducements, whether honorific, symbolic or material. Accordingly, political leaders will always be on the lookout for ways to increase their stockpile of such voter inducements, and will respond to opportunities to trade in influence with those who have the wealth, social standing or popular appeal out of which to cull voter inducements.

Second, authority in government is fragmented, and often not even commensurate with policy responsibility. Officials often require certain cooperative acts from each other, and from non-governmental groups, in order to effectuate any policy. One of the primary resources for an official's influence is the decisions within his formal jurisdiction. Reciprocal bargaining and accommodation with special groups, with the substance of public-policy decisions as the means of influence, therefore characterize official decision-making. Finally, the inevitable voter apathy on many issues, and the ambiguity of voter preferences, will result in slackened control, permitting officials to respond to those who offer nonelectoral inducements without suffering losses in voter support.

Political influence can be viewed, therefore, in terms of analytically distinct systems resting on different resources. The formal system, dependent on the vote, tends toward an egalitarian distribution of influence. It is only one aspect, however, of the total system of influence in which a range of unequally distributed social and economic resources are effective. This abstracted and simplified analysis suggests that political influence will tend to distribute along lines consistent with the general distribution of resources in a society. Can electoral arrangements offset this tendency for the accumulation of political power? This question has guided a considerable body of empirical investigation by sociologists and political scientists.

## STUDIES OF COMMUNITY POWER STRUCTURE

How does the pattern of influence actually develop in American communities? Who really rules? Two major schools of thought have emerged among the students of community power structure, the one generally labeled "stratificationist," the other "pluralist."

The stratification theorists are primarily sociologists, and most of their work was done between 1929 and 1956. According to their view, local communities are characterized by a closed monolithic structure of political power, joined with and derived from the structure of social and economic power in the community. This view of power concentrated at the apex was depicted most vividly in Hunter's study of Atlanta and the Lynds' studies of Middletown. It was elaborated by Warner's studies of Yankee City, Hollingshead's study of Elmstown, and Baltzell's of Philadelphia, and was crowned by C. Wright Mills's sweeping depiction of a national power structure in *The Power Elite.*[2]

More recent studies by political scientists have reached a rather different conclusion, notably Robert Dahl's study of New Haven, Banfield's study of Chicago, and the Sayre and Kaufman study of New York City.[3] Political power in local communities is depicted as relatively dispersed. Not only are a range of actors said to affect any policy decision, but different actors predominate in different policy areas, employing different resources in the process. An urban-renewal decision may arouse builders and the residents designated for dislocation, a school-site decision may arouse competing parents' groups, or a highway decision may arouse construction unions and the homeowners in the path of demolition. Each of these groups may have different channels to influence, whether personal contacts with officials, party affiliations or access to the media. And each may be influential through different inducements: the votes they represent, the publicity they threaten or the legitimation they confer. Power is thus said to be dispersed, for it is based on a great variety of resources, widely distributed through a community. The uncertain and entrepreneurial process through which effective influence is organized under these circumstances is said to make for a relatively open political system. The conclusion, qualified to be sure, is that those who *want* to influence generally *can* influence.

However, the question of who does not participate in political decisions, and why they do not, is not frontally addressed. This is partly attributable to the principle methodology the pluralists employ (and which Polsby justifies as the only methodology for the study of power that conforms to the strictures of empirical science). The method is to focus on selected contests or issues, to identify the contestants and the means of influence they employ, and then to observe who prevails. Those who win have influence. Whatever the usefulness of this method in generating knowledge of the relative influence of identified contestants in a given issue, it falls far short of yielding knowledge of community power structure, in several ways. Most to the point for our analysis, this method can tell us nothing directly about the influence, actual or potential, of those groups who do not become involved in the selected contests. The pluralists tend to be satisfied, however, that nonparticipants are those who are not interested in the issue.

Limited information regarding nonparticipants may inhere in the methodology that the pluralists insist upon, but their sometimes breezy dismissal of this matter is made possible by an implicit conceptual assumption about the nature of Political Man—a concept somewhat analogous to the rationalistic Economic Man of laissez-faire theorists. The political actor, whether an individual or an organized group, is treated virtually as Man-in-Space, uninfluenced by a social environment, and discrepancies between what he does and what he is able to do, between his actual and potential influence, tend to be regarded only as qualifications which follow in a less than perfect world.

But surely such an assumption is untenable, reviewed in the light of even the most elementary knowledge of social stratification. It is obvious that some groups in a community are without material resources to offer as political inducements to decision-makers. Some groups are separated by social location from the possibility of exercising personal influence on decision-makers. And some groups suffer educational disadvantages so that they have less knowledge of political issues and are less expert at political strategy. It is equally obvious that these political deficits are not randomly distributed. Those who are without material resources are also those who are without personal access to decision-makers or other resources for influence. Finally, *those who are without power feel and think themselves to be powerless and act accordingly.*

Dahl's study of New Haven, arguing essentially the pluralist perspective, nevertheless presented evidence showing that participation increases with income, with social standing and with formal education. Participation was greater among professional, business and white-collar occupations than among working-class occupations, and greater in better residential areas than in poorer areas.[4] Dahl takes pains to point out that since there are so many more "worse-off" citizens, their aggregate participation is still considerable—a circumstance which does not quite satisfy democratic norms, however. Further evidence on the relationship between effective influence and social class can be drawn from the forms which participation took among the "worse-off." They were most active in the footwork of campaigning—a kind of participation which is not usually recompensed with public-policy concessions. On the other hand, the "worse-off" appeared least frequently in the classification showing the highest index of local activity, the group that also might be expected to be politically most effective.

It does not seem reasonable, therefore, to ascribe the low level of participation among the poor to lack of political interest or lack of political will. It is more likely due to a lack of political power. The syndrome among the poor that some call apathy is not simply a state of resignation; it is a definite pattern of motivated inaction impelled by objective circumstances. People who know they cannot win do not often try.

In short, while sociologists and political scientists differ regarding the structure of power in American communities, their disagreement is actually about the question of how influence is distributed within the middle and upper levels of the social order. The pluralists may have succeeded in casting some doubt on simple conceptions of a monolithic community power structure, but the evidence that they present demonstrates at most the lateral dispersion of influence among the upper and middle classes. Whether or not such lateral dispersion exists, it argues nothing about the power of the lower class. If our analysis so far suggests that the poor have few resources for regular political influence, the weight of empirical evidence surely does not dispute it.

## THE ROLE OF ORGANIZATIONS
## IN THE POLITICAL PROCESS

Our discussion so far has been conducted in terms of a quaint, but not very useful, artifice. We have examined the capacity of low-income people for regular political influence by discussing the attributes of individuals and groups. But the political process does not consist primarily in the relations between disparate individuals and official decision-makers.

Large, rationalized organizations have come to dominate both governmental and private spheres, each development reinforcing the other. And for a whole range of issues that are not precipitated into public prominence so as to become significant electoral issues, the political dialogue is carried on between organizations. A planning commission deals with organizations or realtors and homeowners; a board of education with teachers' unions and parents' associations; a department of commerce with chambers of commerce. Similarly, on the federal level, regulatory agencies negotiate with the industries they regulate; the Department of Labor negotiates with unions; and the Department of Health, Education and Welfare with professional and scientific societies and philanthropic federations.

Large organizations bring to the political process a superior capability for influence; they have the resources to engage in regular surveillance of the processes of government and to initiate issues.[5] Where individuals are aroused to political action only at periodic elections or through the occasional congruence of awareness and interest, rationalized organizations are able to maintain a steady watch on the political process and to maintain the resources for regular participation and influence. Large organizations are capable of rationalizing and capitalizing the use of resources for influence, both among their participants and over time, thus developing capabilities commensurate with a complex and bureaucratic society and a complex and bureaucratic government. They can keep abreast of the maze of actual and proposed legislation and procedures, decipher their implications and exploit many informal and formal occasions for negotiation and bargaining. They have the ability to generate public issues through regular organizational liaisons and to gain access to the media and political parties. In addition they can offer public institutions the support and technical capability of their own organizations, permitting them to become regular contributors to governmental action and thus extending both the occasions and the means of influence.

Lower-class people have not developed large-scale formal organizations to advance their interests. The reasons are not mysterious. To be poor means to command none of the resources ordinarily considered requisites for organization: money, organizational skill and professional expertise, and personal relations with officials.[6] The instability of lower-class life[7] and the character of lower-class beliefs also discourage the poor from organizational participation.

But of far greater importance, most organizations are generated by the functions they perform in the economic structure, functions having to do with the protection and enhancement of either profits, property or occupational roles. Engagement in the economic structure makes interaction and association—whether through a labor union, a merchants' association or a professional society—profitable or potentially profitable. Most of the poor, being more or less out of economic structures, are not in a position either to create such organizations or to profit from them. It is thus not simply that the poor do not have the necessary attributes for participation in organizations; more to the point, they are not located in economic institutions which facilitate interaction and organization, nor would they have much to gain from participation in organizations not linked to the economic structure.

One of the chief historical examples of low-income organization is the industrial union. Unions developed by exploiting features distinctive to the factory structure in order to secure adherents and to force in their name certain institutional accommodations, first in private spheres and then through the electoral process during the New Deal. It is our view that this organizational form is not available to the contemporary poor.

One feature that made union organization possible and enabled leaders to sustain it was the structural context of the factory itself. Men and women were already assembled and regularly related to each other. The factory was thus a framework for organizing activity which directly paralleled the scope of common grievances and potential benefits for which men and women were being induced to join together. Moreover, once the union was established in the factory, the shared and structured work setting considerably lessened the task of sustaining the organization. The union could bring to bear group sanctions on the worksite to insure participation by workers (and subsequently the legal sanction of the union and closed shops), and dues could be collected through the factory payroll department. Because union organizational structure paralleled factory structure, it could utilize the formal and informal processes of the functioning factory to its own advantage. As a consequence, only limited participation by workers was actually required in the union itself. The union could be sustained without intensive investment in organizing activity which characterized the early days of the industrial union movement and the initial organization of each factory. Thus, not only was the initial assertion of union power possible because men and women were already engaged together in a common structure and could, therefore, be organized, but the initial task of organizing did not have to be repeated for successive assertions of power to be made. The union was able to regularize its organization on the basis of limited contributions from participants, and it was able to do this by relying on the developed structure of the factory system itself.

By contrast, today's poor are relatively dispersed, without patterns of regular interaction. Without such interaction, a sense of common group problems and common group interests is much less likely to develop, especially among a mobile and culturally heterogeneous poor. And even when such shared perspectives do emerge, they are not likely to result in regular participation. Factory workers were first drawn together by the factory; it is a moot question whether organizers could have done it by themselves. Today's poor have to be drawn together by sheer organizer

grit, and the group can be sustained only by enormous investments of organizing effort.

Another feature of the factory situation that made organization
possible was that union membership paid off in material benefits.
The unions developed in the context of profitable enterprises.
Workers were essential to these enterprises; their labor was therefore a source of potential leverage with owners and managers. If
organized, workers could bring the factory to a halt, and press
for improvements in wages and working conditions which management was in a position to grant. It was the expectation of
material incentives that led men and women to join the union,
and the continued ability of the union to produce these incentives that led workers to stay in the union.

The contemporary poor, however, are not located in positions
that can yield economic incentives. They do not fill roles essential to profitable enterprises. If they work at all, it is in marginal
jobs, often for employers who are themselves marginal. They
therefore would have little leverage to force economic concessions,
even if they were organized.

Recent efforts to organize a rent strike in New York City illustrate the difficulties of creating and sustaining an organization
when a structural context promoting regular interaction is lacking and when there are few concrete gains to be made. The rent
strike was initiated by activists, many of whom were drawn from
or inspired by the civil-rights movement. They attempted to
develop organizations among people who, although living together in the same physical locale, were not otherwise engaged
in much regular interaction. On the face of it, the rent strike
seemed to offer a compelling strategy: It singled out the landlord as a clear-cut and inciting target of action; it took place in
the ideological glow of the civil-rights movement; and it promised
concrete improvements in housing conditions. Nor was there a
great deal of risk in rent strikes. In New York, tenants could not
be legally evicted if they followed the procedures in which the
organizers instructed them.

An enormous organizing task was required, however, to compensate for the absence of an existing substructure of interaction
among the tenants. Nor, as it turned out, were housing improvements easy to achieve, for slumlords operating on narrow profit
margins used every legal and illegal evasion to avoid investments

in repair, and if all else failed, simply deserted their buildings. In spite of considerable public sympathy for the rent strikers, the movement was soon exhausted. It was exhausted by the unceasing and overwhelming efforts required to organize in the absence of any existing substructure, and in the absence of economic incentives.

It is difficult to identify an actual or latent structure of interaction which might be exploited to organize today's poor. Many of the poor are unemployed, or employed in irregular jobs in small and marginal enterprises. They will not, therefore, be heirs to the unions which secured both economic benefits and political influence for some of the poor of an earlier era. Lacking substantial economic incentives and an institutional context of interaction, the vague promise of benefits from organized political action will probably not be sufficient to overcome historic barriers to group cohesion within America's lower class: race and ethnic tensions, geographical mobility (increased by renewal and dislocation in our cities), the actuality and ideals of occupational mobility, a style of elite rule that is conciliatory and encased in democratic ritual, and, surely not least important, hopelessness—hopelessness based on the realities of power, for poor people do not stand to gain very much from the frail organizations they form.

## THE ELECTORAL PROCESS

What emerges so far in this review of the distribution of political resources is the conclusion that whatever capacity low-income people may have to influence public policy through regular political processes must rest singularly on the formal mechanism of the vote. Votes must be organized in large and disciplined blocs around policy issues for effective influence. To what extent, then, have the voting resources of low-income groups been organized successfully for this purpose?

Historically, the chief example of low-income electoral organization has been the political machine. The machine was characterized by the use—or misuse—of public power by political leaders to provide private rewards, which in turn served to elicit the votes by which public power was gained and retained. Workers on the machine payroll lent the immigrant poor a sympathetic ear, helped them out when they were in trouble with the police, provided occasional jobs and services—and registered them to vote for machine candidates. Given the deprivations of the immigrant slum, such private rewards were extremely effective in organizing votes. Since these votes were traded for private rewards, however, and *not for the substance of public policy*, the impact of the "river wards" on policy was small. The poor got something, to be sure, but what they got also vitiated their potential for political influence, ensuring they would not get more. Machine leaders grew rich on the public treasury, and so did the business interests to whom they gave away the city's franchises and contracts. Meanwhile, low-income constituents made their primary mark on public life through the rise of ethnic representatives to government positions.

The nature of the political machine is, however, now largely an academic question; its decline has been widely remarked upon and generally applauded. But the decline was hardly a gain for low-income people. The machine's exploitation of the public domain for private ends strained the interests of the growing middle class and "respectable" business groups in the city, while satisfying, if in private terms, low-income groups. Battles for "reform" generally revealed lower-class wards on the side of the machine, in opposition to more prosperous segments of the community. Over time, reform won out.

The urban political parties which are the successor to the machines rely on a variety of methods to organize voters. The important characteristic of the party in this context is that it strives to maintain the coalition of diverse interests and groups whose support is required for the accession to power. The parties strive, therefore, to select issues for public airing that will permit them to maintain the broadest possible coalition of supporters.[8]

Public-policy issues that reflect low-income interests, however, tend to be divisive. They are divisive partly because the contemporary poor are isolated and marked off as deviant by a predominantly middle-class political culture. Such issues are also divisive because they are thought to be compensatory in character, taking from some groups in the community and giving to

others. The parties will therefore tend to avoid issues which reflect the interests of the poor, preferring to deal in policies that
can be interpreted as being to the mutual benefit of a wide array
of groups. The votes of the poor are no longer bought with private rewards, and they are not solicited with public rewards
either.

## DISRUPTION AS POLITICAL INFLUENCE

The chief point that emerges from this analysis is that low-income
people have no regular resources for influencing public policy.
It is obvious that they are without power as individuals. Nor are
they significant participants in the large formal organizations that
keep watch on government, bringing to bear the leverage made
possible by organizational stability, staff and money. Nor did the
machine, nor its remnants that survive in some of our larger
cities, nor the political parties, provide an effective vehicle for
low-income political influence.

What political options then exist? When discontent about public policy from time to time arises among the poor, new resources and channels must be created—an imperative that
inevitably leads to aggressive and deviant action, if it leads to
any action at all. This is illustrated by recent developments in
the civil-rights movement, and particularly by the tactics of the
younger and brasher leaders who draw some support from low-
income groups. The ideological appeals through which these
leaders attract followers reflect many of the precepts attributed
to the lower-class view of the society: The emphasis is on the
"power structure," and the use of pressure to move the power structure; the motives of those in power are impugned; problems which
in other circles are said to be complicated are said to be very
simple; and an almost total irreverence is shown for professional
and bureaucratic concerns. The strategies of these leaders also
reflect the limited resources of their lower-class following. They
rely on demonstrations, on calling out large numbers of people.
Not only does their influence as leaders depend on the support
of large numbers of people, but the unstable character of this
support is such that it must be made visible—it cannot merely

be represented to the power structure as a roster of organizational memberships.

These tactics of demagoguery and demonstration are not without precedent—particularly in the street politics of black ghettos —and politicians have occasionally risen to power by their use. The careers of such politicians as Adam Clayton Powell reveal, however, the strains between the tactics of "the street" and the requirements of regular political stratum in which they come to participate.

Even more striking and revealing than street-style politics is the use of tactics of disruption. Some "extremist" leaders have gone beyond rallies and denouncements of the power structure and have begun mobilizing militant boycotts, sit-ins, traffic tie-ups and rent strikes. The effectiveness of these tactics does not depend only on dramatic presentations. They are intended to command attention and to win concessions by the actual trouble they cause in the ongoing operations of major institutions—by interfering with the daily business of city agencies or with the movement of traffic or the profits of businessmen. Such disruptions cause commotion among bureaucrats, excitement in the media, dismay among influential segments of the community and strain for political leaders.

When people sit in, or refuse to pay the rent, they are breaking the rules. This means that effective disruption depends on the ability of leaders to induce people to violate norms of conduct that are ordinarily deeply ingrained. Somehow the normal pieties, and the normal mechanisms of social control that enforce these pieties, must be overcome. Moreover, to break the rules ordinarily involves some danger; people must be induced to run the risk of provoking coercive and repressive forces.

All of which is to say that it is probably only at certain times in history that the legitimacy of regular political processes is so questioned that people can be mobilized to engage in disruption, for to do so is to violate the implicit "social contract" of major institutions and often to violate the explicit social contract of the law as well. That people are sometimes led to this, and to run the risks involved, only signifies the paucity of alternatives. If our analysis is correct, disruptive and irregular tactics are the only resource, short of violence, available to low-income groups seeking to influence public policy.

## NOTES

[1] See Robert A. Dahl, *Who Governs? Democracy and Power in an American City*, p. 226, for another "common sense" listing. (New Haven, 1961.)

[2] See Floyd Hunter, *Community Power Structure*, Chapel Hill, University of North Carolina Press, 1953; Robert S. Lynd and Helen M. Lynd, *Middletown*, New York, Harcourt Brace, 1929; Robert S. Lynd and Helen M. Lynd, *Middletown in Transition*, New York, Harcourt Brace, 1937; W. Lloyd Warner et al., *Yankee City Series*, 1–5, New Haven, Yale University Press, 1941, 1942, 1945, 1947, 1959; August B. Hollingshead, *Elmtown's Youth*, New York, Wiley, 1949; E. Digby Baltzell, *Philadelphia Gentlemen*, Glencoe, Free Press, 1958; C. Wright Mills, *The Power Elite*, New York, Oxford University Press, 1956.

[3] Dahl, *op. cit.*, Edward Banfield, *Political Influence*, Glencoe, Free Press, 1962; Wallace L. Sayre and Herbert Kaufman, *Governing New York City*, New York, Russell Sage Foundation, 1960. The controversy has also generated a considerable body of critical literature. Two of the best are by Nelson Polsby and Peter H. Rossi. Polsby presents an examination of the logic and method of the stratification theorists. His main argument speaks to the impossibility of summoning empirical evidence to bear on the main propositions of stratification theory. If stratification theorists are global in their purview, however, and depend upon processes which are not accessible to research, it is also true that the pluralist approach of studying the participants and outcomes of selected contests produces knowledge far short of describing community power as such. Rossi makes the case for more extensive comparative studies in order to identify some of the bases for differences in conclusions. (See Nelson W. Polsby, *Community Power and Political Theory*, Yale University Press, 1963, and Peter Rossi, "Community Decision-Making," *Administrative Science Quarterly*, March 1957).

[4] Dahl, *op. cit.*, pp. 284–301.

[5] Edward Banfield, in a study based on Chicago, concluded that civic controversies "are not generated by the efforts of politicians to win votes, by differences of ideology, or group interest, or by the behind-the-scene efforts of a power elite. They arise, instead, because of the maintenance and enhancement needs of large formal organizations" (*op. cit.*, p. 263).

[6] For a discussion of the requirements for organizational influence in city affairs, see Wallace L. Sayre and Herbert Kaufman, *op. cit.*, pp.

481–515. Sayre and Kaufman identify the following means by which nongovernmental groups influence public officials in the resolution of issues: appearances at public hearings; informal consultations; personal relations with group leaders and officials; the provision of advice and services of expert character; conducting studies or making reports; influencing party nominations or invoking party intervention (largely through the inducement of donations and publicity, or by means of personal relations with party leaders); arousing public opinion, mostly through the mass media (and therefore available primarily to the newspapers themselves or to groups with professional staff); and recourse to the courts.

[7] Instability in occupational and family life has frequently been the criteria used to distinguish the lower class or the poor from the working class. See, for example, S. M. Miller, "The American Lower Classes: A Typological Approach," in *Mental Health of the Poor: New Treatment Approaches for Low-Income People,* edited by Frank Reissman, Jerome Cohen and Arthur Pearl, Free Press, 1964, pp. 139–154; also S. M. Miller and Frank Reissman, "The Working-Class Subculture: A New View," *Social Problems,* IX (Summer, 1961), pp. 86–97.

[8] Party organizations are also able to a degree to neutralize policy interests by converting public power to private rewards. They do this far less effectively or extensively than the machine, however, and so must take account of policy interests in holding together voter coalitions.

# A Strategy to End Poverty

RICHARD A. CLOWARD AND
FRANCES FOX PIVEN

How can the poor be organized to press for relief from poverty? How can a broad-based movement be developed and the current disarray of activist forces be halted? These questions confront, and confound, activists today. It is our purpose to advance a strategy which affords the basis for a convergence of civil-rights organizations, militant antipoverty groups and the poor. If this strategy were implemented, a political crisis would result that could lead to legislation for a guaranteed annual income and thus an end to poverty.

The strategy is based on the fact that a vast discrepancy exists between the benefits to which people are entitled under public-welfare programs and the sums which they actually receive. This gulf is not recognized in a society that is wholly and self-righteously oriented toward getting people *off* the welfare rolls. It is widely known, for example, that nearly 8 million persons (half of them white) now subsist on welfare, but it is not generally known that for every person on the rolls at least one more probably meets existing criteria of eligibility but is not obtaining assistance.

The discrepancy is not an accident stemming from bureaucratic inefficiency; rather, it is an integral feature of the welfare system which, if challenged, would precipitate a profound financial and political crisis. The force for that challenge, and the strategy we propose, is a massive drive to recruit the poor *onto* the welfare rolls.

Originally published in the *Nation*, May 2, 1966. Copyright by the authors.

The distribution of public assistance has been a local and state responsibility, and that accounts in large part for the abysmal character of welfare practices. Despite the growing involvement of federal agencies in supervisory and reimbursement arrangements, state and local-community forces are still decisive. The poor are most visible and proximate in the local community; antagonism toward them (and toward the agencies which are implicated with them) has always, therefore, been more intense locally than at the federal level. In recent years, local communities have increasingly felt class and ethnic friction generated by competition for neighborhoods, schools, jobs and political power. Public-welfare systems are under the constant stress of conflict and opposition, made only sharper by the rising costs to localities of public aid. And, to accommodate this pressure, welfare practice everywhere has become more restrictive than welfare statute; much of the time it verges on lawlessness. Thus, public-welfare systems try to keep their budgets down and their rolls low by failing to inform people of the rights available to them; by intimidating and shaming them to the degree that they are reluctant either to apply or to press claims; and by arbitrarily denying benefits to those who are eligible.

A series of welfare drives in large cities would, we believe, impel action on a new federal program to distribute income, eliminating the present public-welfare system and alleviating the abject poverty which it perpetrates. Widespread campaigns to register the eligible poor for welfare aid, and to help existing recipients obtain their full benefits, would produce bureaucratic disruption in welfare agencies and fiscal disruption in local and state governments. These disruptions would generate severe political strains and deepen existing divisions among elements in the big-city Democratic coalition: The remaining white middle class, the white working-class ethnic groups and the growing minority poor. To avoid a further weakening of that historic coalition, a national Democratic administration would be constrained to advance a federal solution to poverty that would override local welfare failures, local class and racial conflicts and local revenue dilemmas. By the internal disruption of local bureaucratic practices, by the furor over public-welfare poverty and by the collapse of current financing arrangements, powerful forces can be generated for major economic reforms at the national level.

The ultimate objective of this strategy—to wipe out poverty by establishing a guaranteed annual income—will be questioned by some. Because the ideal of individual social and economic mobility has deep roots, even activists seem reluctant to call for national programs to eliminate poverty by the outright redistribution of income. Instead, programs are demanded to enable people to become economically competitive. But such programs are of no use to millions of today's poor. For example, one-third of the 35 million poor Americans are in families headed by females; these heads of family cannot be aided appreciably by job retraining, higher minimum wages, accelerated rates of economic growth, or employment in public-works projects. Nor can the 5 million aged who are poor, nor those whose poverty results from the ill health of the wage earner. Programs to enhance individual mobility will chiefly benefit the very young, if not the as yet unborn. Individual mobility is no answer to the question of how to abolish the massive problem of poverty now.

It has never been the full answer. If many people in the past have found their way up from poverty by the path of individual mobility, many others have taken a different route. Organized labor stands out as a major example. Although many American workers never yielded their dreams of individual achievement, they accepted and practiced the principle that each can benefit only as the status of workers as a whole is elevated. They bargained for collective mobility, not for individual mobility; to promote their fortunes in the aggregate, not to promote the prospects of one worker over another. And if each finally found himself in the same relative economic relationship to his fellows as when he began, it was nevertheless clear that all were infinitely better off. That fact has sustained the labor movement in the face of a counterpull from the ideal of individual achievement.

But many of the contemporary poor will not rise from poverty by organizing to bargain collectively. They either are not in the labor force or are in such marginal and dispersed occupations (e.g., domestic servants) that it is extremely difficult to organize them. Compared with other groups, then, many of today's poor cannot secure a redistribution of income by organizing within the institution of private enterprise. A federal program of income redistribution has become necessary to elevate the poor en masse from poverty.

Several ways have been proposed for redistributing income through the federal government. It is not our purpose here to assess the relative merits of these plans, which are still undergoing debate and clarification. Whatever mechanism is eventually adopted, however, it must include certain features if it is not merely to perpetuate in a new guise the present evils of the public-welfare system.

First, adequate levels of income must be assured. (Public-welfare levels are astonishingly low; indeed, states typically define a "minimum" standard of living and then grant only a percentage of it, so that families are held well below what the government itself officially defines as the poverty level.) Furthermore, income should be distributed without requiring that recipients first divest themselves of their assets, as public wefare now does, thereby pauperizing families as a condition of sustenance.

Second, the right to income must be guaranteed, or the oppression of the welfare poor will not be eliminated. Because benefits are conditional under the present public-welfare system, submission to arbitrary governmental power is regularly made the price of sustenance. People have been coerced into attending literacy classes or participating in medical or vocational rehabilitation regimes, on pain of having their benefits terminated. Men are forced into labor on virtually any terms lest they forfeit their welfare aid. One can prize literacy, health and work, while still vigorously opposing the right of government to compel compliance with these values.

Conditional benefits thus result in violations of civil liberties throughout the nation, and in a pervasive oppression of the poor. And these violations are not less real because the impulse leading to them is altruistic and the agency is professional. If new systems of income distribution continue to permit the professional bureaucracies to choose when to give and when to withhold financial relief, the poor will once again be surrendered to an arrangement in which their rights are diminished in the name of overcoming their vices. Those who lead an attack on the welfare system must therefore be alert to the pitfalls of inadequate but placating reforms which give the appearance of victory to what is in truth defeat.

How much economic force can be mobilized by this strategy? This question is not easy to answer because few studies have been conducted of people who are *not* receiving public assistance even though they may be eligible. For the purposes of this presentation, a few facts about New York City may be suggestive. Since practices elsewhere are generally acknowledged to be even more restrictive, the estimates of unused benefits which follow probably yield a conservative estimate of the potential force of the strategy set forth in this article.

*Basic assistance for food and rent:* The most striking characteristic of public-welfare practice is that a great many people who appear to be eligible for assistance are not on the welfare rolls. The average monthly total of New York City residents receiving assistance in 1959 was 325,771, but according to the 1960 census, 716,000 persons (unrelated or in families) appeared to be subsisting on incomes at or below the prevailing welfare-eligibility levels (e.g., $2070 for a family of four). In that same year, 539,000 people subsisted on incomes *less than 80 percent* of the welfare minimums, and 200,000 lived alone or in families on incomes reported to be *less than half* of eligibility levels. Thus it appears for every person on welfare in 1959, at least one more was eligible.

The results of two surveys of selected areas in Manhattan support the contention that many people subsist on incomes below welfare-eligibility levels. One of these, conducted by Greenleigh Associates in 1964 in an urban-renewal area on New York's Upper West Side, found nine percent of those *not* on the rolls were in such acute need that they appeared to qualify for *emergency* assistance. The study showed, further, that a substantial number of families that were not in a "critical" condition would probably have qualified for supplemental assistance.

The other survey, conducted in 1961 by Mobilization for Youth, had similar findings. The area from which its sample was drawn, 67 square blocks on the Lower East Side, is a poor one, but by no means the poorest in New York City. Yet 13 percent of the total sample who were not on the welfare rolls reported incomes falling below the prevailing welfare schedules for food and rent.

There is no reason to suppose that the discrepancy between those eligible for and those receiving assistance has narrowed much in the past few years. The welfare rolls have gone up, to be sure, but so have eligibility levels. Since the economic circumstances of impoverished groups in New York have not improved appreciably in the past few years, each such rise increases the number of people who are potentially eligible for some degree of assistance.

Even if one allows for the possibility that family-income figures are grossly underestimated by the census, the financial implications of the proposed strategy are still very great. In 1965 the monthly average of persons receiving cash assistance in New York was 490,000 as a total cost of $440 million; the rolls have now risen above 500,000, so that costs will exceed $500 million in 1966. An increase in the rolls of a mere 20 percent would cost an already overburdened municipality some $100 million.

*Special grants:* Public-assistance recipients in New York are also entitled to receive "nonrecurring" grants for clothing, household equipment and furniture—including washing machines, refrigerators, beds and bedding, tables and chairs. It hardly needs to be noted that most impoverished families have grossly inadequate clothing and household furnishings. The Greenleigh study, for example, found that 52 percent of the families on public assistance lacked anything approaching adequate furniture. This condition results because almost nothing is spent on special grants in New York. In October 1965, a typical month, the Department of Welfare spent only $2.50 per recipient for heavy clothing and $130 for household furnishings. Taken together, grants of this kind amounted in 1965 to a mere $40 per person, or a total of $20 million for the entire year. Considering the real needs of families, the successful demand for full entitlements could multiply these expenditures tenfold or more—and that would involve the disbursement of many millions of dollars indeed.

One must be cautious in making generalizations about the prospects for this strategy in any jurisdiction unless the structure of welfare practices has been examined in some detail. We can, however, cite other studies conducted in other places to show that New York practices are not atypical. In Detroit, for example, Greenleigh Associates studied a large sample of households in a low-income district in 1965. Twenty percent were already receiving assistance, but 35 percent more were judged to need it. Although the authors made no strict determination of the eligibility of these families under the laws of Michigan, they believed that "larger numbers of persons were eligible than receiving." A good many of these families did not know that public assistance was available; others thought they would be deemed ineligible; not a few were ashamed or afraid to ask.

Similar deprivations have been shown in nationwide studies. In 1963 the federal government carried out a survey based on a national sample of 5500 families whose benefits under Aid to Dependent Children had been terminated. Thirty-four percent of these cases were *officially in need of income at the point of closing:* This was true of 30 percent of the white and 44 percent of the Negro cases. The chief basis for termination given in local department records was "other reasons" (i.e., other than improvement in financial condition, which would make dependence on welfare unnecessary). Upon closer examination, these "other reasons" turned out to be "unsuitable home" (i.e., the presence of illegitimate children), "failure to comply with departmental regulations" or "refusal to take legal action against a putative father." (Negroes were especially singled out for punitive action on the ground that children were not being maintained in "suitable homes.") The amounts of money that people are deprived of by these injustices are very great.

In order to generate a crisis, the poor must obtain benefits which they have forfeited. Until now, they have been inhibited from asserting claims by self-protective devices within the welfare system: its capacity to limit information, to intimidate applicants, to demoralize recipients and arbitrarily to deny lawful claims.

Ignorance of welfare rights can be attacked through a massive educational campaign. Brochures describing benefits in simple, clear language, and urging people to seek their full entitlements, should be distributed door to door in tenements and public housing projects, and deposited in stores, schools, churches and civic centers. Advertisements should be placed in newspapers; spot announcements should be made on radio. Leaders of social, religious, fraternal and political groups in the slums should also be enlisted to recruit the eligible to the rolls. The fact that the campaign is intended to inform people of their legal rights under a government program, that it is a civic-education drive, will lend it legitimacy.

But information alone will not suffice. Organizers will have to become advocates in order to deal effectively with improper rejections and terminations. The advocate's task is to appraise the circumstances of each case, to argue its merits before welfare, to threaten legal action if satisfaction is not given. In some cases it will be necessary to contest decisions by requesting a "fair hearing" before the appropriate state supervisory agency; it may occasionally be necessary to sue for redress in the courts. Hearings and court actions will require lawyers, many of whom, in cities like New York, can be recruited on a voluntary basis, especially under the banner of a movement to end poverty by a strategy of asserting legal rights. However, most cases will not require an expert knowledge of law, but only of welfare regulations; the rules can be learned by laymen, including welfare recipients themselves (who can help to man "information and advocacy" centers). To aid workers in these centers, handbooks should be prepared describing welfare rights and the tactics to employ in claiming them.

Advocacy must be supplemented by organized demonstrations to create a climate of militancy that will overcome the invidious and immobilizing attitudes which many potential recipients hold toward being "on welfare." In such a climate, many more poor people are likely to become their own advocates and will not need to rely on aid from organizers.

As the crisis develops, it will be important to use the mass media to inform the broader liberal community about the inefficiencies and injustices of welfare. For example, the system will not be able to process many new applicants because of cumbersome and often unconstitutional investigatory procedures (which cost 20¢ for every dollar disbursed). As delays mount, so should the public demand that a simplified affidavit supplant these procedures, so that the poor may certify to their condition. If the system reacts by making the proof of eligibility more difficult, the demand should be made that the Department of Health, Education and Welfare dispatch "eligibility registrars" to enforce federal statutes governing local programs. And throughout the crisis the mass media should be used to advance arguments for a new federal income-distribution program.[1]

Although new resources in organizers and funds would have to be developed to mount this campaign, a variety of conventional agencies in the large cities could also be drawn upon for help. The idea of "welfare rights" has begun to attract attention in many liberal circles. A number of organizations, partly under

the aegis of the "war against poverty," are developing information and advocacy services for low-income people [see "Poverty,
Injustice and the Welfare State" by Richard A. Cloward and
Richard M. Elman, the *Nation,* issues of February 28 and March
7]. It is not likely that these organizations will directly participate
in the present strategy, for obvious political reasons. But whether
they participate or not, they constitute a growing network of
resources to which people can be referred for help in establishing
and maintaining entitlements. In the final analysis, it does not
matter who helps people to get on the rolls or to get additional
entitlements, so long as the job is done.

Since this plan deals with problems of great immediacy in the
lives of the poor, it should motivate some of them to involve
themselves in regular organizational activities. Welfare recipients,
chiefly ADC mothers, are already forming federations, committees
and councils in cities across the nation; in Boston, New York,
Newark, Cleveland, Chicago, Detroit and Los Angeles, to mention
a few. Such groups typically focus on obtaining full entitlements
for existing recipients rather than on recruiting new recipients,
they do not yet comprise a national movement. But their very
existence attests to a growing readiness among ghetto residents
to act against public welfare.

To generate an expressly political movement, cadres of aggressive organizers would have to come from the civil-rights movement and the churches, from militant low-income organizations
like those formed by the Industrial Areas Foundation (that is, by
Saul Alinsky) and from other groups on the Left. These activists
should be quick to see the difference between programs to redress
individual grievances and a large-scale social-action campaign
for national policy reform.

Movements that depend on involving masses of poor people
have generally failed in America. Why would the proposed
strategy to engage the poor succeed?

First, this plan promises immediate economic benefits. This
is a point of some importance because, whereas America's poor
have not been moved in any number by radical political ideologies, they have sometimes been moved by their economic interests.
Since radical movements in America have rarely been able to
provide visible economic incentives, they have usually failed to
secure mass participation of any kind. The conservative "busi-

ness unionism" of organized labor is explained by this fact, for
membership enlarged only as unionism paid off in material benefits. Union leaders have understood that their strength derives
almost entirely from their capacity to provide economic rewards
to members. Although leaders have increasingly acted in political
spheres, their influence has been directed chiefly to matters of
governmental policy affecting the well-being of organized workers. The same point is made by the experience of rent strikes in
northern cities. Their organizers were often motivated by radical
ideologies, but tenants have been attracted by the promise that
housing improvements would quickly be made if they withheld
their rent.

Second, for this strategy to succeed, one need not ask more of
most of the poor than that they claim lawful benefits. Thus the
plan has the extraordinary capability of yielding mass influence
*without* mass participation, at least as the term "participation" is
ordinarily understood. Mass influence in this case stems from
the consumption of benefits and does not require that large
groups of people be involved in regular organizational roles.
Moreover, this kind of mass influence is cumulative because benefits are continuous. Once eligibility for basic food and rent grants
is established, the drain on local resources persists indefinitely.
Other movements have failed precisely because they could not
produce continuous and cumulative influence. In the northern
rent strikes, for example, tenant participation depended largely
on immediate grievances; as soon as landlords made the most
minimal repairs, participation fell away and with it the impact
of the movement. Efforts to revive tenant participation by organizing demonstrations around broader housing issues (e.g., the
expansion of public housing) did not succeed because the incentives were not immediate.

Third, the prospects for mass influence are enhanced because
this plan provides a practical basis for coalition between poor
whites and poor Negroes. Advocates of low-income movements
have not been able to suggest how poor whites and poor Negroes
can be united in an expressly lower-class movement. Despite
pleas of some Negro leaders for joint action on programs requiring integration, poor whites have steadfastly resisted making
common cause with poor Negroes. By contrast, the benefits of
the present plan are as great for whites as for Negroes. In the big

cities, at least, it does not seem likely that poor whites, whatever their prejudices against either Negroes or public welfare, will refuse to participate when Negroes aggressively claim benefits that are unlawfully denied to whites as well. One salutary consequence of public information campaigns to acquaint Negroes with their rights is that many whites will be made aware of theirs. Even if whites prefer to work through their own organizations and leaders, the consequences will be equivalent to joining with Negroes. For if the object is to focus attention on the need for new economic measures by producing a crisis over the dole, anyone who insists upon extracting maximum benefits from public welfare is in effect part of a coalition and is contributing to the cause.

The ultimate aim of this strategy is a new program for direct income distribution. What reason is there to expect that the federal government will enact such legislation in response to a crisis in the welfare system?

We ordinarily think of major legislation as taking form only through established electoral processes. We tend to overlook the force of crisis in precipitating legislative reform, partly because we lack a theoretical framework by which to understand the impact of major disruptions.

By crisis, we mean a *publicly visible* disruption in some institutional sphere. Crisis can occur spontaneously (e.g., riots) or as the intended results of tactics of demonstration and protest which either generate institutional disruption or bring unrecognized disruption to public attention. Public trouble is a political liability; it calls for action by political leaders to stabilize the situation. Because crisis usually creates or exposes conflict, it threatens to produce cleavages in a political consensus which politicians will ordinarily act to avert.

Although crisis impels political action, it does not itself determine the selection of specific solutions. Political leaders will try to respond with proposals which work to their advantage in the electoral process. Unless group cleavages form around issues and demands, the politician has great latitude and tends to proffer only the minimum action required to quell disturbances without risking existing electoral support. Spontaneous disruptions, such as riots, rarely produce leaders who articulate demands; thus, no terms are imposed, and political leaders are permitted to respond in ways that merely restore a semblance of stability without offending other groups in a coalition.

When, however, a crisis is defined by its participants—or by other activated groups—as a matter of clear issues and preferred solutions, terms are imposed on the politicians' bid for their support. Whether political leaders then design solutions to reflect these terms depends on a two-fold calculation: first, the impact of the crisis and the issues it raises on existing alignments, and, second, the gains or losses in support to be expected as a result of a proposed resolution.

As to the impact on existing alignments, issues exposed by a crisis may activate new groups, thus altering the balance of support and opposition on the issues; or it may polarize group sentiments, altering the terms which must be offered to insure the support of given constituent groups. In framing resolutions, politicians are more responsive to group shifts and are more likely to accommodate to the terms imposed when electoral coalitions threatened by crisis are already uncertain or weakening. In other words, the politician responds to group demands, not only by calculating the magnitude of electoral gains and losses but by assessing the impact of the resolution on the stability of existing or potential coalitions. Political leaders are especially responsive to group shifts when the terms of settlement can be framed so as to shore up an existing coalition, or as a basis for the development of new and more stable alignments, *without* jeopardizing existing support. Then, indeed, the calculation of net gain is most secure.

The legislative reforms of the Depression years, for example, were impelled not so much by organized interests exercised through regular electoral processes as by widespread economic crisis. That crisis precipitated the disruption of the regionally based coalitions underlying the old national parties. During the realignments of 1932 a new Democratic coalition was formed, based heavily on urban working-class groups. Once in power, the national Democratic leadership proposed and implemented the economic reforms of the New Deal. Although these measures were a response to the imperative of economic crisis, the types of measures enacted were designed to secure and stabilize the new Democratic coalition.

The civil-rights movement, to take a recent case, also reveals the relationship of crisis and electoral conditions in producing legislative reform. The crisis in the South took place in the context of a weakening North-South Democratic coalition. The strains in that coalition were first evident in the Dixiecrat desertion of 1948, and continued through the Eisenhower years as the Republicans gained ground in the southern states. Democratic party leaders at first tried to hold the dissident South by warding off the demands of enlarging Negro constituencies in northern cities. Thus for two decades the national Democratic party campaigned on strongly worded civil-rights planks but enacted only token measures. The civil-rights movement forced the Democrats' hand: A crumbling southern partnership was forfeited, and major civil-rights legislation was put forward, designed to insure the support of northern Negroes and liberal elements in the Democratic coalition. That coalition emerged strong from the 1964 election, easily able to overcome the loss of southern states to Goldwater. At the same time, the enacted legislation, particularly the Voting Rights Act, laid the ground for a new southern Democratic coalition of moderate whites and the hitherto untapped reservoir of southern Negro voters.

The electoral context which made crisis effective in the South is also to be found in the big cities of the nation today. Deep tensions have developed among groups comprising the political coalitions of the large cities—the historic stronghold of the Democratic party. As a consequence, urban politicians no longer turn in the vote to national Democratic candidates with unfailing regularity. The marked defections revealed in the elections of the 1950s and which continued until the Johnson landslide of 1964 are a matter of great concern to the national party. Precisely because of this concern, a strategy to exacerbate still further the strains in the urban coalition can be expected to evoke a response from national leaders.

The weakening of the urban coalition is a result of many basic changes in the relationship of local party leadership to its constituents. First, the political machine, the distinctive and traditional mechanism for forging alliances among competing groups in the city, is now virtually defunct in most cities. Successive waves of municipal reform have deprived political leaders of control over the public resources—jobs, contracts, services and favors —which machine politicians formerly dispensed to voters in return for electoral support. Conflicts among elements in the urban Democratic coalition, once held together politically because each secured a share of these benefits, cannot now be so readily contained. And as the means of placating competing groups have diminished, tensions along ethnic and class lines have multiplied. These tensions are being intensified by the encroachments of an enlarging ghetto population on jobs, schools and residential areas. Big-city mayors are thus caught between antagonistic working-class ethnic groups, the remaining middle class and the rapidly enlarging minority poor.

Second, there are discontinuities in the relationship between the urban party apparatus and its ghetto constituents which have so far remained unexposed but which a welfare crisis would force into view. The ghetto vote has been growing rapidly and has so far returned overwhelming Democratic majorities. Nevertheless, this voting bloc is not fully integrated in the party apparatus, either through the representation of its leaders or the accommodation of its interests.

While the urban political apparatus includes members of new minority groups, these groups are by no means represented according to their increasing proportions in the population. More important, elected representation alone is not an adequate mechanism for the expression of group interests. Influence in urban politics is won not only at the polls but through the sustained activity of organized interests—such as labor unions, homeowner associations and business groups. These groups keep watch over the complex operations of municipal agencies, recognizing issues and regularly asserting their point of view through meetings with public officials, appearances at public hearings and the like and by exploiting a whole array of channels of influence on government. Minority constituencies—at least the large proportion of them that are poor—are not regular participants in the various institutional spheres where organized interest groups typically develop. Thus, the interests of the mass of minority poor are not protected by associations which make their own or other political leaders responsive by continuously calling them to account. Urban party organizations have become, in consequence, more an avenue for the personal advancement of minority political leaders than a channel for the expression of minority-group interests. And the big-city mayors, struggling to preserve an uneasy urban consensus, have thus been granted the slack to evade the conflict-generating interests of the ghetto. A crisis in public welfare would expose the tensions latent in this attenuated relationship between the ghetto vote and the urban party leadership, for it would thrust forward ghetto demands and back them with the threat of defections by voters who have so far remained both loyal and quiescent.

In the face of such a crisis, urban political leaders may well be paralyzed by a party apparatus which ties them to older constituent groups, even while the ranks of these groups are diminishing. The national Democratic leadership, however, is alert to the importance of the urban Negro vote, especially in national contests where the loyalty of other urban groups is weakening. Indeed, many of the legislative reforms of the Great Society can be understood as efforts, however feeble, to reinforce the allegiance of growing ghetto constituencies to the national Democratic administration. In the thirties, Democrats began to put forward measures to circumvent the states in order to reach the big-city elements in the New Deal coalition; now it is becoming expedient to put forward measures to circumvent the weakened big-city mayors in order to reach the new minority poor.

Recent federal reforms have been impelled in part by widespread unrest in the ghetto and instances of more aggressive Negro demands. But despite these signs that the ghetto vote may become less reliable in the future, there has been as yet no serious threat of massive defection. The national party has therefore not put much pressure on its urban branches to accommodate the minority poor. The resulting reforms have consequently been quite modest (e.g., the war against poverty, with its emphasis on the "involvement of the poor," is an effort to make the urban party apparatus somewhat more accommodating).

A welfare crisis would, of course, produce dramatic local political crisis, disrupting and exposing rifts among urban groups. Conservative Republicans are always ready to declaim the evils of public welfare, and they would probably be the first to raise a hue and cry. But deeper and politically more telling conflicts would take place within the Democratic coalition. Whites—both working-class ethnic groups and many in the middle class—would be aroused against the ghetto poor, while liberal groups, which until recently have been comforted by the notion that the poor are few and, in any event, receiving the beneficent assistance of public welfare, would probably support the movement. Group conflict, spelling political crisis for the local party apparatus, would thus become acute as welfare rolls mounted and the strains on local budgets became more severe. In New York City, where the mayor is now facing desperate revenue shortages, welfare expenditures are already second only to those for public education.

It should also be noted that welfare costs are generally shared by local, state and federal governments, so that the crisis in the cities would intensify the struggle over revenues that is chronic in relations between cities and states. If the past is any predictor of the future, cities will fail to procure relief from this crisis by persuading states to increase their proportionate share of urban welfare costs, for state legislatures have been notoriously unsympathetic to the revenue needs of the city (especially where public welfare and minority groups are concerned).

If this strategy for crisis would intensify group cleavages, a federal income solution would not further exacerbate them. The demands put forward during recent civil-rights drives in the northern cities aroused the opposition of huge majorities. Indeed, such fierce resistance was evoked (e.g., school boycotts followed by counterboycotts) that accessions by political leaders would have provoked greater political turmoil than the protests themselves, for profound class and ethnic interests are at stake in the employment, educational and residential institutions of our society. By contrast, legislative measures to provide direct income to the poor would permit national Democratic leaders to cultivate ghetto constituencies without unduly antagonizing other urban groups, as is the case when the battle lines are drawn over schools, housing or jobs. Furthermore, a federal income program would not only redeem local governments from the immediate crisis but would permanently relieve them of the financially and politically onerous burdens of public welfare[2]—a function which generates support from none and hostility from many, not least of all welfare recipients.

We suggest, in short, that if pervasive institutional reforms are not yet possible, requiring as they do expanded Negro political power and the development of new political alliances, crisis tactics can nevertheless be employed to secure particular reforms in the short run by exploiting weaknesses in current political alignments. Because the urban coalition stands weakened by group conflict today, disruption and threats of disaffection will count powerfully, provided that national leaders can respond with solutions which retain the support of ghetto constituencies while avoiding new group antagonisms and bolstering the urban party apparatus. These are the conditions, then, for an effective crisis strategy in the cities to secure an end to poverty.

No strategy, however confident its advocates may be, is foolproof. But if unforeseen contingencies thwart this plan to bring about new federal legislation in the field of poverty, it should also be noted that there would be gains even in defeat. For one thing, the plight of many poor people would be somewhat eased in the course of an assault upon public welfare. Existing recipients would come to know their rights and how to defend them, thus acquiring dignity where none now exists; and millions of dollars in withheld welfare benefits would become available to potential recipients now—not several generations from now. Such an attack should also be welcome to those currently concerned with programs designed to equip the young to rise out of poverty (e.g., Head Start), for surely children learn more readily when the oppressive burden of financial insecurity is lifted from the shoulders of their parents. And those seeking new ways to engage the Negro politically should remember that public resources have always been the fuel for low-income urban political organization. If organizers can deliver millions of dollars in cash benefits to the ghetto masses, it seems reasonable to expect that the masses will deliver their loyalties to their benefactors. At least, they have always done so in the past.

## NOTES

[1] In public statements it would be important to distinguish between the income-distributing function of public welfare, which should be

replaced by new federal measures, and many other welfare functions, such as foster care and adoption services for children, which are not at issue in this strategy.

[2] It should also be noted that the federal government, unlike local jurisdictions, has taxing powers which yield substantially increased revenues as an automatic by-product of increases in national income.


Strategy of Crisis:
A Dialogue

A NOTE BY THE EDITORS
OF THE AMERICAN CHILD.


*A new force is being mobilized for the people in poverty. The force is the people themselves. And the strategy is to precipitate a crisis in local welfare systems throughout the nation by having all who qualify demand full payment. The goal: a federally financed guaranteed income.*

*Richard A. Cloward and Frances Fox Piven, who advanced the strategy in the Nation on May 2, 1966, assert that for every*

Reprinted with permission of the *American Child*, Vol. 48, No. 3 (Summer 1966).

*one of the nearly 8 million persons now on welfare, at least one more "probably meets existing criteria of eligibility but is not obtaining assistance." The widespread financial crisis in welfare that would result from a campaign to enroll the eligible poor and to help existing recipients win their full benefits would force Washington to institute a guaranteed income, they say.*

*Reaction to the proposal has ranged from the support of many activists—welfare-rights demonstrations have already been scheduled—to the skepticism of others who believe a bombardment of welfare claims may accomplish little more than disruption.*

*In an effort to put the issue in perspective,* American Child *arranged the following dialogue among proponents and critics.*

*The participants:*

RICHARD A. CLOWARD

FRANCES FOX PIVEN

EDGAR CAHN, *special assistant to the director, Office of Economic Opportunity*

GEORGE A. WILEY, *director, Poverty/Rights Action Center*

ROBERT SCHRANK, *director, Urban Youth Work Corps, Mobilization for Youth*

ELI E. COHEN, *executive secretary, National Committee on Employment of Youth (moderator)*

## THE DIALOGUE

CLOWARD: Across the United States today a tentative movement is beginning to emerge in the slums and ghettos of the big cities. Groups of welfare clients are beginning to organize to demand from the public-welfare system benefits of which they have been deprived and some surcease from the intimidating procedures which govern this program. There is, in short, the possibility that the emergence of these grassroots groups poses the basis for a new freedom movement in the United States.

To use the word "freedom" is to allude to at least two separate meanings:

On the one hand, these tentative stirrings in the ghetto represent an effort on the part of people to free themselves from the "tyranny" of government—and there is no other term by which to characterize the public-welfare system. It is without doubt the most barbarous and savage governmental program in our history. Its procedures are based on the assumption that low-income people are not capable of managing their own affairs, must be subjected continually to various forms of surveillance, not a few of them probably unconstitutional. In this sense, then, the embryonic movement which we see in Los Angeles, Detroit, Chicago, Cleveland, Boston, New York and elsewhere represents a new surge on the part of people for freedom and dignity.

Secondarily, this movement represents an effort on the part of people to free themselves from the tyranny of poverty. For our public-welfare system, although it may have been created with the intent of lifting people to some minimal level of subsistence, has everywhere failed to do so. The groups of welfare people organizing in the ghetto are the beginnings of a movement to alter both of these conditions.

There are several elements of the strategy which has been proposed by Dr. Piven and me. In the first instance, it takes account of the fact that low-income people have enormous latent economic leverage in the public-welfare system. One of the most significant characteristics of the welfare system is that it has systematically and unlawfully deprived people of economic benefits to which they are entitled; and these economic deprivations in the aggregate represent no small amount of money. It is estimated in New York City alone that the conveying to people of their full economic benefits would cost hundreds of millions of dollars, and there is no reason to suppose that in more conservative jurisdictions the aggregate deprivations are any the less.

So the strategy points in the first instance to the political pressure which can be generated by mobilizing people to claim their full economic benefits, either those who are already on the rolls and have failed to secure all to which they are entitled, or the thousands and thousands of people who are not on the rolls but who are eligible.

The second element in the strategy goes to the effect of such a fiscal crisis on the politics of the large cities. The Negro is an increasingly important political element in the large cities, although for various reasons he is not organized to capitalize on his numbers. The strategy which is proposed here, a strategy of enlisting people to claim their full benefits and recruiting large numbers of eligible people to the rolls, would enable the Negro community to create a major political crisis in the cities that are already in a precarious fiscal situation. Faced with such a crisis—one which would exacerbate strains among the Negro and white working-class and middle-class elements in the urban Democratic coalition—the federal government might be moved to institute major new economic reforms to replace the public-welfare system and to distribute income on a more equitable and less tyrannical basis, specifically by establishing a guaranteed annual income.

SCHRANK: It is, of course, very difficult to argue a case against people on welfare getting everything they are entitled to, as it is, I think, very difficult to argue that a movement to help people on welfare get their entitlements does not have great moral value. My basic problem with this concept is that it addresses itself to a much broader question, that of the establishment of a guaranteed annual income. It speaks of a strategy around which the activists in the civil-rights movement will gather themselves, and it is in this sense that I have trouble with the proposal. Because it would seem to me that if we want to use the energy of the civil-rights movement and other activist groups in the United States, then a very close examination of possible alternatives is necessary in deciding what is the best course for these movements to follow.

If we are talking about fundamental changes—and I would say that the guaranteed annual income is a very fundamental change—then I have doubts as to whether the proposed welfare route will get us on the road to a guaranteed annual income. I say these things because there are fundamental social and economic problems involved in this proposal. One is that the protestant ethic is still very much in effect in this country. Working is still very much part of our culture, and I don't think a decision can be taken that we simply ignore this factor of work and concentrate our efforts on marginal people who are not working and who are on welfare.

People on welfare are marginal people in our society simply because they don't function in the main social institution of work. To take a decision of this kind implies that we're going to build a movement around marginal people, and I have great trouble in seeing where such a movement will go. It would be a mistake for the civil-rights movement to put its main emphasis in the welfare direction, because it implies that all we have to offer in our society is welfare. And welfare is looked on negatively whether those of us in this room look on it that way or not.

Doesn't this suggest that we close the door to hundreds of young people who really want jobs and want careers and tell them to look to welfare? As a matter of fact, I see the activist in the civil-rights movement as organizing around the right to participate in society, and it seems to me that what your strategy says is that what we need to do is legitimize no participation. There is a big issue involved as to whether welfare really is considered a part of our dominant institutions in our society. If it were, and if nonwork were part of our life, then I think that issue would be a kind of a reasonable one. That there are people who would remain on welfare, particularly the aged and disabled, I have no problem about that—that they should get whatever they are entitled to there is no question. My trouble is with the strategy of making this a central issue for civil-rights groups.

WILEY: Well, I'd have to say that the appearance of the strategy by Cloward and Piven has represented a shot in the arm to a lot of the civil-rights activists around the country. A lot of us who have come out of the civil-rights movement have been concerned that there develop a significant movement in the northern ghettos, and a lot of people who have been trying to work in the ghettos in major urban areas have been really quite frustrated about finding significant handles for bringing about some substantial change in the living conditions of people there.

This idea of releasing the potential for major economic pressure through trying to encourage people to gain their rights in the welfare system is one that has had immediate response and has been enormously attractive to activists working in urban areas. I may say that a lot of us have been hampered in our thinking about the potential here by our own middle-class backgrounds—and I think most activists basically come out of middle-class backgrounds—that were oriented toward people having to work and that we have to get as many people as possible *off* the welfare rolls. And I think the idea that for millions—particularly people who can't work, people who are senior citizens or female heads of household—just encouraging them to assert their rights is a very attractive thing. I think that this strategy is going to catch on and be very important in the time ahead. In the history of the civil-rights movement the thing that attracted me is the fact that the substantial changes that have taken place such as the Civil Rights Act of '64 and Voting Rights Act of '65 particularly have come about as the result of major drives in one or more cities where substantial confrontations have taken place which have plunged the nation into significant crises. And I think that a crisis strategy has been the only one that has really produced major success in the civil-rights field. Second, the civil-rights movement has been able to move people—among them the most downtrodden, depressed and apathetic people in the country—

around the drive for freedom and human dignity. This driving force for motivating people to get involved in most cases in very dangerous situations has been a towering force that's not sufficiently recognized in developing a political movement. And I think that the potential here for getting the people involved in demanding rights as human beings from a system that doesn't treat them as human beings is enormous.

CAHN: I think the questions raised by this article break down into at least four categories. One is the simple issue of feasibility. The second is what kinds of response from the welfare system can one anticipate. A third is what kinds of net gains, both minimally and maximally, can one hope for. And last is the question of whether the purpose of the strategy is best considered as an end product or simply as a means to something else. And if only a means, what does that imply about the strategy and the ultimate purpose of the immediate goals sought by the proposal?

With regard to feasibility, I think there are a large number of questions, to a certain extent technical questions, that have to be pointed out. As you know, Dick, for instance, to talk about entitlement in New York City would entail problems of residence requirements and proofs and affidavits and the obligation to determine whether there is a man in the house and all these things. Entitlement in the sense of sheer need is one thing. Entitlement in the sense of legal entitlement with or without creative litigation is another. It seems to me that when you are dealing in a field like this, you are going to need lawyers, you are going to need organizers, you are going to need resources in order to do any of the things you have in mind other than help people on a case-by-case basis. And when one talks about drawing upon the resources of either lawyers or churches or civil-rights groups, then one has to pose the question of alternatives in terms of their priorities.

I think there are problems of organization, as opposed to, let's say, dissemination of simple knowledge about welfare rights. There is a question of whether organization based upon a category that a great many people consider to be undesirable or tainted will have appeal. But organization in the context of what the system has determined to be highly individualistic determination is a difficult thing. As soon as you get past the stage of marches or mass protests then the individual has to go through the system. The system then becomes intimately and degradingly personal, and it seems to me that it holds the roots of obstructing any organizational concept that you desire.

It seems to me here that the modes of the system's response will be various forms of palliative reforms as soon as any overall demands can be seized upon, whether it be residency requirements or investigation or the cessation of mandatory house investigations or trying out a rule with regard to father substitutes. You can get palliative reforms, but nonetheless you can also get new rules and new constrictive regulations which operate restrictively while satisfying certain present demands and eliminating certain blatant injustices. This may take the form of decreasing budgets or keeping budgets static in time of inflation. It may take the form of simply proliferating new rules. There will be a premium on delay. And delay will pay off heavily for officials. The critical issue will be whether the right to receive welfare vests when application is made or whether payments must begin only after a final official determination, which may take place months later.

More important, the strategy is significantly deficient in terms of what one might call vectors towards shaping a constructive response. If one, say, looks at Watts, one can say Watts was a riot, Watts was a crisis, Watts precipitated reactions. One of the things that it clearly did *not* do was to provide very much guidance to anybody as to how to respond most constructively in cutting through the gordian knot of agencies and of the programs that were going on and getting help to people.

Now, assuming for the time being all the questions on feasibility can be answered, the problem remains that the strategy contains very few directives right now for providing guidance to decision-makers or opportunities for the poor to begin to assess and express their own sense of priorities and needs. And their own sense of priorities and needs tends not to go, as you pointed out, Bob [Schrank], to welfare, but to "making it" and getting a job.

When one goes to the question of net gains, I suppose one could say: Is this just a means to extend the dole, or to enforce the minimum wage more systematically, or produce simply more people on welfare, or get a negative income tax? I think it may well produce a more clearly differentiated serf class. What seems to be important is that those who will be responding will also have motivation for making sure that there is an income differential or some other sort of status differential between those who work and those who don't in this society. They will do so in an attempt to retain status or power or distinction. As long as the income differential will be used to perpetuate or even increase the distinctions which this society has evolved for marking off the middle class from the poor and the disenfranchised, then the proposals I have seen for a negative income tax and similar program will still allow for a significant absolute differential and by increasingly disproportionate amounts. You know, even if you get a minimum income, that minimum income is going to be increasingly disproportionate to the kind of both income and opportunities available to those who are not the primary beneficiaries of those programs that I've seen. So I am concerned that the strategy itself doesn't contain within it any kinds of factors which might note a true awareness of the kind of responses needed in order not to perpetuate the existing situation and entrench it even further.

And there is also the question of means and ends. Right now there is a lot of money in ghetto communities—the mean income in, say, Harlem, Bedford-Stuyvesant of families approaches thirty-five hundred dollars a year. What this means is that within the ghetto community there are considerable financial resources. One might increase that pool of money by various means, by increasing welfare benefits, by getting more people on welfare or by negative income taxes. It seems to me that at least as important or even a more important question is how one begins to use that pool of money as an economic base for significant community activity, for community-governed enterprises, in such a way that issues of housing and jobs and unions and education are taken care of. Right now if one says we'd like to increase the pool of money within the ghetto community we can all agree on that proposition.

Right now the decision as to how that pool of money is used is a decision jointly shared by governmental officials and the poor (to a certain extent) and by slumlords, merchants and lenders and so forth. One of the most important things would be if the decision of how to use those existing resources were to rest primarily with the poor—with poor persons having access to experts who might be of use in an employee role rather than in an enlightened-dictator capacity.

Finally with respect to means and ends I want to note that one of the most significant strategies for change has been the force of competition. We know that public education is a monopoly, and welfare is a monopoly too. Pressure from within has not been as effective a force for changing monopolistic systems as competition has been. In assessing the Cloward and Piven proposal, we should consider whether it would not be more productive to create alternative competitive institutions which prod the welfare monopoly into being more responsive to its clientele. Now I don't know what alternative or competitive systems there might be for welfare. But I expect that if a community were to set up, using its present pool of money, a sort of community corporation structure, it would begin to make its own decisions with regard to its own destiny, in regard to the fundamental aspects of community life, law protection, services and so forth. And it could even evolve a substitute of alternative to welfare to accomplish both income distribtuion and socially useful tasks.

PIVEN: It seems to me that the criticisms in your presentation and in Bob's [Schrank] presentation raise two kinds of questions —one as to the legitimacy or value of the goal sought by this strategy of the minimum-income program, and the other as to the feasibility of the strategy. I think that some of the criticisms of the goal have to do with imputing to it more than it sets out to do.

It isn't a recommendation for comprehensive and all-embracing reform of the society. It talks about assuring to the very poor a minimally decent income. It doesn't have anything to say about —and certainly nothing to say against—rehabilitation programs for people. It doesn't close the door on strategies or proposals for increasing the minimum wage or whatever. It doesn't say that people should not work, that we shouldn't also at the same time seek to expand the opportunities for people who want to work. Those are other issues, and ones we do not address.

The fact of the matter is that most of the people whom we

now call very poor are not going to participate in occupational roles, at least not in this generation. And so, therefore, to say that this strategy doesn't give people jobs, which everybody really wants, is to forfeit the income goal for an aspiration which isn't going to be realizable for most of the very poor. Edgar's [Cahn] remarks that the sharp differential between classes in our society will be maintained are I think true. The question really is not what does this strategy fail to do, measured by some vision of the egalitarian utopia. I don't think the serf class will be created by a guaranteed income; I think it's created by the fact that people are dependent on state agencies for assistance now. The question, therefore, is how to mitigate this serf role that the poor are cast into—and certainly it will be less serfdom when people have as a matter of rights some sort of guaranteed income. You don't compare it with an egalitarian ideal. I don't think that's fair.

There were objections raised as to the strategy's feasibility. The question of what good it would do the civil-rights movement arose from the sense that Americans don't believe in giving people money—they believe in giving people an occupation, a working role, and therefore the civil-rights movement would suffer from being associated with this welfare strategy. And then there were a number of good organizing questions that you raised, Edgar, but again I think we have to compare this strategy with what we now have in the way of opportunities for forcing change. What does the civil-rights movement now have and what will it be giving up? How strong is the civil-rights movement? How well has it been able to move in the northern ghettos in enlisting support from the ghetto itself, or in enlisting allies from other powerful groups? It has not been able to do well at all.

What does this strategy pursue and how does it differ from civil-rights action on school-integration issues, or residential-integration issues or job-integration issues? What does this strategy offer that others have not? I think there are two fundamental advantages. The first is the effort to capitalize on benefits legally available through the governmental system that can be released through organizing activity; we feel people will respond. The second is that a guaranteed income, the end product sought, is not likely to offend other groups in the city in the way the strategies that have been pursued by the civil-rights movement in the northern ghetto until now have offended other groups in the cities.

This doesn't mean, I don't think, that there aren't still many questions having to do with the tactics of organizing. From what studies we have done, it seems to us that the extent of unused welfare entitlement, which is a measure of the extent of economic pressure that can be brought to bear against the welfare system and city and state government systems by releasing these benefits, is great. The question is how to release them, and Edgar speaks quite convincingly of the difficulty of making welfare a proud thing that people will claim. Perhaps people who are already on welfare have been in a sense politically damaged by this experience, and this, I think, is one of the advantages of the guaranteed income. But people can nevertheless be aroused to claim benefits withheld from them, or to protest the withdrawal of benefits, when they are told this is their right and given help in doing it.

And if you talk about enlisting people who are eligible, yet not on welfare, who in some cases don't know about it, who in other cases are ashamed to ask for the dole, it seems to me that you're confronting organizers with tasks which are less formidable than asking them to develop organizations modeled on images of participatory democracy, which it seems to me you're suggesting when you talk about the community corporations in the ghetto. It's hard to do. People move and act in patterned ways in organizations in response to compelling incentives. Everywhere else in society they do it this way. They don't participate for remote ideals, and the singular advantage in this strategy is that we can offer to people concrete and simple incentives. It's this, I think, that distinguishes the strategy as an organizing strategy.

SCHRANK: Just a couple of things that I wanted to respond to: One is a kind of pragmatic approach that I pick up from both Dick [Cloward] and Frances [Piven] that says, "Well, we don't know what else to do anyhow, so why not do this?" And, of course, that troubles me right away, because if that's the reason—you have nothing else to do—then, I think, there are dangers involved with that kind of strategy. Simply out of desperation you have to do something, so this seems like as good a thing to do. Now I may be vulgarizing that a little bit, but I would suggest that you have to do more than create a crisis. And this is what troubles me. I think that this is the greatest problem of the civil-rights movement—it created a number of crises and then didn't know what to do after the crises.

Having spent a lot of years both in the labor movement and political movements that were expert at creating crises, I know that the whole problem in creating a crisis was to have alternatives for what happens after the crisis. That's the key, and I don't think that you can have an alternative unless you have an ideological base.

There's this one more point, and this is that I think that a strategy for change must involve allies within the society. When I talk of allies I mean a variety of institutions. I don't see, for instance, the lay—or white—movement responding to this at all. I don't know whether the middle-class groups are going to respond to any extent as an ally around this particular issue. So I don't know from whence you're going to get support from the other sections of society, which I think is critical.

WILEY: Bob and Edgar raise several questions. To respond to the first one first—the basic question of using crisis as a strategy: It is wrong to use the analogy of Watts, because of the kind of crisis that Watts was. It was a wholly spontaneous event. One day it happened, and who was in a position to deal with it? The kind of crisis we mean is what happened in the South around the civil-rights issues. There were appeals to sympathetic groups in the North, appeals to the federal government, various kinds of tie-ins to a greater movement. The point is that a crisis in which important issues are clearly confronted can power a movement.

The question is whether or not this strategy is harnessable. I think that this is a strategy that can release energy and be harnessed to power a movement. The appeal of this as far as the civil-rights forces are concerned is that there are really relatively few alternatives that can release energy on a significant scale. I think this has a potential for generating steam, and the question is then how we harness that steam to motivate the involvement of church, labor and other sympathetic groups into a drive for a guaranteed-income plan.

CLOWARD: On Bob's points about the importance of ideology, particularly in the early days of the American labor movement, I would certainly agree that there was an enormous amount of altruism. It's also true, however, that the labor movement would be nowhere if it had not offered economic incentives. It would never have motivated masses of men.

It seems to me that both points hold in the strategy which we are proposing. As I said before, the public-welfare system is one of the most coercive systems that has ever been forced on low-income people. We have in our earliest writings stressed not merely the economic incentives to organization but we have tried to convey the sense of fear which this system generates in people, the degree to which they are intimidated by all manner of policy and procedure, the routine invasions of their households by case-workers under the guise of rehabilitation when, in fact, they are there to perform the function of surveillance, and all of the other mechanisms by which people feel that big brother is watching them.

So we are arguing here not merely from the point of view of narrow self-interest but more basically from the feeling that low-income people do value dignity, do—like their brothers in the labor movement—value freedom from coercion, whether it's by the institution of private property or by government.

A strategy based solely on ideology is, we have argued—Dr. Piven and I—not enough! In addition to the ideology, the urge for freedom, the urge for dignity, one does have to have some significant economic incentive.

CAHN: But how large are those economic incentives you offer? How many people conform to the class of presently eligible for welfare but not receiving it? I'm told that the stack of welfare regulations in Los Angeles weighs a hundred and sixteen pounds —and I assume a goodly portion of the hundred and sixteen pounds is devoted to making a distinction between those who are poor and those who are entitled to welfare. What will be the effect organizationally of motivating people who aren't qualified? And how much energy is released when you do get on welfare in, say, Florida where the most a family can get is eighty-one dollars a month? That happens to be the worst of the maximums allowed in any state, but a great many states certainly have maximums significantly below what is needed for a living income.

WILEY: Edgar, the question of increasing benefits, say, five dollars a month or going about to get someone a winter coat may seem pretty small—but it really can be the spark to power a movement, because the very small things can be big to the people who need them. The problem hasn't been how you can keep people interested in programs that give them small gains; it's been how can you connect that program to a movement that will make substantial social change. For example, Saul Alinsky in Chicago has been very effective in involving people around local issues, but not around larger issues. And this is one of the most attractive parts of the Cloward-Piven strategy: It does tend to make the connection between problems of immediate concern to the poor and the larger questions of income maintenance, guaranteed income, etcetera.

SCHRANK: I'm worried that a strategy to get small gains might also end up preventing you from getting really broad sweeping changes which another strategy would go to and really create an important crisis. I don't see how your tactics will lead to a guaranteed income. I see the strategy when it comes to getting people their entitlements on welfare. And I'm for it. But I don't see that as a movement. How you then organize them around a broad program for change—I don't see that in the strategy. I would suggest—and it would be hard to document it, I know—that the energies would be much better spent in trying to build a broad ideological movement and not with a program of you-give-me-this and I'll-give-you-that. I think, by the way, that that's what has gone wrong with the labor movement today. It operates that way—for small gains—and it doesn't have any ideology.

And just one other point, Dick. In making analogies, you have to recognize that workers do have power over the economy—namely, they can shut it down. They have the power of strikes, and without it I think they wouldn't have anything. I don't see how welfare people can shut down the economy. I don't really even see how they can disrupt it. The welfare institution will react to pressure just as the employers reacted to the workers. It just wasn't a matter of strike-and-you-have-it. It was a matter of strike and a total process taking place, and in many instances being able to wait it out. I don't see how welfare people will be able to wait it out.

I'm concerned that welfare people can be easily victimized, and I think a movement such as yours has to have a good per-

spective on how it's going to take care of the victims. What are
you going to do with welfare people when the welfare system
reacts? What if the officials say we won't give you more, we'll
give you less? Are welfare people in a position to cope with that
kind of strategy? I don't think you can expect that kind of commitment from them.

CLOWARD: Let me make a brief comment on the issue of small
gains. It's certainly true that in many southern districts welfare
benefits are minuscule, but we have stressed in our proposals that
this is a strategy for the large northern cities where benefits are
not so minuscule. In New York City, for example, a family of
four gets not an eighty-dollar-a-month allowance as is the case in
some southern areas, but more nearly twenty-five hundred a year,
over $200 a month, and that's not including eligibility for special
allowances for heavy clothing, household furnishings and the
like, which could bring the total for a family of four up to the
vicinity of three thousand dollars a year. So the economic potential of these allowances is much bigger in the northern cities.
Secondly, the deprivations are big. In New York City special
allowances amount to a mere forty or fifty dollars per person a
year; under the pressure of a movement, this small amount could
be multiplied many, many times. Given the five hundred thousand people already on welfare, this accelerated cost could
amount to millions and millions of dollars. And only half the
eligible people are on welfare at all. Billions of dollars are involved here.

Now to get to Bob's point on the power of ghetto people. I
quite agree that welfare people can't organize against employers
precisely because they don't have the economic leverage. What we
are suggesting, however, is that they do have a form of power in
government itself, in making it adhere to its own laws. It will
not amount to the same continuing power that labor has, but it
will amount to sufficient power to create a crisis, a crisis that
could lead to some kind of reform of the traditional means of
distributing income in the country.

That brings me to one final point. The question of employment and training is constantly posed as an alternative to an income-distribution push. I don't see them as polar opposites. As
Dr. Piven pointed out, we do not suggest that the emphasis on

employment and training should be diminished. What we do say is that the question of poverty and the question of individual mobility should be to some extent separated. A great many poor people are not going to become economically mobile, and I refer to the aged, the disabled, female-headed families, et cetera. It may be true that many of these women would like to work, but it's also true that many would just like to be mothers. The problem is how to provide a minimum condition of subsistence for them without governmental coercion, intimidation and degradation.

COHEN: We were talking for the most part about the question of feasibility and obviously we are not going to resolve that. I wonder whether we couldn't spend some time on the issue of alternative strategies. What are the alternative strategies for the group of whom Dick just spoke? No one's questioned the goals—giving welfare people their entitlements—and also the large issues of some new income-maintenance program, such as the guaranteed income. What would be the alternative ways of achieving some kind of income redistribution?

CAHN: When we talk about poverty as a monetary thing, I think sometimes we're wrong. . . . Welfare people have in common a number of things with a great many other people in the ghetto. They have some kind of income—it's not enough, but together that may constitute a composite pool of resources. I'm in favor of increasing that pool. But when we get to the problem of bridging the strategy between getting increments of income and organizing a movement that has an affirmative thrust toward contribution, it seems to me that we ought to look at the problem of how increasing the money in that pool can be made to create a sufficient economic base for other forms of democratic participation and community control of educational, recreational and cultural enterprises.

COHEN: But do you have some specific alternatives in connection with what you are saying? If you have criticisms about what Dick and Fran are saying, what would you have in its place?

CAHN: The criticism does not rule out the strategy. There is nothing wrong and everything right with getting people on welfare who are entitled to welfare. The question is in what perspective does one view the strategy, how one uses the resources—real and monetary and physical resources of the poor—in such a manner as to create the possibility for participation and realization that just does not exist for the poor in this society.

WILEY: I have to interrupt. I have a real problem. When one talks about the "pool of resources" and so forth—you know, I am a Ph.D., but I don't understand anything you are saying. I don't know how to translate it into some effective program in the ghetto. Unless someone can do that for me, I don't know what to do. But I do know what to do tomorrow and this afternoon about getting some people in motion around the welfare and income issue.

That gets me to another point. I'm very concerned about the strategy of the war on poverty in the Economic Opportunity Act. The basic premise of that strategy is that we must direct programs at reconstructing individual people toward some kind of an adjustment or accommodation to the current institutions of the society. Now you'll say that's a gross oversimplification, that we're doing other kinds of things. But in a sense the main thrust of the program is toward retraining, rehabilitative and palliative services to poor people. I question that strategy, based on the fact that it is degrading to the people served.

The difference in this strategy is that it builds dignity in the people that it deals with. So this is my point, that the poverty program degrades the people it serves. Instead of trying to change the institutions that create and sustain poverty, it seeks to change the victims of poverty.

Now another thing about Edgar's "pool of resources." It sounds to me like something that isn't going to rock the boat. I have a feeling that the more one directs himself to not rocking the boat, the more you tend to emphasize that there is nothing wrong with the society that produced the problem and that poverty is the fault of poor people themselves.

CAHN: I disagree with you that the main thrust of the war on poverty is individual change or a means of escaping from the critical need for institutional change. I would also say that there have been programs implemented that have institutional change as one of the top priorities. But I think it would be inappropriate in the context of what we are discussing here to try and pervert this discussion into an apologia for the war on poverty.

WILEY: I don't think that one should expect Drs. Cloward and Piven to elaborate a complete diagram on how to mobilize various forces, how to build alliances, et cetera. There is need for a lot of discussion on how the strategy could be implemented. And I might mention that I am now in the process of developing a center in Washington that we're calling the Poverty/Rights Action Center. The Center is going to devote a major part of its energy toward working on the development and elaboration of this strategy. As to whether it's feasible: I am not one of the people saying that all in a community should go out tomorrow and try to precipitate a crisis around welfare. I suggest instead that a lot more people and organizations begin helping poor people secure the rights and benefits that are due them under the welfare laws. This is necessary preparation for a massive assault on the welfare system.

PIVEN: When Edgar invokes the ideal of creating participation and dissent in ghetto communities, I think he overlooks the way in which a decent income underlies participation; thirty-five hundred dollars a year doesn't often permit it. The poverty program's way of developing low-income participation—it's programs for credit unions and co-ops—ignores two overriding problems.

First, when you try to achieve *significant* economic change, politically dominant groups will fight it. The trouble is that the poor are not a majority and no amount of participation or re-adjusting will make them into one. Second, our strategy is a more realistic reflection of the way other groups have their interests represented: through organized pressures that generate change in major institutions. There are tactical problems that need to be worked out, but it doesn't seem to me that these problems are in any way to be resolved by a more idyllic mode of participation and organization.

SCHRANK: I didn't say it at the beginning, so I'll say it now at the end. I think Dick and Frances are to be given a lot of credit for developing this document, although I have disagreements with it, and I don't have my alternative strategy ready. But I think the problem is the definition of the problem. Dick and Fran have defined *part* of the problem. Let's call it the welfare piece of it, that's one thing. I think the problem, though, is much broader. There's the whole question of youth unemployment. I would hate to have to say to youth who are unemployed today that our program for you is to get you on welfare or to get you entitlements. Or how about the seventeen million workers today who are still exempt from the minimum-wage law and are very much a part of poverty? You have to direct yourself to their problem.

The point is there are a lot of different pieces to this problem, and this is my trouble with the proposal. It doesn't consider the other pieces. I get a sense that it is another gimmick that says if we do this, we'll start something going that will change the whole ball of wax.

CLOWARD: I would like to object to some of this discussion on the ground that no strategy can solve everything. The question is: Can we find a strategy to solve anything? That is the criterion by which this strategy should be judged.

I agree with Ed that there is a whole set of questions in this society about participation in a great many institutional areas, and I also agree with Bob that the guaranteed minimum income is not a program for comprehensive economic reform or comprehensive institutional reform. But it also strikes me that by posing all of these requirements for dealing with all the problems, you can vitiate what viability this strategy may have to deal with some of the problems.

One can talk about all kinds of social change, one can state all kinds of desirable goals, but in the final analysis one has to come down to the question of where the political muscle is going to come from to force these ends. If the crisis we are advocating can be created, hopefully some form of economic reform will come.

Bob speaks of people who are employed but below the minimum wage. The guaranteed income would solve that problem by stating that no man would have to work for less than some specified amount. And I don't think that men should have to work for exploitative wages, any more than I think a woman in

Louisiana or Michigan or Florida should be struck from the welfare rolls because she has an illegitimate child. I think people ought to be unconditionally guaranteed a minimum subsistence. And the question today is how we can at least find the pressure to deal with that single problem.

COHEN: Let me just give several closing notes: It's perfectly clear that everyone around the table would like the people on welfare and others who should be on welfare to get everything they are entitled to. And I would assume that almost all are agreed that whatever we can do to achieve a guaranteed income would be very worthwhile.

Where we seem to start parting company is on this particular method and its feasibility. On the one hand, the proponents are talking about using the only leverage that the low-income people in the ghetto have to achieve a crisis that will, in George Wiley's words, release energies and lead to small gains and hopefully then lead to larger change. On the other hand, there are those who are saying that you are working with a group that isn't going to respond, and even if they do, the establishment will react in such a way that they'll curtail what you are trying to do; there are not the allies or the resources to cope with what would follow the crisis. We've had no definitive discussion on alternatives except to say this is a strategy for one group and there are other strategies needed for other groups.

I think the discussion has been good not only in terms of ventilating views but I think it's been enlightening in the sense of understanding what this is and what it is not. If Bob hadn't stolen my thunder, I'd want now to thank Dick and Frances for an exciting new idea that could have a great deal of significance.

# Birth of a Movement

RICHARD A. CLOWARD
AND FRANCES FOX PIVEN

It is never easy to fix the beginnings of a movement, but participants in the emerging welfare-recipients movement will probably remember the last days of June 1966. On June 20 about forty men and women on relief left Cleveland on the first lap of a 155-mile march to Columbus, there to present complaints about public welfare to Governor Rhodes. As the marchers passed through cities and towns on the route, local recipients, ministers, social workers and other sympathetic citizens, sometimes hundreds of them, fell in line for a short distance. (But in the town of Creston a cross was burned.) On the morning of June 30, when they finally reached Columbus, the forty marchers were joined by busloads of recipients from all over Ohio. Some 2000 protesters paraded down Broad Street to the capitol to argue the case against Ohio's welfare system. Dick Gregory, one of those who addressed the crowd, announced: "This is not a civil-rights movement; it's a human-rights movement."

Ohio was not the only scene of demonstrations that day. In New York 2000 pickets, most of them on welfare, marched in the hot sun while their children played in City Hall park. And in fifteen other cities, including Baltimore, Washington, Los Angeles, Boston, Louisville, Chicago, Trenton and San Francisco, 2500 more people in groups of 25 to 250 simultaneously demonstrated against "the welfare."

A great variety of demands were put forward on June 30 and continue to be reiterated in subsequent demonstrations. Chief

Originally published in the *Nation*, May 8, 1967. Copyright by the authors.

among them is the call for higher grant levels. In Ohio, for example, recipients receive only seventy percent of what the state itself has declared to be the minimum subsistence income by 1959 standards—73¢ per day per person for food, clothing and all other expenses except rent. The June marchers wanted the state to use its $30 million budget surplus to raise grant levels. Recently, 2500 people in Greensboro, N.C., signed petitions to the state legislature calling for increases in grant levels; the maximum monthly payment which can be given a family of four is $152.50, but the actual average payment is only $96.00. Nationally, we spend about .7 percent of our personal income for welfare. The average annual payment for an AFDC (Aid to Families with Dependent Children) family of four is about $1800, ranging from $380 in Mississippi to about $2700 in New York.

"Snooping" by welfare investigators is a bitter and constant grievance. In Cleveland the police department's Bureau of Special Services (BOSS), whose main function is to hunt out "subversives," cooperates with the welfare department. A favorite BOSS tactic is to interrogate the children of AFDC families about undeclared family income or the male companions of their mothers. Similar invasions of privacy occur regularly throughout the country, and welfare recipients are beginning to resist them. At neighborhood meetings in the South Bronx, for example, one AFDC mother after another will rise to vow that she will no longer teach her children to lie to the investigator about having seen their father.

Women predominate at demonstrations, but some men turn out, and their numbers may increase. Unemployed single men rarely succeed in getting on the rolls, even though in many places they are eligible for general assistance. Welfare officials say it is not good for able-bodied men to be on relief; it undermines their initiative. Being chronically unemployed, one might counter, is not character-building either, especially if there is no other source of income. Men on the picket lines carry signs reading: JOBS OR INCOME. Since many welfare departments also refuse (often contrary to their own regulations) to provide benefits to supplement low wages, other signs call for DECENT WAGES OR WELFARE.

The establishment of day-care centers for children, so that their mothers can work, is among the most popular demands, although its popularity may decline when recipients actually experience the type of employment, and the wage level, society has in store for them.

Some groups seek improvements in food-distribution programs which are administered locally by welfare departments. The Food Stamp Act of 1964 prohibits distribution of free surplus commodities in areas where bonus food stamps are sold. In the South many people lack the money to buy food stamps, partly because they are illegally kept on welfare. Nevertheless, county after county is now switching from the distribution of free surplus commodities to the food-stamp plan. The result has been near-starvation for tens of thousands. Two million Negroes left rural areas between 1960 and 1965 alone—driven out by traditional welfare policies and the unemployment produced by federal agricultural subsidies which reward mechanization by big landholders. When the Mississippi Advisory Committee held hearings in Jackson last February to investigate the food-distribution problem, 800 poor Negroes crowded in. At one point they seized the microphones and held them for two hours to condemn welfare and food-distribution practices.

Recipients are also plagued by restrictions in the food-stamp program, particularly prohibitions on the use of stamps to buy such items as soap powder, toilet paper, cigarettes and beer. Merchants in big cities do a thriving business by selling forbidden items (including toys at Christmas) at a high premium in extra stamps. And they'll oblige only if the recipient is a regular purchaser of their typically shoddy goods at inflated prices. More "ethical" merchants limit themselves to hiking prices twice a month, on "check days." In some places welfare groups are joining forces with consumer-boycott groups to combat these practices.

But of the many motives leading recipients to band together, none is more powerful than the hope of obtaining some relief from the distress of poverty. The most persistent theme of the movement is the demand that welfare departments abandon the widespread practices of rejecting legitimate applicants, summarily terminating the benefits of others and failing to provide the full benefits prescribed by law to those who remain on the rolls. Groups which have concentrated on this issue have shown the most dramatic growth and the most stable membership.

Local groups have mounted a colorful variety of demonstrations to press their demands. Last September nearly 1000 recipients picketed the welfare department in New York, demanding increased grants for school clothing; the protest culminated in a three-day sit-in by AFDC mothers. Some 200 in Cleveland staged a "buy-in" at a local department store, carefully selecting children's books, scarves, winter coats and other items of children's clothing, for which they instructed the store manager to bill the department of welfare. In California recipients have organized "job-ins" to demand suitable employment at regular wages for men who are able to work. The state currently forces male heads of families to "work off" their grants by cutting brush in municipal and county drainage and irrigation ditches. If they refuse this peonage, they are dropped from the rolls. "Cook-ins" have been used. At a demonstration in Baltimore a meal prepared from surplus foods was served the mayor in his office; he declined to eat it. California officials and their wives, attending a "banquet" organized by recipients, were embarrassed when presented with a meal composed solely of varieties of beans. In some places the names of especially punitive welfare workers are compiled and distributed on "louse lists"; elsewhere, their pictures are blown up in the style of "wanted" posters and nailed to telephone poles and tenement doors. By such techniques, private shame is being converted into public indignation.

In the past, welfare clients have not often dared to taunt the system, its retributive powers being what they are. Even though the risks to individuals are still great, groups are now holding firm in the face of harassment. Recipient organizers have been struck from the welfare rolls in some places, and this practice may spread if the movement grows sufficiently powerful to cause political difficulties. Demonstrators have been arrested in a dozen cities. In Washington, welfare investigators photograph pickets from ground-level office windows; they follow demonstrators on marches, taking motion pictures through small squares left in the paint-darkened windows of their station wagons. (These practices ceased, at least temporarily, when they were the subject of a *Washington Post* article, illustrated by a large picture of a welfare investigator photographing pickets.) Police photographers in New York (who also work for a division called BOSS) erect tripods in the midst of picket lines. Wiley stresses to local groups the critical importance of making alliances with lawyers who will defend recipients against retaliation.

### NATIONAL LINK-UP

If the demonstrations on June 30 and subsequently result in the organization of some segment of the poor, much of the credit will belong to a national body formed in the spring of 1966—the Poverty/Rights Action Center. It is headed by George A. Wiley, a former professor of chemistry who joined CORE and later became its associate national director. After leaving CORE, Wiley wanted to promote organizations of the poor focused on economic deprivations; he recognized such possibilities in the proposal to build a movement by mobilizing people to claim benefits due them under law. Wiley now believes that "the welfare movement is the most important development among low-income people since Rosa Parks refused to move to the back of a bus in Montgomery, Alabama."

Wiley's achievements are worth noting. The simultaneous demonstrations in June were the result of strenuous efforts to establish links with the few scattered groups that already existed around the country and to spur local activists (many of whom were in limbo after the civil-rights movement passed its peak) to begin organizing new groups. In August about 100 recipient leaders attended a meeting convened by the Center to lay the groundwork for a national movement. As new groups develop, Wiley maintains contact, provides program materials and offers advice on organizing strategies, fund-raising techniques and ways of dealing with intractable public-welfare bureaucracies. Recently, a national newsletter was started. In February of this year 350 people, representing more than 200 welfare groups in seventy cities of twenty-six states, attended a second national meeting of leaders. Participant groups ranged from the "Mothers of Watts" to "Mothers for Adequate Welfare" in Boston; from Chicago's "Welfare Union of the West Side Organization," composed of unemployed Negro males, to eastern Kentucky's "Committee to Save Unemployed Fathers," consisting of white ex-miners. Wiley has also helped to develop a National Coordinating Committee of Welfare Rights Organizations.

### PROFESSIONALS KNOW BEST

Figures prominent in the social-welfare establishment are cautioning civil-rights leaders, foundation officials and other potential supporters of the movement that political controversy created by welfare groups may impel state legislators to retaliate, as by lowering grant levels. Welfare reform, they say, is best left to the professionals and other experts who know their way about the legislative corridors. By coincidence, recently increased federal payments to localities for professionally staffed rehabilitative programs have produced better salaries, higher standards of training and various professional embellishments; they have not provided much additional in the way of funds for food, clothing and household furnishings—at least not for recipients.

The unions of public-welfare employees also think clients should defer to their leadership, on the ground that unions fight for reforms that will benefit everyone. Some unions have given modest aid to recipients' organizations, and recipients have joined picket lines during union strikes. However, the alliances have been uneasy. In labor-management negotiations, the unions concentrate on wages and working conditions and do not push hard on issues of concern to recipients. During the Depression, unemployed men demanding relief and welfare employees joined in the Workers' Alliance, but today's recipients are not primarily unemployed workers, and welfare employees now want to be professionals. Unions of investigators bargain to be called "case workers" and to be relieved of paper work so that they can practice "rehabilitation." Most recipients do not need rehabilitation and submit to it only when it is made a condition for continuing to receive benefits. Recipients, in short, cannot expect the social-welfare establishment to advance their interests.

### WHO WILL HELP?

Organizing takes money. For even minimal national leadership, the Poverty/Rights Action Center needs $5000 per month. But fund raising has been slow in the welfare movement. People who gave to the civil-rights movement remember the drama of Selma:

The need to help unemployed men and welfare mothers to organize seems far less compelling.

It is remarkable that so much has been done thus far with so little money. The organizing accomplished by groups affiliated with the New York City-Wide Coordinating Committee of Welfare Groups is a case in point. Neighborhood units raise money where they can, mainly from dues, socials and occasional contributions. The City-Wide body, which now has a telephone and a one-room office donated by a protestant church, has financed its nine months of operation with less than $5000. Nevertheless, it staffs its office, holds biweekly meetings of neighborhood representatives, sends out a weekly newsletter, sponsors citywide demonstrations (some of which have involved several thousand people) and cooperates with member groups in numerous local demonstrations. The chief accomplishment of the City-Wide Committee, however, is the millions of dollars in benefits it has procured for members, mostly through "minimum standards" campaigns.

In New York, as in many other states, people get money from welfare in two ways. Once certified as eligible, they are supposed to receive a regular "food and rent" check every fifteen days. Because the law recognizes that people also need clothing and household furnishings in order to live at a minimum standard, provision is made for special grants on an "as needed" basis. But the system does not inform people of this entitlement, it does little to help those who do know of it to make application and it frequently turns down (or trims down) legitimate requests. A massive campaign has been under way since last summer to inform recipients about their right to these benefits and to overcome the reluctance of the system to make grants. Simple forms have been prepared, in English and Spanish, listing the many items to which people are entitled (e.g., galoshes and a bed and mattress for each child), with spaces left for people to check the items they need. Tens of thousands of these forms have been circulated in the welfare ghettos, along with fliers telling people to bring the completed checklists to the meeting place of a local recipients' organization. When the forms have been collected, a demonstration is held at the district welfare center in support of a delegation delivering the forms in bulk to the administrator. Some 10,000 families have participated in these minimum-

standard campaigns, and have received checks averaging about
$300. This represents a total of $3 million wrested from the system. Nor does this large sum take account of the indirect results
of the minimum-standards campaign: Client organizing has encouraged well-motivated social investigators to fight harder for
approval of minimum-standards applications (procedures for administrative approval become more cumbersome with the size
of the request) and has prodded their unmotivated colleagues
into being more attentive. The workers, it is said, reflect this new
climate in the handling of their entire case loads, not just the
cases of clients known to be members of recipients' organizations.
It is impossible to estimate how many additional millions in
benefits have been released in this fashion.

Although cash resources have been hard to find, welfare organizing has been supported by contributions of other kinds, mostly
from antipoverty agencies and churches. The Office of Economic
Opportunity, with its rhetoric about community action, attracted
hundreds of activists to its payrolls, and then harnessed them to
traditional social-service programs. However, at least a few of the
antipoverty agencies have taken up welfare abuses as part of their
programs. What usually happens is that alert staff members, once
in contact with poor people, perceive that injustices perpetrated
by welfare departments, especially the illegal withholding of financial benefits, must be remedied before other family problems
can be attacked. And so the staff of a Head Start or youth-
employment program may begin to ask the welfare department
to "adjust" individual cases. As the volume of cases grows and
the workers become more expert as advocates, a community of
recipients sometimes emerges—stimulated, often, by news of the
national movement. OEO money has been particularly instrumental in assisting welfare organizing in New York, Washington,
St. Louis, New Orleans, Newark and Paterson, N.J., Pittsfield,
Mass., and various cities in California and Kentucky. In addition, a number of VISTA members have become active organizers, and very effective ones.

A good many neighborhood ministers and priests have joined
their welfare constituents on the picket lines and in sit-ins. In
Chicago, churchmen have also given outright gifts of money to
groups, and in Cleveland the Council of Churches is contributing
to the support of welfare organizing by Students for a Democratic

Society (SDS). In addition, the Council has sponsored a series of arresting ads in local newspapers. One shows only the distended belly of a pregnant woman, with the caption in one-inch type, LET 'EM STARVE. The text then describes the niggardly sums available to Ohio's welfare families. And although it has contributed no funds, the National Council of Churches has been extremely helpful to Wiley in a number of ways; indeed, without its assistance the Center might not have survived.

Civil-rights groups are slowly becoming involved. A few Urban League groups have been organizing; the NAACP Legal Defense Fund is taking test cases in the welfare area and is helping organizers in the South. National CORE, its financial resources badly depleted, has been unable to do much, but local chapters in Providence, Baltimore, Newark, Lexington and Denver have been active. SDS has done intensive organizing, especially in Cleveland, Newark, Chicago, Baltimore, Jersey City and Boston, and there are signs that other SDS units may include this issue in their broader organizing programs. Organizations directed or influenced by Saul Alinsky have been effective in some places, especially Syracuse and Chicago (where The Woodlawn Organization has built a welfare union with ten "locals"). And Martin Luther King announced in March the beginning of an intensive organizing drive in the Chicago slums to build "a base of power in order to bring about a guaranteed annual income."

Some settlement houses—University in New York, Southside in Columbus, and Southeast Neighborhood in Washington—have been very active. Individual social workers (some of them public-welfare employees) are affiliated with welfare groups in most cities. The young professionals organized in New York as "Social Workers for Civil Rights Action" are raising funds for the city-wide welfare groups. A few local chapters of the National Association of Social Workers have provided travel money for recipient leaders to attend national organizing meetings. In late February a consortium of students from the schools of social work in the New York metropolitan area sponsored an eight-hour teach-in on the welfare movement, attended by some 1500 persons. The speakers included James Farmer, Kenneth Clark, George Wiley, Robert Theobald and several recipient leaders. The Poverty/Rights Action Center is raising money for students to do welfare organizing in the urban ghettos as "summer" projects, somewhat along the lines of projects previously sponsored by the civil-rights movement in the South.

## WELFARE IN THE COURTS

Concomitant with the development of a recipients' movement, an assault is being mounted in the courts against the laws, rules and procedures of public welfare; each drive has been reinforcing the other. The Scholarship, Education and Defense Fund for Racial Equality has been active in the courts. Its legal staff, headed by Carl Rachlin, advises welfare groups on strategy, represents individuals who have been arrested in demonstrations and tries to persuade other lawyers to join the struggle. Last summer the Law Students Civil Rights Research Council placed dozens of law students in Chicago, Cleveland, New York and throughout the South, many of them assigned to work exclusively with welfare groups. The program will be repeated next summer, with a much sharper focus on welfare issues. A number of the legal-service projects sponsored by OEO are at work on welfare problems. The California Rural Legal Assistance Project, for example, moved vigorously against the welfare departments and has itself been attacked by the California bar.

A leader in the drive to establish the rule of law in the welfare field is Edward Sparer, director of the "law and social welfare center" of the Columbia University School of Social Work. Sparer and a large staff of lawyers try to persuade legal organizations and private attorneys throughout the country to take pivotal test cases against the system. They do exhaustive legal research and advise on the preparation of briefs. Several critical cases are now being taken by such organizations as the Legal Defense Fund and various OEO legal-service projects. One crucial case, now in the federal courts, is a test of Georgia's "employable mother" rule, which permits administrators to deny AFDC benefits to any mother who is deemed eligible for employment and whose children are older than three years, whether or not jobs are to be had. The rule also prohibits the payment of supplemental benefits to a mother who is employed at wages falling well below scheduled grant levels. By thus forcing people to take any job at any wage, this rule and similar practices in other southern states encourage exploitation. Another matter, now being considered by the United States Supreme Court, deals with the question of whether a tenant can be evicted from a public-housing project without being given a statement of cause or a hearing; the implication for the thousands of recipients involuntarily dropped from the welfare rolls is clear. Indeed, many of the cases now being taken could substantially increase the number of people eligible for initial or continuing benefits. If the "employable mother" case is won, Georgia's rolls could double. But welfare departments will not comply with new rulings unless they are pressured to do so. The task of a movement is to organize that pressure.

## ORGANIZING FOR CRISIS

What does the future hold for a movement of the welfare poor? Much depends on their ability to endure the frustrations of organizing, the drudgery of pounding the pavements and knocking on doors. Recipients want to bring the welfare system to its knees, here and now. Delegates to the national meeting in Washington last February, on hearing reports of starvation in Mississippi, were ready to abandon the conference and march on Jackson. Workshops on the details of organizing techniques turn into rallies where people rise one by one to "tell it like it is."

But marches, rallies and exhortations are not what has fueled the movement thus far and made it grow. Its appeal lies, rather, in its tangible achievements: extracting benefits prescribed by law, and giving protection against the untrammeled . . . power of "poor law" agencies. Welfare recipients share with people everywhere a tendency to affiliate with organizations that can hold out the promise of economic gains. Nor is anything else likely to induce mass participation.

However, merely drawing people into organizations will not yield much power, for welfare recipients are a numerical minority, and what little strength of numbers they have is diluted by racial divisiveness. Like organized labor, welfare recipients need a source of strength that goes beyond their numbers. Labor exerts economic leverage through the strike; welfare recipients can exercise power by claiming benefits held back by the system.

To wield this power, however, the movement must mobilize

with single-minded determination to obtain benefits for its members—for those now eligible who have been illegally rejected or discharged from the rolls, and for those on the rolls who are not receiving the full benefits prescribed by law. Naturally, it must also begin recruiting the huge new groups which will become eligible if various test cases are won in the courts.

Each time a welfare group turns to some other issue—such as agitating for a day-care center—it wastes its one source of potential power. Campaigns to get benefits will produce pervasive and persistent turmoil: bureaucratic turmoil because cumbersome (and unconstitutional) procedures for review and surveillance will break down; fiscal turmoil as welfare costs rise in localities where existing sources of tax revenue are already overburdened; and political turmoil, especially within the urban Democratic coalition, as an alerted electorate divides on the question of how to overcome this disruption in local government. Reverberations of local trouble will be felt at the national level, and in the ensuing debate over remedies to relieve local conflict, the poor and their allies can press for fundamental reforms.

Such reforms could extend to a variety of economic policies. Unemployed men are usually turned away from "home relief" offices, even in jurisdictions where they are legally eligible for aid. If they confine themselves to protests and rallies they won't get much, if anything. But if they organize to demand legal benefits, local costs will mount sharply, and that may focus national attention on the need for a program of full employment. Similarly, when low-wage earners organize to get the supplementary welfare benefits to which they are entitled in many places, a new force for higher minimum wages will be felt. If recipient groups (and lawyers) can prevent southern welfare departments from dropping thousands of families at cotton-chopping time, so that they may be exploited in the fields, pressure to review agricultural policies may mount. And the breakdown of welfare's archaic procedures may help draw attention to the need for a simplified, federally administered guaranteed income for those who should not work (e.g., mothers with small children) or cannot work (e.g., the disabled or those made temporarily unemployed through recession, automation or plant relocation).

Will current organizing strategies produce the massive benefits which are the movement's chief source of leverage for reform?

The answer is mixed. Thus far, organizing has mainly concentrated on processing individual complaints. This method is useful in building core groups, but it cannot be employed to reach large numbers, for it requires virtually boundless manpower and patience. Organizing by this method requires that grievance committees of recipient groups first study the complex manuals which specify entitlements. But in many places officials must go to court or find sympathetic investigators who will steal copies. Furthermore, the welfare system can forget, stall, harass and intimidate. It can correct an error one month and repeat it the next. It can resist interference on a case-by-case basis in dozens of ways.

Part of the answer to these problems is to make recipients themselves more effective plaintiffs by informing them of their rights. Simplified manuals, prepared by social workers and lawyers, are now available in about twelve northern cities and in several southern states. A broad distribution of such documents will go a long way toward overcoming the ignorance of entitlements by which recipients are now victimized. But had labor confined itself to negotiating for individual workers, it would have obtained little more than minor concessions from management. It took the economic power of the strike to bring about more substantial reforms. Unless welfare groups do more than adjust individual grievances and hold rallies, they too will obtain only minor concessions. These token concessions will weaken the movement by creating a momentary sense of victory, leaving untouched the real sources of poverty: unemployment and low wage levels, agricultural subsidies which enrich large landholders and drive small farmers and rural workers into the urban ghettos, and the lack of a guaranteed income to protect people against a variety of misfortunes.

A more efficient strategy to increase participation, and also to build toward a crisis in the welfare system, focuses on some common deprivation that affects many people and involves much money. The minimum-standards campaign in New York City is the best example, but even there the potential has hardly been tapped, for only about five percent of the city's 650,000 recipients have so far been reached by the movement. In each jurisdiction, organizers need to study local rules to determine whether a given category of benefits is being regularly withheld, and then must mount mass campaigns to unlock these benefits. Such campaigns bring organizers into contact with a good deal of money. A fair proportion of those helped maintain an affiliation with core organizing groups; some become formal members, others stand by to support mass meetings and demonstrations.

*The movement's full impact will be felt when it turns to recruiting eligible persons to the welfare ranks. The reservoir is enormous, since only about half of those now eligible are on the rolls. Philadelphia groups are planning to station members in welfare centers to offer help to applicants who are rejected. (In Philadelphia, as in many other places, the department turns down half of all who apply, and lawyers estimate that half of these rejections are illegal.)*

*The recruitment potential is suggested by the experience of an antipoverty agency in Baltimore. Having opened a new office in a ghetto area, agency staff members set out to do "case-finding" for their services by knocking on doors. In the process, they uncovered hundreds of poverty-stricken people whom they routinely referred to welfare, with the result that the AFDC rolls in the neighborhood doubled. When interviewed by newspapermen, the director of the Maryland state board of social welfare insisted: "It's not our responsibility to inform people of their entitlements." This is precisely government's responsibility, but it will not meet that obligation. An energetic recruitment campaign will have at least the same effect in other areas, and a public crisis will result.*

Some participants in the movement (and some of its supporters) are offended by talk of creating a "crisis." What they fail to see is that the system has already been subverted by its continuous accommodation to powerful groups arrayed against the poor and the minorities in the local community. Consequently, recipients are victimized by the discrepancy between the statutes governing the system, which are bad enough, and day-to-day rules and practices, which are far worse. The purpose of a recipients' movement is not to subvert government any further but to reveal how other political forces have already succeeded in subverting it, and then to press for major economic reforms. The legitimacy of disrupting a system that is already so corrupt is unassailable.

# Workers and Welfare: The Poor Against Themselves

RICHARD A. CLOWARD
AND FRANCES FOX PIVEN

The New York City Coordinating Committee of Welfare Groups, which mainly represents mothers and children, has just announced a major campaign based on our proposal to recruit poorly paid male workers and their families onto the relief rolls to obtain substantial wage supplements. If the campaign succeeds, it could spread to other cities, providing the basis for a political alliance between the working and nonworking poor. Such a coalition of poor people would be a defense against the mounting attacks on the welfare system—attacks spearheaded by better-paid segments of the working and middle class.

Behind these attacks is a growing political agitation for a "solution to the welfare problem." The white working class is especially angered by the rising rolls. To white workers, welfare is a "black problem"—arising from the softheadedness of liberals in dealing with the black poor, or the opportunism of politicians in dealing for the black vote. And so . . . a new battle is about to take place between the white working class and the black (and in New York, the Puerto Rican) poor.

The sources of the controversy are easy to see. Welfare rolls are escalating, especially the AFDC rolls. Taking all categories together, the rolls in New York City have almost trebled since 1960, are now rising by about 20,000 each month and will reach 1 million by the first of the year. Considering the vast migrations of

Originally published in the *Nation*, November 25, 1968. Copyright by the authors.

the poor from Puerto Rico and the southern United States, these figures are not surprising. Furthermore, tens of thousands of families who are eligible for assistance are not yet receiving it, so the rise can be expected to continue—that is, unless new restrictions result from the upcoming investigations.

Relatively speaking, the cost of public assistance in America is quite modest—far less than the subsidies to better-off groups. But if welfare accounts for a small percentage of federal outlays, it is often a very large percentage of local expenditures. Even though New York City pays only about twenty-five percent of welfare expenses (fifty percent is reimbursed by the federal government, and another twenty-five percent by the state), welfare will cost the city about one-third of a billion dollars this year. That seems an intolerable burden in a city already teetering at the edge of bankruptcy.

The working poor carry a disproportionate share of the tax burden, given the regressive character of our tax system (especially local sales and property taxes). A broader view of class inequities would lead working-class leaders to mount an attack on a tax structure which benefits the affluent and victimizes the working class; instead, they attack the welfare poor. For to white working-class people, and even to many black workers, it appears that the welfare recipient is enjoying a free ride on their hard-earned tax dollars, meanwhile scorning the value of work and the self-esteem of workers.

Nor is that the worst of it. The welfare recipient seems to be undermining the financial rewards of work as well. In several northern states, among them New York, a worker earning the minimum wage who has a nonworking wife and one child takes home less money than is allotted to a comparable family on welfare. For larger families the advantage of being on welfare is even greater. That this issue provokes intense feeling is clear. "It doesn't pay to work anymore!" is the angry complaint. The value of work is being affronted, and that value is deeply ingrained. How else explain the persistence with which those who do the dirtiest work at the most exploitative wage levels apply their shoulders to the wheel? If the working poor are victimized by their pride, they are also embittered by their lot, and it is upon the nonworking underclass that they vent their anger.

Nothing offends working-class spokesmen quite so much as

demands by organized welfare recipients for higher levels of benefits, or for full entitlements. Needless to say, they find even more
infuriating efforts by client groups to enroll the hundreds of
thousands of eligible poor who have not been receiving benefits
(usually because they do not know of their entitlements or have
been illegally rejected). Welfare supplicants are supposed to be
meek and grateful; instead they are confronting their benefactors
with aggressive demands. The angry protests of the workers today
echo the outrage voiced by the defenders of private property when
these same "ungrateful" workers began to organize. Just as those
workers, being the victims of the propertied, no longer held property rights to be sacrosanct, so welfare recipients now question
the inviolability of work values, for the bulk of them, being the
very old or the very young, or mothers or disabled, either cannot or should not work. Each phase of the struggle by the poor
for some measure of justice is also a struggle against the cate-
chisms which legitimate exploitation.

The welfare issue is contributing to the polarization of black
and white in the cities, for the welfare rolls in the cities are
disproportionately black. (Nationally, the AFDC rolls are half
white.) But polarization is also partly the legacy of a long history
in which blacks were used by employers to depress wages and
retard unionization. The black scab is an old enemy—the central figure in a labor lore that goes back to a stevedores' strike in
New York in 1855, to a miners' strike in Alabama in 1894 and
to a factory strike in East St. Louis during World War I. The
hatred lingers, for it is deeply imprinted. Other groups—
Chinese, Japanese, Mexicans—have also been made to play the
scab role, especially in efforts to break agricultural strikes, but
none was used so regularly as the black. With the success of
large-scale unionization, white workers had less to fear from
strikebreaking. By excluding the blacks from union membership,
they were able in many cases to exclude blacks from employment
altogether. The New Deal even brought the blacks and whites
of the cities together in a political coalition. A brief but uneasy
peace followed.

Now the dislocation of blacks from agriculture has aroused
the old antagonisms once more. The New Deal coalition, always
tenuous, is fragmenting as blacks flood into the cities to threaten

working-class residential areas, schools, services and jobs. Black
and white are again being turned against one another in competition for scarce resources. And white workers are once again
fixing blame on blacks, not on those above them. Once more,
the black is cast as scab, not least in the emerging welfare controversy.

One working-class solution to welfare scabbing is to reaffirm
the imperative of work—the slogan will be "Put them to work!"
Congress already sensed this rising sentiment a year ago when it
enacted provisions requiring the states to train and assign mothers
and children older than sixteen to employment, unless there is
"good cause." A few congressmen opposed the measure, arguing
properly that a society which has never provided full employment for men had no right to force work upon women and children, but the argument did not carry. In the wake of the debate,
one satisfied senator was heard to say, "We've solved the maid
problem." And so perhaps they have, for compulsory work programs may succeed in removing large numbers of women and
teen-agers from the welfare rolls. Then perhaps Congress will
contemplate extending the same remedy to the aged, to young
children and to the disabled.

But just how the lower stratum of the working class will benefit from these measures is difficult to see. At best, competition for
low-paying jobs will intensify, and whatever leverage workers
have in bargaining with employers will be undercut. For in many
states women and children will be discharged from the rolls to
take any work at any wage and on any employer's terms. One
can say this with certainty, since some of the states had one
variation or another of "employable mother" rules long before
the new federal requirement, and the experience with these rules
has been dismal indeed. Together with a multitude of kindred
rules (like "man-in-the-house" and "substitute parent" regulations), such provisions have always been used to maintain an
exploitable labor supply.

To keep ahead of welfare-payment levels, the working-class
will probably also call for an increase in the minimum wage of
$1.60. But it is by no means clear that the better-paid segments
of organized labor are committed to raising minimums in more
than principle, for they generally resist any diminution of dif-

ferentials between them and lower-paid workers. There is also a great deal of evidence to suggest that lower-paid workers are hurt when minimum wage levels are raised. Labor-intensive industries migrate to low-wage areas or accelerate efforts to automate, or go out of business altogether. The result is fewer jobs for marginal workers. All in all, the popular solutions to the so-called welfare problem will not benefit the working poor—except, that is, as workers derive satisfaction from punishing nonworkers.

Ironically, it is the *working* poor who may be the chief losers in the present controversy, especially if welfare-payment levels are scaled down to a point below the minimum wage. For it is not generally understood that some states have a wage-supplement program through which low-paid workers can claim hundreds of millions of dollars, even raising their incomes above the levels now received by nonworking welfare recipients. These supplements may be jeopardized if welfare programs are made more restrictive.

In New York State, supplements now bring the annual income of a worker earning the minimum wage ($3120) to as high as $6000, $7000 or $8000, depending on the number and ages of family members. For example, a minimum-wage worker with a wife and four children receiving a wage supplement grosses $6264. Furthermore, his wage supplement of $3144 is not subject to federal, state or local income taxes. To achieve the same after-tax income from wages, this worker would have to be raised from $1.60 to $3.50 per hour. Between 150,000 and 300,000 working families in New York City alone are entitled to wage supplements; a mere 12,000 now claim them.

How is it that hundreds of millions of dollars in available wage supplements continue to go unclaimed by thousands of working poor? The answer is that the payments are not called wage supplements but "home relief," and they are not distributed by the Labor Department but by the Welfare Department. Union leaders have traditionally resisted encouraging their members to apply for welfare wage supplements, believing this an admission of their failure to obtain higher wages through collective bargaining. Welfare departments cannot be relied upon to inform people about benefits; quite the contrary. Consequently, many workers simply do not know that these payments are available or how to calculate their eligibility. Some workers who do know shy away because of their traditional contempt for the dole and for those who subsist on it.

In truth, low-paid families which fail to claim wage supplements are being taken in by the "free enterprise" ideology of the private economy, although that ideology bears little relation to what has become the reality. Ours is a "subsidy enterprise" economy, and the subsidies go to those who are enterprising in the use of their political influence. The low-paid alone seem not to realize this. Farmers receive wage supplements—we call them agricultural subsidies. The construction unions enjoy high incomes partly because of government subsidies to builders who are required to pay the "prevailing wage." Large numbers of middle-income people enjoy the benefits of a host of housing and transportation and tax subsidies. And these are merely a few of the items on a very long list of government giveaways, both direct and indirect, which support the standard of living of the more affluent in America. In a subsidy economy, the singular faith of the working poor in advancement through wages alone is pathetic, to say the least.

The magnitude of supplemental income relinquished by the working poor is both staggering and sobering. In New York, wage supplements are determined by a simple calculation of the difference between what welfare calls the worker's "net income" and the scheduled welfare-grant level. Net income is calculated by deducting a series of work-related expenses from gross earnings. For a typical male worker, these expenses over the course of a full year might be:

| | |
|---|---:|
| Carfare (40¢ per day) | $104 |
| Lunch ($1.15 per day) | 299 |
| Social Security (on minimum wage) | 137 |
| Union dues | 40 |
| Flat allowance of $20 per month | 240 |
| (for other work-related expenses) | $820 |

In addition, income taxes are deducted. For a worker, his wife and one child at the minimum wage, federal and state taxes would be $140, yielding a total wage-related deduction of $960 and a net income of $2160. With two children, taxes would be

$20, which yield a deduction of $840 and a net income of $2280. Workers with three or more children pay no income taxes, so their total deduction is $820 and their net income is $2300.

Column A in the following chart shows the payments that nonworking welfare families receive. (In each family category, the smallest payment is made where the oldest child is under six and the largest payment where the oldest child is in college or equivalent institution.) Net incomes for working families earning the minimum wage are shown in Column B. The difference (Column A minus Column B) is the wage supplement to which the worker is entitled, as shown in Column C. The worker's new income (his earned income of $3120 plus the wage supplement) is shown in Column D. Thus, a worker with five children, the oldest of whom is in college or vocational school, would receive $6968 *even though he earns only $3120.* As noted earlier, his wage supplement of $3848 is not taxable. Furthermore, we have assumed that all workers are paying a modest $100 monthly rental. Many pay more, especially those with large families, and the wage supplement calculated by welfare can be adjusted upward (or downward, if the rent is lower) to cover the actual cost of rent, within certain limits.

So far we have assumed that the worker earns only the minimum wage. Higher-paid workers are also eligible for wage supplements, up to the maximum incomes shown in Column E. Families at the maximum are entitled to the wage supplements in the amounts shown in Column F, which are also nontaxable.

To calculate the wage supplement available to a worker whose earned income falls between the minimum wage and the maximums shown in Column E, one must first subtract $3120 from the gross earned income, then subtract the remainder from the appropriate figure in Column C (determined by the number and ages of children). The difference is the wage supplement, assuming a rental of $100 per month.[1]

As for the frequent charge that welfare destroys the incentive to work, it can readily be seen that those who work are better off. How much better can be calculated by comparing Column A (what nonworking welfare families receive) with Column D (the worker earning at the minimum wage with a wage supplement). The difference is equivalent to the work-related deductions described earlier. Furthermore, workers who claim wage supple-

WAGE SUPPLEMENTS AVAILABLE IN NEW YORK STATE

| Worker and Housewife and | (A) Nonworker Welfare Budget (1) ($100 Rent) (2) | (B) Estimated "Net Income" of a Worker Earning Minimum Wage ($3120 per year) | (C) Annual Wage Supplement To Minimum Wage Worker | (D) Annual Total Income (Minimum Wage and Wage Supplement) | (E) Maximum Earned Income for Those Eligible for Wage Supplement | (F) Annual Wage Supplement to Maximum Wage Worker |
|---|---|---|---|---|---|---|
| 1 Child | | | | | | |
| —Under 6 years | 3204 | 2160 | 1044 | 4164 | 3804 | 360 |
| —In College (3) | 3564 | 2160 | 1404 | 4524 | 4164 | 360 |
| 2 Children | | | | | | |
| —Older Child Under 6 Years | 3616 | 2280 | 1336 | 4456 | 3996 | 460 |
| —Older Child In College | 4264 | 2280 | 1984 | 5104 | 4644 | 460 |
| 3 Children | | | | | | |
| —Oldest Child Under 6 Years | 4052 | 2300 | 1752 | 4872 | 4312 | 560 |
| —Oldest Child in College | 4916 | 2300 | 2616 | 5736 | 5176 | 560 |
| 4 Children | | | | | | |
| —Oldest Child Under 6 Years | 4340 | 2300 | 2140 | 5260 | 4500 | 660 |
| —Oldest Child in College | 5444 | 2300 | 3144 | 6264 | 5604 | 660 |
| 5 Children | | | | | | |
| —Oldest Child Under 6 Years | 4900 | 2300 | 2600 | 5720 | 4960 | 760 |
| —Oldest Child in College | 6148 | 2300 | 3848 | 6968 | 6208 | 760 |

Note (1): The "flat grant" of $100 per person per year for replacement of heavy clothing and household furnishing has been included in estimating payment levels, but excluded from calculations of eligibility in accord with welfare regulations.

Note (2): All calculations assume a monthly rent of $100; if the actual rent is higher or lower, all columns except (F) would be adjusted by the difference, within limits prescribed by welfare regulations.

Note (3): Or in any legitimate institution of learning or vocational training beyond high school.

ments also become eligible for Medicaid, a considerable benefit in itself.

Unions could help the working poor to obtain these extraordinary supplements, perhaps by distributing brochures . . . explaining why workers are entitled to these benefits in a subsidy economy and how to claim them. The unions are not likely to do this, hemmed in as they are by old prejudices and by a rank-and-file version of an obsolete entrepreneurial ethic. But were low-paid workers to coalesce with nonworkers in a fight for decent welfare-payment levels and improved supplementary-wage policies, all could gain. The political and economic stakes are high for all low-income families. It is more likely, however, that the growing attacks on welfare will become just another series of events in the lengthening chronicle of the American poor against themselves.

# NOTES

[1] There is one deterrent in establishing eligibility for wage supplements—the family must first divest itself of most assets. But low-paid families are not likely to have many assets, and these substantial wage supplements would quickly compensate them for the loss.

The assets which must be disposed of are these. If the worker has any equity in a private pension plan, he must borrow half and live on the proceeds at a rate equivalent to the scheduled levels in the chart. At the scheduled levels, workers would use up their equity in a month or two, especially if they pay high rents. The remaining equity must then be assigned to the welfare department. Similarly, workers may not carry life insurance on themselves or any member of their family in excess of $500 face value per person. Equity beyond this amount must be assigned.

If the worker owns a home—as few low-paid workers in New York City do—it must be assigned. However, the family may continue to live in the house, and the mortgage and taxes will be paid in lieu of rent by the welfare department. If and when the house is finally sold, the department will claim the proceeds. Finally, a family is not ordinarily allowed to own an automobile unless it is needed for work.

However, experience shows that the enforcement of this rule is extremely discretionary.

For all of this, welfare departments are very much political animals. They possess considerable discretion in interpreting and enforcing various rules, and they would not be uninfluenced by pressure from unions representing workers. It might also be said that many of these rules about assets are of doubtful constitutionality; some of them are already being challenged by attorneys associated with the National Welfare Rights Movement, a struggle union attorneys could also take up.

# Rent Strike: Disrupting the Slum System

FRANCES FOX PIVEN
AND RICHARD A. CLOWARD

For a few feverish months during the winter of 1963–64, rent strikes broke out in New York's barrios. Activists of various persuasions moved in to canvass the tenements, blending the language of the building codes with the language of direct action. In a short time some 500 buildings were on strike. Then, almost as quickly as it had erupted, the movement subsided. By late spring there were few traces to be seen.

The rent strike of 1963–64 was not the first. In the 1890s, after a half-century of turbulence among the urban poor, rent strikes were common in New York. They occurred again after World War I and during the early years of the Depression. Accused of bolshevism and threatened with reprisals, tenants nonetheless compelled government to limit rent increases and curtail evictions. These earlier strikes usually began spontaneously, often leading to massive street violence. Radicals tried to capitalize upon these uprisings to build permanent "peoples' organizations," hoping by education and exhortation to turn the seemingly incoherent energy of the mob into consistent pressure for continuing reform through the electoral process. And this is ironic, for the reforms produced by rent strikes resulted from the disruptions themselves, not from the influence of tenant organizations which, if they emerged at all, were small and unstable. In retrospect, the rent strike of 1963–64 was probably the least disruptive in history; it was also the least successful in pro-

ducing any important reforms. Its failure suggests some lessons
for the future.

By the early 1960s, New York City had been plagued with a
housing shortage for at least two decades. Then, as now, the
shortage took its severest toll on blacks and Puerto Ricans, who
occupied the 550,000 units classified by the census as "deteriorated, dilapidated, or lacking essential facilities" and the 100,000
other units classified as "overcrowded." The hardships created by
inadequate and insufficient housing were intensified by the
destruction and dislocation caused by urban renewal and public-
works programs, which had set the city's low-income neighborhoods on edge. And by the late summer of 1963, after the
civil-rights march on Washington for Jobs and Freedom, activists
were beginning to turn to the ghettos of New York and other
northern cities to stimulate blacks to act on political and economic issues.

In this climate of discontent and protest, a maverick radical
named Jesse Gray announced a Harlem rent strike. On November 1, Gray took out sixteen buildings. A month later the number had risen to fifty. Volunteers from the Northern Student
Movement then joined forces with Gray, and another fifty Harlem
buildings went on strike. On the Lower East Side, a chapter of
the Congress of Racial Equality (CORE) took six buildings out
on strike in the fall, and later its efforts were augmented when
Mobilization for Youth, an antipoverty project sponsored by the
federal and city governments, helped a variety of community
groups to form "The Lower East Side Rent Strike," bringing
about fifty more buildings into the movement. Meanwhile, an
especially effective CORE group in Brooklyn organized 200
buildings. In East Harlem, fifty buildings struck, some organized
by the East Harlem Tenants Council and others by two local
CORE chapters. A union of low-paid blacks and Puerto Ricans,
Local 1199 of the Drug and Hospital Workers, helped put thirty
more buildings on strike by working with tenants who were
union members. With Gray at its head, a massive protest seemed
about to burst forth from the black slum. The civil-rights movement had indeed come North.

But day-to-day organizing had little drama. After the first
flush of enthusiasm, young and inexperienced organizers began
to accept the guidance of the Metropolitan Council on Housing,

an organization of older radicals which had formed during the earlier struggles against urban renewal and whose leaders urged cautious tactics consistent with the complex statutes governing rent withholding. The law prescribed an elaborate bureaucratic course, and the courts interpreted the law rigidly. Judges admitted only the inspection records of the Department of Buildings as evidence of hazardous violations. To obtain those records, organizers had to fill out forms and arrange and follow up appointments for inspections; check agency files to make sure that hazardous violations had been posted; and meanwhile see that rents withheld by tenants were being collected and deposited in a private escrow account. (If the tenants lost in court, these funds were turned over to the landlord; if they won, the money was turned over to the clerk of the court, to be given to the landlord after repairs were made.) Finally, organizers had to shepherd tenants through the courts. And all of this turned out to require enormous effort and expertise.

At the outset, rent-strike cadres were not dismayed by these elaborate procedures. Indeed, they defined them as a means of educating tenants and building tenant associations. Canvassing door-to-door to discover housing violations was a way of making contact with tenants; filing "multiple form" complaints was a way of stimulating building meetings; assigning tenants the responsibility for collecting rents and managing escrow accounts was a way of strengthening building committees and developing leadership. And through these tenant groups, organizers believed the poor could be educated to the larger political issues underlying slum housing. Such "radicalizing" of tenants was presumably to produce mass associations capable of exerting regular influence on government; each arduous bureaucratic task would contribute to the creation of a permanent "peoples' organization." That public agencies were thereby dictating the tactics of the movement struck no one as anomalous.

The emphasis on bureaucratic rules and procedures was also dictated by fear that tenants would be evicted if other tactics were followed. A few evictions did occur, and they sometimes evoked frenzied but haphazard resistance. Early in February, Gray and ten of his aides were arrested for attempting to prevent an eviction by "strong-arming" city marshals. Sometimes, when marshals appeared, organizers sat on the furniture while one of their number hurried to file a stay of eviction with the court. When furniture was already piled on the street, organizers occasionally moved it back to gain time to get the tenant into court. But while such "holding" tactics usually worked, they were not employed regularly, for the organizers concentrated on using legal safeguards. When CORE organizers failed to resist the eviction of a family on the Lower East Side, other striking tenants, fearing that they also would be turned out, hysterically demanded the rent money from their escrow accounts. That event broke the strike in the CORE stronghold on Eldridge Street. Such experiences seemed to affirm the importance of adhering all the more to elaborate bureaucratic procedures. Organizers became clerks, and political action was reduced to bookkeeping.

The test of these tactics was to come in the courts. The first two cases were heard during a barrage of publicity and were won by the tenants. But public interest quickly faded, and in subsequent decisions judges reaffirmed traditional property rights. When—sometimes mysteriously and sometimes because of slip-ups—records subpoenaed from the Department of Buildings failed to show hazardous violations, judges rejected the testimony of tenants or photographs of building conditions and ordered the rents to be paid, often berating the organizers for trouble-making. Landlords frequently asked for adjournments, since they knew that many tenants would prefer to pay the rent rather than spend another day in court. Such failures led organizers to adhere even more rigidly to procedures, to focus more and more energy on fewer and fewer buildings.

But the bureaucratic rites by which repairs were to be exacted, and tenants educated, exhausted organizers and bewildered tenants. To cope with agency procedures required precisely those resources of money and expertise which are scarcest among the poor. Meanwhile, landlords exploited bureaucratic intricacies and corruptibility to evade or overcome the challenge. Even occasional tenant victories in the courts yielded only minor and temporary repairs. Unable to produce repairs quickly and to multiply them widely, tenant affiliation did not expand, and the strike developed little political force. Thus, the movement began to subside a few months after it formed.

At first blush, the rent strike appears to be a simple and powerful strategy to bring about housing reform. It can be just that, but only if it acquires the momentum to compel government action. In the strike of 1963–64 the landlord was the target, and that was the first mistake. Slum landlords generally do not have the resources to rehabilitate their buildings—not, at least, unless rents are substantially increased. The slum is the underbelly of the real-estate market; tenants who cannot compete for housing elsewhere are preyed on by entrepreneurs who lack the capital or competence to compete for profit elsewhere. More prosperous and stable real-estate investors put their capital in the regular market, where money can be made in less demeaning ways, leaving the slum to be exploited by men who seek to gain on dubious speculative exchanges or who, restrained by rent-control laws from levying large increases, shore up their declining profits by skimping on repairs and services. The result is inflated prices and deteriorated buildings—a situation that can be remedied only by public action.

Public programs exist on the books, but are unused. In New York City, for example, low-cost municipal loans can be made to landlords to reduce the burden of undertaking rehabilitation; by 1963, however, only one such loan had been made, because the city was reluctant to become implicated in the shadowy finances of slum housing. The receivership program empowers the city to take over and repair hazardous buildings; after a year of operation, only sixteen buildings had been acquired and, at that, the commissioner of real estate reported indignantly that the city was finding the venture unprofitable! Thus, despite a wide variety of programs and powers available to municipalities, the bulk of slum housing remains and worsens—the rent-strikers of 1963–64 lived in some of the same tenements which inspired the protests of such Nineteenth-Century reformers as Jacob Reis and Lillian Wald.

Political leaders and public agencies never became the target of the 1963–1964 strike. On the surface municipal agencies were conciliatory. The Department of Buildings put an inspector at Gray's disposal, and similar concessions were made to leaders elsewhere. Meanwhile, the mayor and his aides spoke out publicly against the slums, bewailing housing conditions and invoking the villain landlord of ancient myth. They called for more housing inspectors as well as legislation authorizing higher fines and jail sentences. These responses were predictable, if not perennial; the law already permitted considerably higher fines than were being levied by the courts, and housing agencies, we have noted, already had substantial powers and programs they were not employing. In the end, government escaped unscathed, having made only a few meaningless concessions.

How can government be forced to act? One thing is certain: The tactics used in 1963–64 won't do. Organizers reasoned that with the promise of repairs as the initial inducement to participate, stable organizations of the poor would eventually be formed, and that these would influence government. But the continuing emphasis on building permanent associations rests on a mistaken premise: that public decisions are made only in response to organized voting numbers. This view overlooks the impact of crisis as a way of compelling public action. When crisis occurs, many groups are aroused; they view disorder as a failure of governmental responsibility and demand measures (whether concessions or repression) to restore order. Crisis thus has a potential political force far greater than the number of citizens, organized or not, who participate in the disruptive action itself. The legalistic tactics of 1963–64 did not generate a public crisis, but other, more disruptive rent-strike tactics would.

The key to a disruptive rent strike is for tenants to pocket the rent, not place it in escrow. Widespread action of this kind would throw the slum-housing economy into chaos, for many landlords would have to abandon their property, leaving thousands of tenants in buildings without services or even minimal maintenance. As health hazards multiplied and the breakdown of landlord-tenant relations threatened to spread, the clamor would mount for governmental action to solve the crisis.

Pocketing the rent money would mean an immediate gain for tenants—a far more compelling incentive to participate than the vague hope of getting minor repairs. The main job of organizers would be to expand the strike by exciting indignation and urging tenants to spend their rent money for other needs. Such activity is much more compatible with the skills and temperament of organizers than canvassing for violations, filing forms, searching records, maintaining escrow accounts and sitting endlessly in courtrooms. Relieved of these wearisome chores, they should be able to reach far more people than in 1963–64.

What of the dangers? It will be argued that the city can

retaliate—at the very least, evictions might result. To minimize this risk, organizers need to mobilize at least a few hundred buildings to launch the strike, adding more buildings during the two- or three-month period it takes landlords to process evictions. It is unlikely that thousands, or even hundreds, of families would be put out on the streets, especially on the streets of ghettos whose growing and turbulent populations politicians can no longer afford to antagonize flagrantly. Furthermore, mass evictions would be viewed by many in the wider public as an even greater disorder than the breakdown of slum-property relations.

It is important to understand that political leaders can prevent evictions, for the decision to evict is as much political as judicial. City governments, for example, have the legal right to initiate court proceedings against landlords who fail to correct violations. New York City has, in addition, the power to undercut legal actions taken against tenants by such landlords, simply by reducing rents to a dollar a month in buildings with multiple violations. Nor would housing courts in most cities, typically run by politically appointed judges, be so lenient with landlords when pressed by political leaders. Finally, to obtain time to wash out dispossess actions, mayors in most cities can simply order city marshals to delay all evictions, as a New York mayor did during the violent rent strike of 1933. The legalistic tactics employed by the tenants in 1963–64 enabled political leaders to leave the strikers at the mercy of the agencies and the courts. But faced with tactics which ignore bureaucratic procedures and court proceedings, public officials would have to use their powers to forestall mass evictions or risk a major threat to political stability. Except in the face of a crisis, however, chief executives will not use these powers. Even if they did act, organizers would have to develop cadres to resist isolated evictions, defending the lone tenant by pitting the ghetto against the city's marshals and thus raising the specter of large-scale violence. Street action is far easier to mobilize than stable organizations of tenants. In 1963–64, however, organizers did not encourage street action, having pinned hope on the bureaucracies and courts.

By now it should be abundantly clear that the strategy we advocate is in no way limited to those few cities with statutes authorizing rent withholding. These laws are irrelevant, if not diversionary. Our analysis shows the futility of efforts to help

masses of tenants make individual use of cumbersome procedures of legal redress. Disruptive tactics have a different purpose:
to shift the burden of action against slum landlords from tenants
to city governments.

There are measurable gains to be made by a disruptive rent
strike. At the very least, this tactic should impel cities to use such
programs as exist, whether offering low-cost loans to landlords
who are willing to make repairs or making extensive emergency
repairs and billing landlords for the cost. Most important, under
cumulative impact of disruptive actions, thousands of buildings
would be abandoned—left to government to take over. It is
crucial to understand why this result would follow.

Slum housing is rampantly illegal, yet public agencies have
never made much effort to enforce housing codes in New York.
Even in those few cases where landlords were taken to court, the
fines levied per violation averaged only twenty-two dollars in
1963. By 1966 they had fallen to fourteen dollars. Code-enforce-
ment machinery is not allowed to work for good reason: A crack-
down would produce massive dislocation of landlords and
tenants. Repairs are extremely expensive, and building income
is limited by the poverty of the captive tenant market as well as
by rent-control laws. Just a modest step-up in enforcement activity
under a new administration in New York City recently resulted
in a upsurge in the number of foreclosures, tax delinquencies and
vacate orders. If slumlords were pushed out, government would
have to house the minority poor. So the enforcement agencies
use their powers gingerly and selectively, usually paying heed
only when tenants have the tenacity or the "pull" to compel
enforcement.

In other words, slum profits have depended on collusion between city agencies and landlords: In return for nonenforcement
of the codes, the slumlord takes the blame for the slum and en-
ables the city to evade the political ire of the ghetto. But once
municipal agencies are compelled to act on the codes, many
owners of deteriorated buildings will be forced out of business,
unable or unwilling to make the required repairs. Considering
the highly marginal character of the slum market, the rent-strike
tactics we propose could precipitate change no less fundamental
than large-scale public takeover of land and buildings.

What would a city government do with slum buildings? Very

likely it would divest itself as quickly as possible of responsibility for them. To maintain the slums could only be expensive and politically onerous. City officials would run the risk of angering tenants dissatisfied with repairs and services, as well as taxpayers disgruntled by new investments in housing for the black and poor. Under such circumstances, municipalities might well move to sell or lease slum lands and buildings to private redevelopers. New governmental schemes are now in the making to stimulate investments in ghettos by national corporations, with federal subsidies to guarantee profits (e.g., tax benefits, low-cost loans and insurance, and rent supplements). These schemes, if implemented, would provide a way out for municipalities thrust by disruptive rent strikes into the role of slum landlords.

Federally subsidized corporate redevelopment will result in better housing and facilities; it will also bring the ghetto under the hegemony of an alliance of national corporations and federal bureaucracies. Now that blacks are coming into power in many large cities, the ghettos would be much better off with the municipality acting as redeveloper and landlord. Nevertheless, corporate ownership appears to be the wave of the future, and the leverage of the vote will have limited effect on corporate policies regarding location and design, tenant selection or rents.

To deal with corporations on these policies, tenants will need to develop modes of influence beyond the vote. In this connection, corporate ownership might provide a favorable context for organizing mass-based tenant unions. As we noted earlier, most tenants now live in buildings owned by small entrepreneurs who themselves have limited financial resources and so cannot yield to tenant demands; with nothing much to gain, tenants cannot easily be organized. Furthermore, ownership is so fragmented that efficient negotiating is virtually impossible. Under a system of national corporate ownership, however, tenants would confront large-scale landlords with ample resources to be conceded at the bargaining table. Tenant organization would then be comparable to organization of workers in the factory system or in that sector of agriculture controlled by large corporations. Thus rent strikes could be mobilized to demand partial control of management policies and lower rents (so it would fall to large corporations, not the poor, to fight with Congress for higher rent subsidies). Most important, strikers might hold out for concessions which would nurture stable tenant unions—especially collective-bargaining contracts and a dues check-off from rent payments. In Chicago a few tenant groups have used rent strikes as leverage against several large landlords, forcing through contracts which include check-offs. But whether the object is to compel housing improvements in a system of fragmented slum ownership or to create tenant unions in a system of large-scale ownership, disruptive tactics are the key.

There are only certain periods when a disruptive force can be mobilized, for the poor are ordinarily passive, obeisant to the rules prescribed by dominant institutions. But from time to time normative control weakens and unrest mounts, as in 1963–64. Now such a time is upon us again; there is greater turbulence in the ghetto than ever before. Young and aggressive leaders are emerging who are unencumbered by ties to white institutions. Whatever else might be said about the rhetoric of black power, it serves to undermine the legitimacy of established arrangements, freeing people for militant action.

This is also a time when disruption might have unique force in moving government. The black masses are swelling in many cities, and more than a few white municipal leaders remain in office merely because blacks are not yet sufficiently mobilized, or antagonized, to unseat them. Under the impact of disruptive tactics, white politicians wishing to retain control of municipal government would have to make concessions. In New York for example, Mayor Lindsay, a Republican, was assured of election in 1965 because blacks, ordinarily Democratic, gave him an unprecedented forty-two percent of their vote. Were he to permit mass evictions, his subsequent defeat would seem a foregone conclusion. Elsewhere, the potential for black reprisals against white politicians is far greater; blacks compose a mere fifteen percent of New York's population, but they are approaching (or have already reached) a majority in many cities.

Of course, a disruptive strategy is always uncertain because it is not guided by legal and political conventions. But if in violating these conventions the poor are exposed to risk, they are worse off on what may seem less treacherous ground. For in playing by institutional rules, they take on the full complement of inhibiting requirements imposed by powerful groups who make the rules. Unable to meet these requirements, they can only lose.

# Dissensus Politics: A Strategy for Winning Economic Rights

RICHARD A. CLOWARD
AND FRANCES FOX PIVEN

In the week after his death, Martin Luther King was memorialized as both leader and symbol of the southern black confrontation with white America, a confrontation of such moral clarity and intensity that it moved a majority of Americans to unite in support of the civil-rights legislation of 1964 and '65. This interpretation confirms the widely held belief that Negroes cannot obtain justice unless they coalesce with other groups in a majority alliance—which means, of course, the national Democratic coalition. According to this view, it is the wishes of a majority that finally impel political leaders to act. The task, therefore, is to identify the issues and exchanges by which a unified majority can be culled from a people divided by class and region, by race and religion.

But the political dynamics of the southern phase of the civil-rights movement may have been quite the reverse of what is commonly supposed. We would argue that its legislative victories were not the product of a majority consensus but of cleavage in the North-South Democratic coalition. The political impact of nonviolent protests, of "moral confrontations," was to widen that cleavage. The legislative concessions of 1964 and '65 owed less to the numbers of people committed to the civil-rights movement—whether blacks or their white allies—than to the sharply divisive impact the movement had upon an already strained North-South Democratic partnership. And if this theory

Originally published in the *New Republic*, April 20, 1968. Copyright by the authors.

is correct, it may be that blacks and other minorities can also compel future gains from the majority coalition by threatening to disrupt it.

Negroes have been part of the Democratic coalition for almost four decades—that is, beginning with the reorganization of the Democratic party during the elections of 1928 and 1932, when an alliance was struck between urban ethnic groups in the North and the traditionally Democratic South. In 1936 a majority of blacks voted Democratic for the first time. As members of that coalition, blacks have obtained minor concessions. In 1940, for example, a Roosevelt-oriented Supreme Court declared the white primary unconstitutional, and in 1941 FDR established the Fair Employment Practices Commission. Each concession to Negroes was fiercely resisted by southern Democrats who succeeded in warding off civil-rights legislation of any significance for nearly three decades.

The first overt signs that the North-South partnership was in danger of dissolving appeared during the presidential campaign of 1948. Early in February, Truman, responding to the swelling numbers of blacks in the North, urged Congress to act on the recommendations of the President's Committee on Civil Rights, which had reported the previous year. He went on to press for a strong civil-rights plank in the party platform. Incensed, delegates from the southern states convened in July to get a States' Rights party on the ballot. An irate Georgia congressman summed up southern sentiment with the declaration that "Harlem is wielding more influence . . . than the entire white South." In the subsequent election, four Deep South states—Louisiana, South Carolina, Alabama and Mississippi—actually delivered their electoral votes to the States' Rights presidential candidate. The South has not been "solid" since.

At the convention of 1952 and again in 1956, Democratic leaders backed off, trying to placate the Dixiecrat delegates by adopting a watered-down "compromise" civil-rights plank and, after long drawn-out intraparty struggles, seating them without a "loyalty" pledge. The Dixiecrat states duly returned to the Democratic columns in 1952, but South Carolina and Louisiana by very slim majorities. Elsewhere in the South the Republicans made big gains: Florida, Virginia, Tennessee and Texas went for Eisenhower in 1952, to be joined by Louisiana and Kentucky in 1956. Missouri also voted Republican in 1952, although it returned to the Democratic fold in 1956. The party's hold on the South was slipping rapidly.

The South was, of course, provoked by the civil-rights challenges made by the northern wing of the party, however ineffectual those challenges had so far been. Southern opinion was especially aroused by the Supreme Court's landmark decision against segregated education, won by NAACP attorneys in 1954, and which marked the emergence of desegregation as a national issue. But if that issue aroused fury in the South, it evoked considerable sympathy in the North, especially among the growing black electorate of the cities. Nevertheless, conciliation of the South was still the order of the day. Campaigning in 1956, Stevenson called for "slow but deliberate" efforts to desegregate.

It was not until 1955, when Martin Luther King led the Montgomery bus boycott, that organized civil-rights protests seized the attention of the nation. With each wave of protest, northern black voters grew increasingly restive, and the Democratic party could not ignore it. Appeasement of southern racism was becoming a political liability, for Negroes who had been staunchly loyal to the party of the New Deal were beginning to defect. In 1952 Eisenhower won twenty-one percent of the black vote; in 1956 he won thirty-nine percent. And in 1957 and 1960 a Democratic Congress passed the first civil-rights measures of the Twentieth Century.

By 1960, when John Kennedy campaigned on a strong civil-rights platform, the collapse of the southern wing of the party was plainly visible: In the three previous presidential elections only Georgia, Arkansas and North Carolina consistently gave their electoral votes to the Democratic candidate. Convinced that he could not resurrect southern allegiance, Kennedy appealed to black voters in the industrial states. The choice was correct. While the Democratic showing in the South was poor, it was no worse than during the conciliatory Stevenson campaigns. The States' Rights party won Mississippi and Alabama; Florida, Tennessee, Kentucky and Virginia voted Republican. And although Negro skepticism toward Democratic pledges on civil rights persisted, costing Kennedy thirty percent of the national black vote, the ghettos in a number of strategic northern cities turned in extraordinary Democratic percentages, swinging several critical states in very close races to assure his election.

Nevertheless, Kennedy did virtually nothing on civil rights during his first two years. He had won office, but narrowly. Moreover, his overall legislative program was being throttled by the conservative coalition of Republicans and southern Democrats, and the midterm elections of 1962 threatened to further deplete his congressional strength. It was not only that he wished to avoid fanning the fires of white resistance in the South; the racism of the white working class was also beginning to become an unmanageably divisive factor in the Democratic urban coalition. Accordingly, he signed an executive order barring discrimination in federally subsidized housing, but did nothing to implement it; he backed a bill to ease voter-literacy requirements, but sent no substantial civil-rights legislation to Congress. And he waited apprehensively for the midterm election.

However, the Democrats in 1962 won an unprecedented midterm victory, gaining four seats in the Senate and suffering only minimal losses in the House. Significantly, the small Republican advances were in the South, where they added five House seats (and very nearly won a Senate seat in Alabama); thus, southern support was still eroding, despite continuing Democratic efforts at conciliation.

Meanwhile, civil-rights agitation reached its crescendo, with sit-ins, demonstrations and boycotts which southerners repaid with killings, jailings, burnings and bombings. As the drama played itself out, North-South sentiments on civil-rights issues became sharply polarized, creating the political tension that would finally force legislative action. In February 1963, the president informed Congress of new civil-rights proposals, dealing primarily with public accommodations, voting rights and equal employment. He submitted a bill in June.

But the proposed legislation was moderate, and even so it seemed likely to fall prey to the conservative coalition in Congress. Demonstrations escalated. In August several hundred thousand people assembled for the March on Washington, and throughout the fall demonstrations were mounted in hundreds of cities and towns. In November a much strengthened bill was reported out of the House Judiciary Committee, a bill which

Lyndon Johnson, following Kennedy's death, pushed through the Congress, using all the political resources of his office to obtain the necessary Republican support, including votes to shut off a filibuster in the Senate. The 1964 Civil Rights Act became law.

The reasoning underlying Johnson's extraordinary commitment to civil rights is not difficult to deduce. He was bidding for heavy Negro support in the upcoming presidential election. Like Kennedy before him, he judged that the Deep South would defect to the Republican party, as five states subsequently did. But the Negro vote turned out to be decisive in a number of southern states which hung in the balance, such as Arkansas, Florida, Tennessee and Virginia. More important, Johnson received an astonishing ninety-four percent of the national black vote, which helped to give him the largest percentage of the popular vote in history.

A year later, with a voting-rights bill before Congress, Martin Luther King led thousands of supporters in the Selma marches. When Congress enacted the bill, that phase of the civil-rights struggle ended.

We review this history so as to underline the fact that legislative victories were not a simple response to majority sentiments. Left to themselves, labor and liberal and minority groups in the North would not have taken the initiative. Nor was it the sheer numbers involved in the southern movement that yielded those victories; the protesters were too few to compel the administration to champion measures that would fracture the North-South coalition alliance. Rather, it was the divisive impact of protest tactics that produced legislative gains by accelerating defections among southern white voters and threatening to produce defections in the urban ghettos as well.

Legislative concessions were made to mollify pro–civil-rights groups in the North. Notice, however, that the Civil Rights Act of 1965 also laid the groundwork for renewed Democratic strength in the South through provisions to enfranchise southern Negroes. In time, Democratic constituencies may be rebuilt by drawing together white moderates and newly enfranchised Negroes. So far, Negro registration has increased from 856,000 to 1,493,000 in the six states covered by the Voting Rights Act. A few states in the Deep South may remain in doubt (Alabama,

Mississippi, South Carolina, Louisiana and Georgia went Republican in '64), but Negro voter registration (up from eight to forty-seven percent in Mississippi, for example) may eventually restore even these states to the Democratic columns.

Although the civil-rights movement aggravated tensions in the regional coalition of the Democratic party, it did not create them. These tensions were produced by the steady movement of blacks to the North and into the big-city Democratic folds, a process which has slowly shifted the balance of political forces in the North-South Democratic partnership. Disruptive protests made it impossible for majority politicians to persist in placating the South. Thus, although the party platform proposed desegregation of interstate transportation in 1948, it was the freedom-riders and the brutality and public attention they provoked that produced an ICC order desegregating interstate transportation facilities more than a decade later.

The civil-rights movement is therefore an example of what might be called "dissensus politics": A cadre, acting on behalf of a minority within a coalition, engages in actions which are designed to dislodge (or which threaten to dislodge) not only that minority but, more important, *other significant constituent groups in that same alliance*. Through the cadre's ability to generate defections among other groups in a coalition, its impact becomes far greater than the voting power of the minority. If the strategist of consensus looks for issues and actions to bring groups together, then the strategist of dissensus looks for issues and actions which will drive groups apart.

Tactics to provoke dissensus are probably most effective at times when widespread social or economic change has already undermined a majority coalition, making it vulnerable to attack. Since the leaders of the coalition will tend to resist realignments of power and policy as long as possible, the disrupters must expose the underlying political tensions being produced by changing conditions. Then, confronted with actual or threatened electoral realignments, majority leaders will make concessions in an attempt to restore a weakening coalition or reorganize a shattered one.

Nevertheless, most leaders of the civil-rights movement remain committed to a strategy of influence through consensus politics, as advanced by Bayard Rustin in his article, "From

Protest to Politics" (*Commentary*, February 1965). With the passage of the Voting Rights Act, Rustin called for blacks to move from the streets to the polls, especially in alliance with other voting blocs in the traditional liberal-labor-minorities coalition. He pointed to the potential power of newly enfranchised southern blacks and to the growth of Negro electoral power in northern cities. But Mr. Rustin does not see that mass action in the streets *did* produce mass action at the polls—*not merely by blacks but also, and primarily, by whites.* If this interpretation has merit, then Rustin was not recommending a shift "from protest to politics" so much as a shift from one political strategy to another—in effect, from dissensus politics to consensus politics.

In the interim between Selma and King's assassination, the central concern of civil-rights forces shifted from legal rights to poverty. King himself began to work in the urban ghettos and to prepare plans for a poor-people's campaign for jobs and income. Implicit in this shift is the belief that the tactics which produced legal victories in the South can produce economic gains in northern cities, and for the same underlying political reasons.

In the past, the Democratic coalition was based on the state parties of the rural South and the big-city parties in the urbanized North. And while southern defections have lent greater weight to the big-city organizations, the cities have become more important in their own right. Two-thirds of our population now live in metropolitan areas. The regional configurations which formerly dominated national politics are rapidly giving way to urban configurations.

Race and class conflict in the cities is partly being played out in the arena of public services. But because blacks are newcomers, and not well organized, policies have not generally been much modified in response to them. When existing policies blatantly ignore changing constituencies, disruptive tactics can expose them as anachronisms and force new accommodations. Public-welfare practices are a prime example of such outmoded adaptations, and a national movement of welfare recipients is now growing whose strategy is to disrupt and expose them. In response to older constituent groups—the white working class which is concerned about taxes, and many in the middle class who suppose that poverty is better solved by "rehabilitating" the poor than by redistributing income—the administrators of public-welfare agencies keep the rolls low and budgets down. They refuse to inform the poor of their eligibility for assistance, erect a tangle of bureaucratic barriers against those who do apply, and simply reject many eligible applicants illegally. The public-welfare system distributes its meager benefits to but half of those who are legally eligible.

The welfare-recipients movement is disrupting this pattern by mobilizing many of the poor to claim their entitlements under the law. Mounting claims mean higher costs and higher taxes. Predictably, spokesmen for the working classes are already showing alarm and indignation, liberals are troubled; but the masses of the black poor are also becoming aroused. Welfare reforms are to be a major demand of the "poor-people's campaign" this summer.

In the short run, the result will be chaos in the welfare program. But that chaos will expose the ways in which the poor have been sacrificed to more-powerful groups in the Democratic coalition. To cope with the resulting dissensus, the national Democratic party might try to lessen welfare costs to localities, while also liberalizing the entire program. Relieving localities of the financial burden would placate the working class and others in the urban coalition, and a more liberal income-maintenance system (a federally guaranteed income, perhaps) would be a major concession to the black poor.

Similar dissensual strategies can be employed to force concessions in other areas—for example, in housing, which for the black poor in the cities is substandard, overcrowded and overpriced. Small-time landlords grub a profit from slum housing by shortcutting on repairs and services, buying "political insurance" against code enforcement with active support of local Democratic clubs. Liberals and "good government" groups, for their part, are satisfied with perennial reforms of the housing codes, to which political leaders acquiesce, knowing that cumbersome procedures of legal redress will do little except to satisfy the reformers. And even when legislation for new construction or rehabilitation is passed, only token funds are appropriated out of deference to other groups.

Housing agencies are thus the managers of a system of collusion; they do not enforce codes because to do so would bankrupt the slumlords and compel government to house the minority poor—a circumstance that would entail either diverting funds from programs serving other groups or raising local taxes. To avoid the ire which such actions would evoke, municipal government uses its enforcement powers gingerly and selectively, content to let the slumlord reap the fury of the ghetto.

These arrangements could be disrupted through massive withholding of rent, with tenants advised to spend the money instead for food and clothing. City governments would then be under great pressure to forestall evictions for fear of provoking widespread violence in the ghetto. Considering the marginal character of the slum market, many owners of deteriorated buildings, unable or unwilling to make the required repairs, would be forced out of business, propelling government into taking over slum housing. The consequent drain on municipal revenues and the conflicts engendered among urban groups would intensify local political conflict. But local conflicts reverberate in the national Democratic party, generating pressure for federal subsidies for low-income housing in large U.S. cities.

As the foregoing examples suggest, to effectively disrupt the coalition in the cities, something more than the marches, demonstrations and sit-ins of the southern movement will be required. Segregation in the South was an entrenched symbolic system, and tactics of moral confrontation were sufficient to provoke pervasive electoral discord, particularly since it cost the North little to support the extension of constitutional rights to southern Negroes. But in the era which Martin Luther King foresaw, blacks will be making economic rather than legal demands, and so challenging major class interests in the city. These interests will not be overcome by protests alone. They will be overcome, for example, by enrolling the poor to bankrupt the welfare system or inciting rent revolts to close down the slum system.

It will be said that dissensual politics may so aggravate the working class that it will move further to the right, or even out of the Democratic coalition altogether. While this danger exists, it must be said that the working class is now being held securely in coalition by policies which work against the black poor. It has opted only for specific and limited economic reforms, and has now become a major impediment to economic advances by the Negro.

It will also be said that disruptive tactics may spur greater violence in the cities, arousing so strong a backlash that politicians can no longer ease conflict by making concessions to different groups in a coalition. Violence *is* a danger, but since the conditions which breed violence already exist, the occasions which provoke it are manifold. To assume the burden for keeping the peace by refraining from disruptive tactics may be to forego the major reforms upon which a more enduring, less volatile peace depends.

A dissensual political strategy is risky for another reason. The poor who generate disruption have little control over the responses to it. Still, the only recourse of an impoverished minority is to create the kinds of crises to which political leaders must respond, hoping that reforms will follow. In Martin Luther King's words, "We are aware that we ride the forces of history and do not totally shape them."

# PART

Blacks and
the Cities:
The Prospects for
"Black Power"

Introduction

By the midsixties, blacks appeared to be gaining political power, and black leaders were becoming more intrepid. Several developments gave them heart. First, the new concentrations of black voters raised expectations of electoral influence. Second, the civil-rights movement was commanding widespread sympathy and support outside of the South; it was even commanding concessions from the federal government. Third, the ghetto masses were beginning to stir, joining in organized protests and in riots. These new possibilities for power helped to thrust up an insurgent group of younger and more militant black leaders who challenged the most central tenets of the older civil-rights organizations, mainly the century-old conviction held by black leaders and liberal whites that integration was the solution to the blacks' quest for justice in America.

The integrationist doctrine had different dimensions, for integration was at once an end to be valued in itself, a means to other ends, and a political strategy. Blacks and whites ought to reside in the same neighborhoods, go to the same schools, work together and play together simply because it was right; people ought to live together without regard to race and, for that matter, without regard to religion, ethnicity or class. This was the ideal of universal brotherhood, supported by the notion that the United States had achieved at least a degree of universality in the treatment of other groups. The blacks' turn in the melting pot was past due.

But it was also believed that integration in neighborhoods, schools, work and play would yield blacks other, more practical benefits. If blacks lived in white neighborhoods they would share in neighborhood amenities; if they went to white schools they would share in the superior staff and facilities of these schools; if they worked side by side with whites they would participate in the occupational benefits that white workers had gained. And if all this were achieved, blacks would virtually lose their identity as blacks, and by losing that identity be relieved of the psychological burden of socially defined racial inferiority.

Finally, the integrationists were also committed to coalition politics. Specifically, they believed that integration or any other set of goals could only be achieved by working with whites, a strategy that in practice meant working through organizations dominated by whites.

The "separatist" challenge which emerged in the mid-1960s represented an attack upon all of these tenets. Integration was denounced as a goal and the melting pot as an ideal, in part because integration was not as much to be valued as cultural distinctiveness, and in part because the melting pot was judged, correctly, to be less reality than myth. After a century of melting, other class and ethnic groups still did not, by and large, live in the same neighborhoods or go to the same schools. The separatists also questioned the benefits that would presumably result from integration, particularly the psychological benefit of denying black identity. And they eschewed coalition politics, calling for the development of independent black political organizations instead of relying on liberal and labor allies who, they argued, had always sold out blacks in the end.

We supported the separatist challengers. We shared some of their skepticism about the benefits to be gained from integration, and we did not think that blacks would get very much beyond tokenism from their white allies without independent political organization. But what seemed most to the point was that whether or not integration was a desirable goal, it was not going to be achieved, at least not in the foreseeable future, for reasons we spelled out in "The Case Against Urban Desegregation." To attempt integration, particularly in housing, schools and voluntary associations, was to pit limited black power against the most hardened antagonism of white majorities. We thought the record of the integrationist struggle spoke for itself; the concessions that had been made had been almost entirely symbolic, in no way curbing the accelerating pattern of segregation in the cities.

Moreover, the struggle to win these integrationist concessions had probably helped to defeat efforts to expand other programs for the black poor. Efforts to integrate housing, for example, had not only failed, but blacks had actually been harmed by the attempt. The bitter struggles to locate public housing projects in white neighborhoods had virtually halted the construction of public housing in many cities and had generated popular fears of such proportions that the public-housing program could not be used to improve conditions in the ghettos either. Meanwhile, housing segregation was increasing, for if black political power was not sufficient to overcome resistance to neighborhood integration, it surely could not stem the flight of more affluent whites to the suburbs, or quickly yield blacks the incomes necessary to follow in their wake.

Despite the furor created by the integrationist-separatist debate, the more basic question was the prospect for black progress, and increasingly that question seemed to hinge on the development of black political power in the big cities. When blacks migrated in such large numbers during and after World War II, they concentrated mainly in the central-city ghettos of the most populous northern industrial states. Coincidentally, this demographic shift allowed blacks to become voters, to become a modest electoral force for the first time in their history. It seemed only a matter of time before they would become a decisive influence in mayoralty and statewide contests in the most important cities and states in the nation. Moreover, the demographic shift gave blacks influence beyond their numbers in presidential contests, for the particular states in which they settled were crucial to the election of any president.

The new possibility for black political power in the cities was quick to be noted, for it suggested parallels with the experience of other newcomers to the city. It is generally believed that earlier groups, particularly the Irish, managed to enter the mainstream of American life by capitalizing on their voting power in the cities. Votes became the currency that ethnic leaders exchanged for jobs, services and sympathetic treatment from city bosses. In 1960 it appeared that the blacks' turn had come in the historic process of urban political assimilation.

We did not entirely share this optimistic view. We agreed that blacks would slowly come to be the dominant voting bloc in many cities, but the prospects for converting those votes into gains of the kind achieved by other groups seemed less likely. One reason was that the political organization of the cities had changed; the ethnic machine had been superseded by the professional bureaucracies. With that change, the opportunities for political leaders to dispense benefits in return for allegiance had been diminished, partly because employees entrenched in the bureaucracies now controlled many of the benefits that machine leaders once dispensed to their followers. Civil-service associations and unions of public employees were both ready and able to defend their hard-won terrain, and they were doing so at the expense of blacks, as we pointed out in an article entitled "Militant Civil Servants."

Not only had changes occurred in the political infrastructure of the cities, but there were signs of innovations in federal and state policies that would further diminish the gains to be made through urban electoral ascendancy, in part because the influence of big-city government was itself being diminished. In "Black Control of the Cities: Heading It Off by Metropolitan Government," we summarized some of the skeletal beginnings of one such innovation, which consisted of new arrangements for the administration of federal programs in metropolitan areas. Through requirements already being attached to federal grant-in-aid programs, an instrumentality for the expansion of federal control was slowly being built that threatened to encroach upon the powers of local governments in metropolitan areas, especially upon the powers of the big cities where blacks were concentrating.

These articles were written as warnings. Blacks had come to be city dwellers, and the opportunity for a measure of power in the cities had to be defended both against the groups which would resist black gains and against the structural changes which would weaken the power of city governments. It was not that earlier immigrant groups had in fact advanced very far through city politics; it was rather that even these limited opportunities were becoming more restricted for blacks. That warning was summed up in "What Chance for Black Power?"

# The Case Against Urban Desegregation

Frances Fox Piven
and Richard A. Cloward

For years the chief efforts of a broad coalition of liberals and reformers, in dealing with the problems of the Negro, have been directed against segregation. Some significant gains have been made, particularly in the laws governing Negro rights in certain institutional spheres, such as voting and the use of public accommodations. But in some areas the thrust for integration seems to have worked against Negro interests. This is especially true with regard to housing and education of the black poor in large cities.

There are two main reasons for this: (1) Efforts to ameliorate basic social inequities, such as deteriorated ghetto housing and inferior educational facilities, have been closely linked to the goal of integration, and, since integration measures arouse fierce resistance, proposals to redress these social inequities have usually failed. It is for this reason that after several decades of civil-rights struggle the lot of the black urban poor has actually worsened in some respects. (2) If the Negro is to develop the power to enter the mainstream of American life, it is separatism

Reprinted with the permission of *Social Work*, Vol. 12, No. 1, (January 1967). As reprinted here, we substituted for the first section of the article an earlier but longer article dealing with the same subject matter, "Desegregated Housing: Who Pays for the Reformers' Ideal?" which appeared in the *New Republic*, December 17, 1966. The material toward the close of the present article on the relationship of ethnic separatism and political power was taken from Richard A. Cloward, "The War on Poverty: Are the Poor Left Out?" which appeared in the *Nation*, August 2, 1965. The latter articles are copyrighted by the authors.

—not integration—that will be essential to achieve results in certain institutional arenas. Both of these points have implications for both public policy and political action.

## DESEGREGATING HOUSING

Reformers oriented to the urban ghetto have generally sought two objectives that they have seen as closely linked—to promote desegregation and to obtain better housing and education for the poor. Efforts to desegregate housing, however, have been roundly defeated by massive white opposition. Indeed, residential segregation is increasing rapidly.[1] Moreover, because provision of decent housing for the poor has been tied to desegregation, this end also has been defeated. Despite the huge congressional majorities enjoyed by President Johnson in the 89th Congress, not much was done for the slums of our cities. Some promising legislation was enacted: the Housing Act of 1965, the rent-supplement bill, the demonstration-cities bill. But in each case the issue of racial integration endangered the passage of bills, then emasculated them by the meagerness of appropriations. And now, with the 90th Congress, we have probably lost the small margins by which most of the housing legislation survived, and we may forfeit the small gains already made. It is time, therefore, to reexamine the relation, if any, between racial dispersion and decent housing for the slum poor.

Restricted housing is regarded by reformers as the key factor in creating and maintaining racial barriers, and in turn racial barriers are said to force Negroes into the deteriorated slum; therefore, it is felt that desegregation should be a central objective of housing-and-redevelopment programs for the poor. But since there is, at best, little public support for low-income-housing programs, and this tenuous support has been overwhelmed by fierce opposition to residential integration, the struggle for residential integration has cost the poor, especially the black poor, dearly. In effect, the desperate need for better housing and facilities in the ghetto has been and continues to be sacrificed to the goal of residential integration—a goal which, given the political realities of racial conflict in urban areas, can only be said to be receding from view. And as this goal recedes, so too does decent low-income housing.

In fact, segregation has increased! Nor is there any reason to believe that this trend will abate. For one thing, differential birthrates reinforce existing patterns of segregation, concentrating larger and larger numbers of blacks wherever they live. Between 1950 and 1960, for example, the nonwhite population of the nation increased by 26.7 percent and the white population by only 17.5 percent. For this reason, as well as because of the relatively higher rate of movement of nonwhites toward central cities, the black population in urban areas is growing more rapidly than the white. During the decade which ended in 1960, the nonwhite population in American cities increased by half, urban whites by one-fourth.

As the urban black population rises, segregation is intensified. The most dramatic separation by color *within* the urban area has taken place between the central city and suburban ring. Between 1950 and 1960 the nonwhite population in the central cities *swelled by sixty-three percent,* while the number of whites continued to decline.[2] Central cities now contain less than half the urban white population, but eighty percent of urban nonwhites. One-third of urban blacks are in the nation's ten largest central cities. Within a decade or two, blacks will probably constitute a majority in a dozen or more of our largest cities. (The nation's capital is already sixty-three percent black.)


WHAT WOULD INTEGRATION REQUIRE?

In view of these trends, the task of maintaining racial balance in the city seems insuperable; to offset them, huge numbers of families would have to be shuffled about by desegregation programs. This point was spelled out last spring by George Schermer at a "national housing workshop" sponsored by the National Committee Against Discrimination in Housing. Schermer estimated the numbers of people who would have to be moved each year in order to insure a fifty-fifty population balance in Washington, D.C., in the year 2000. Assuming that migration trends and birthrates remain constant, 12,000 nonwhite families would have to be dispersed to suburban areas and 4000 white families induced to return to the District *every year until 2000.*[3]

Even if whites could be induced back to the city and blacks accommodated in the suburbs, residential integration would not result. For within the central city itself, residential concentration by color is on the upswing. In 1910, for example, sixty percent of New York City's blacks lived in assembly districts which were less than five percent black; by 1960, sixty-two per-cent were in districts over half black. In southern cities, which traditionally have tended toward more dispersed patterns of settlement (with black servants and artisans living near those they serve), ghettos are being formed by the concentration of growing black populations.

Again, assuming that present trends persist, Schermer estimates that to achieve integration neighborhood-by-neighbor-hood in Philadelphia by the end of the century, 6000 Negro families would have to go to the suburbs and 3000 whites settle *exclusively in ghetto areas* each year. The numbers, of course, would be infinitely greater in cities like New York and Chicago, which have much larger aggregations of Negroes. Little wonder that the staff of the New York City Department of City Planning concluded in an unpublished report last year that even if all current housing and planning programs were directed to the goal of desegregation, the city could at best only halt the spread of ghettoization, not reverse it.

Our experience with a variety of approaches to desegregating housing has not been in the least encouraging. The most popular approach is legal reforms, coupled with information and education programs. Legislation is sought which prohibits preju-dicial treatment of blacks, whether by deed restrictions, by dis-criminatory actions of private realtors or landlords, or by governmental policies themselves (such as the FHA mortgage-underwriting policy, rescinded in 1945, which prescribed racially homogeneous housing). These reforms reflect an essentially lib-ertarian ideal: a legal structure which ensures the individual rights of minority-group members. But it is by now self-evident that such reforms have little actual impact on urban segregation in housing (or in education or employment).

Substantial legal gains in the housing field were made years ago, long before the recent "activist" phase of the civil-rights movement. Indeed, the very proliferation of legal-reform measures may account for the prevalence of the view among liberals that there has been progress in desegregating housing. Racial zoning ordinances, for example, were struck down by the courts in 1917; race-restrictive deeds (covenants), which were developed to serve the same function as racial zoning, were declared unconstitutional in 1948; and in 1958 New York City developed the nation's first statute outlawing discrimination in housing financed wholly with private funds. Legal reforms proliferate, but patterns of segregation widen.

Part of the reason that legal reforms have had little effect is the weakness of the laws themselves. Many of the discriminatory acts which produce segregation in private housing involve the sacred precincts of property and domicile. Efforts to protect by law the rights of minorities shade into infringements of the rights of others and may even be contrary to other laws which protect rights of property and privacy.

Legal reforms are further weakened by the reluctance to provide for effective enforcement. New York has both a State Commission on Human Rights and a parallel City Commission. The procedures for securing redress, however, ordinarily require knowledge and patience on the part of the plaintiff which cannot in fairness be expected of someone merely looking for a decent place to live. Moreover, although one apartment may be "opened" after tortuous procedures, there is no deterrence to further violations, no carryover effect. Each negotiated enforcement of the law remains an isolated event, and so members of a minority have little confidence in the efficacy of registering complaints. Recently, New York's two agencies proudly announced a "great increase" in complaints received, but the *total* amounted to a mere 528 complaints during the first half of 1966.[4] Philadelphia's counterpart agency, the Commission on Human Relations, has received only 466 complaints in the entire three years since a fair-housing ordinance was adopted.

Broad educational efforts are intended to change discriminatory attitudes in the white community. "Fair-housing committees" in receiving communities are intended to overcome hostility toward entering blacks. Information and broker services are designed to remedy communication gaps, such as lack of information about housing opportunities outside the ghetto and difficulties in gaining access for inspection. The Urban League's "Operation Open City" combines all these strategies to help Negro families find housing.

Housing opportunities are still, however, overwhelmingly controlled by the regular institutions of the private real-estate market, and the mores of the market have been only incidentally affected by legal advances and desegregation programs. Private real-estate agents reflect the inclinations of the vast majority of housing consumers, and so they distribute information concerning available housing and provide access for inspection in ways that accord with existing class and racial neighborhood patterns. Projects like Operation Open City and fair-housing committees have at best opened just a few housing opportunities beyond the ghetto. Operation Open City reports, for example, that only 300 of the persons registered since February have moved into predominantly white areas. Furthermore, these efforts reach predominantly middle-class Negroes: Housing in outlying communities generally requires at least a lower-middle income. The ghetto poor are resisted by white neighborhoods generally, but the most furious opposition comes from white working-class neighborhoods—the very ones with housing many blacks might be able to afford.

## IF NEGROES HAD MORE MONEY

Eliminating the poverty of the ghetto masses is the basis of a second general approach to residential integration. Proceeding from our belief in individual opportunity and the "open" society, the argument is that Negroes will be able to bid competitively for housing outside the ghetto once they have better jobs and incomes. There are a number of fallacies here.

First, programs intended to advance blacks economically—by education and job training—currently reach a mere one in ten of America's poor, white as well as Negro. Even if the scope of these programs were vastly expanded, millions of the poor would still not be helped. Of the 35 million people below the federal poverty line (e.g., $3100 per annum for an urban family of four), several million are aged and are permanently unemployable. One-third of the poor are in families headed by females, and it does not seem reasonable to expect this group to raise itself from poverty by entering the labor force. Many of the remaining poor are ill; others are permanently noncompetitive for a host of additional reasons, not the least being the debilitating effects of years of chronic unemployment and underemployment.

More than half of the poor are under eighteen. Presumably, the optimists who advocate skills-enhancement as a solution to poverty have the potential of this group in mind. But in the past the upward journey to the middle class has taken low-income groups as much as three generations. Negroes are handicapped at the outset by chronic deprivation; they confront persisting barriers of economic and social discrimination; they must surmount new barriers posed by automation and the professionalization of occupations. Under the circumstances they can hardly be expected to lift themselves, one by one, more rapidly than members of groups before them which had much greater economic opportunity. For most poor of the present generation, and perhaps for many in the next, a strategy of individual mobility is irrelevant.

Even if large numbers of Negroes are lifted either to or somewhat above the poverty line, their chance of getting decent housing will not greatly improve. In urban areas adequate housing is hard to come by for families with annual incomes of less than $7000; in 1960, only 3.4 percent of Negroes had such incomes. Indeed, middle-class whites have obtained huge governmental subsidies to bring decent housing within their reach (e.g., urban-renewal land write-downs, low-cost government-insured mortgages, special federal tax advantages for builders and realtors, as well as local tax abatements).

Furthermore, because of discriminatory patterns, blacks in effect pay more for housing than whites. Although in most metropolitan areas Negroes pay slightly lower rentals than whites in each income group, they get vastly inferior housing. Income gains will continue to be partly dissipated in excessive rentals.[5]

We must also stress that resistance in the receiving community persists, whatever the incomes of potential black invaders.

Karl and Alma Taeuber conclude after extensive analysis of census data that "residential segregation prevails regardless of the relative economic status of the white and Negro resident."[6]

## CONSEQUENCES OF OUR GOOD INTENTIONS

The myth that integrationist measures are bringing better housing to the Negro poor comforts liberals; it placates (and victimizes) the Negro masses; and it antagonizes and arouses the bulk of white Americans. The "backlash" is part of its legacy. While turmoil rages over integration, housing conditions worsen. They worsen partly because the solution continues to be defined in terms of desegregation, so that the energies and attention of reformers are diverted from attempts to ameliorate housing in the ghetto itself.

By being linked to the goal of integration, traditional programs for low-income housing (e.g., public housing) have become so controversial that appropriations are kept low and in many places are not even used. Although the 1949 Housing Act alone authorized 810,000 units of low-rent housing, a mere 600,000 units have been constructed since the first National Housing Act in 1937. During the past few years we have constructed only about 26,000 units annually or about half of what could have been built under existing legislation. The ghetto poor have paid in this way for the struggle over whether black and white shall mingle, neighborhood by neighborhood.

Public housing was intended, by at least some of its proponents, to facilitate integration as a by-product of rehousing the poor. And it has always been plagued by that secondary goal. Integrated projects have been thwarted because, as Negroes move in, low-income whites leave or are reluctant to apply. (The Federal Public Housing Agency classifies only twenty-seven percent of its projects as integrated and these include an unspecified number which have only one or two Negro families.) The resulting high-rise brick ghettos offend liberals, and they attack. But when housing officials attempt to bring about integration by such devices as quota systems, other critics are offended on the ground that such procedures are discriminatory. The New York City Housing Authority has been alternately forced to "reform" by making commitments to foster integrated projects, only to be asked to "reform" again by abolishing its color-conscious procedures.

Efforts to further integration by locating housing projects in white neighborhoods have provoked far more serious opposition than efforts to integrate the projects themselves. Only when white tenants predominate is there any degree of tolerance for public housing in these communities. In Newark, for example, the racial balance in projects ranges from over ninety percent white in outlying "country club" areas to over ninety percent Negro for projects located in central-ghetto wards. Because this accommodation was made from the outset, Newark has been able to win support for public housing and hence to build relatively more units than most other cities. Similarly, the New York City Housing Authority has long accommodated to the wishes of borough presidents in site selections (and is much criticized for it), and has also used its full share of public-housing subsidies. But in many localities disputes over the location of public housing projects have evoked furious controversy, often leading to the reduction of the program and surely making its political future shaky. In a study of public-housing decisions in Chicago, Martin Meyerson and Edward Banfield showed how volatile the site-selection issue is. By proposing locations which raised the integration issue, the public-housing authority provoked a two-and-a-half-year struggle which not only defeated the site proposal but consolidated opposition to public housing itself. A similar struggle is now going on in New York City; the Lindsay administration has insisted that public housing be located on vacant land in outlying areas, and so the current sites have still not been approved.

The new rent-supplement law bears the same political onus as public housing. The current appropriation of $20 million will permit only a few showpiece displays. If experience with public housing is any predictor, the opposition which rent supplements provoked in Congress and which almost defeated it will be repeated in each local community as efforts are made to implement the plan. White majorities will veto any project they feel will threaten their neighborhood and will eventually ban the program that raises the threat. Public subsidies, in short, have failed to reverse the trend toward segregation in urban areas and have not produced new or rehabilitated housing for the poor.

While the poor are left with token programs and token funds ("demonstration" projects for rehousing the poor have become a favorite device), huge new subsidies have been finding their way into the hands of middle- and upper-class interests in the central city. These programs, put forward as attempts to serve "the city as a whole" by clearing slums, improving the tax base, or retrieving the middle class from the suburbs, have had the effect of intensifying ghetto deterioration. We have spent some $3 billion on urban-renewal programs, and in the process whole low-income communities have been destroyed, including some 328,000 units of housing (most of them low rental). Only some 13,000 units of low-rent public housing have been constructed on the area sites. Luxury apartment houses, stadiums, coliseums, auditoriums and office buildings now stand where the poor once lived.[7] (Highway development has had equally devastating effects.) Curiously, these measures are sometimes justified by the goal of integration, for it is hoped they will lure middle-class whites back from the suburbs.

Nor has much been done to mitigate the cruel cost to ghetto residents of clearance and redevelopment. Procedures for interim management on sites scheduled for clearance place owners and tenants in a prolonged state of uncertainty, making them either the agents or the victims of quick exploitation. The effects on those eventually dislocated, about seventy percent of whom are nonwhite, are only partially tempered by relocation provisions.[8] The stalemate we now see in some urban-renewal programs (e.g., as a result of Saul Alinsky's activities in Chicago and Rochester) represents an achievement for the poor: They have finally been spurred by the accumulated abuses of years of dislocation to protest against the further destruction of their homes and communities.[9]

In the housing act of 1949, Congress asserted a national responsibility to provide a decent dwelling for every family. The nation, however, has not progressed very far. In New York City, for example, Mayor Lindsay's housing task force recently reported that there were half a million unsound units currently occupied (roughly the same number reported through years of new public assaults on the slums) and that the number was on

the increase even though *the number of low-rental units* has de-
creased more than thirty percent since 1960.[10] In Boston, the
last family-size public-housing unit was built in 1954; the city's
nationally acclaimed urban-renewal effort diminished by twelve
percent the supply of low-rental housing (less than $50 a month)
between 1960 and 1965.[11] The federal public-housing program
has produced only 600,000 low-income dwelling units in the
three decades since it was initiated. The federal urban-renewal
program and the federal highway program have together demolished close to 700,000 units, most of which were low rental,
in less than half that time. Meanwhile, private builders, spurred
on by federal tax incentives and mortgage programs designed
to encourage construction, have made still further inroads on
the supply of low-income housing by reclaiming land to erect
middle- and upper-income units. The cheap accommodations
that remain in large cities are in buildings that have been permitted to run down without maintenance and repairs or in
which rents are pushed to the limit the captive slum market
can afford. High-minded public policies notwithstanding, the
dimensions of housing needs among the nonwhites in big cities
have, in fact, enlarged.


## TAKING ACCOUNT OF WHITE HOSTILITY

The Achilles heel of housing programs has been precisely
our insistence that better housing for the black poor be achieved
by residential desegregation. This ideal glosses over the importance of the ethnic community as a staging area for groups to
build the communal solidarity and power necessary to compel
eventual access to the mainstream of urban life. If the ideal of
heterogeneity has led reformers to press for measures which
threaten to bring Negroes into white neighborhoods, the force
of separatism has consistently won out—and housing in the
ghetto has worsened.

If group conflict is at the root of past failures, strategies must
be found to improve ghetto housing without arousing the ire
of powerful segments of the white community. In managing this
conflict, politicians try to make concessions to contending groups.
But this is possible only if significant groups in the political

majority remain unaroused or relatively indifferent to what has been conceded. As we have shown, the prospect that Negroes might invade white neighborhoods generates such intense opposition that politicians, in the interest of self-preservation, are forced to avoid any action except to promote token measures to placate reformers. Hostile feelings created by the struggle over integration tie the hands of political leaders who might otherwise give their support to less controversial concessions, such as subsidies for low-income housing in the ghetto.

It seems clear, then, that reformers must apply what political pressure they have to secure relief in the ghetto itself. We already have the legal and administrative channels, but we have put virtually no funds into them. The most urgent need is for subsidies, for both new housing and the interim rehabilitation of existing structures, and for vigorous intervention in the ownership and management of slum buildings.

Current estimates of the costs of rehousing the residents of central-city ghettos are very large and hence tend to deflect attention from proposals. Commissioner Gaynor of the New York State Division of Housing and Community Renewal says it will take $14 billion to replace New York City's half-million substandard units with public housing; Senator Robert Kennedy's slum proposal for the city would cost about $15 billion in the next ten years. These figures are misleading, however. Government subsidies are needed essentially to cover the interest and amortization on bonds or mortgages. Since development costs are paid over long periods, the annual outlay (in public housing, for example) is only 4.5 or five percent of the original amounts (in addition to local contributions in the form of tax abatement). Moreover, the huge estimates being given are for long-term building programs; during the initial years, subsidies are needed for debt service on only a fraction of the amount eventually invested.

## WAYS OF REHABILITATING THE SLUMS

New housing can be built under the public-housing program, or through the use of rent supplements and low-cost government mortgages. These programs do not fix and limit the form of low-rental housing—public-housing authorities can use their subsidies to buy or to lease privately built dwellings, for example; they are not restricted to barren high-rise projects. Because overcrowding is at a critical peak in most central city ghettos, new housing should be used to augment the supply of dwelling units and neighborhood space. We should not tear down any but the most hazardous slum housing. We should build either in marginal and underused areas, where it is possible to extend ghetto boundaries without excessive neighborhood friction, or in more outlying ghetto enclaves.

Slum housing can also be substantially upgraded by repairs, new wiring and plumbing (estimated by housing experts at about $1500 per unit) or gutting and rebuilding a structure (which can cost as much as eight times that amount). Because it is cheaper and does not require neighborhood upheaval, various kinds of rehabilitation should be given priority, even if eventual demolition and rebuilding are contemplated.

Incentive schemes in the form of loans and grants can be offered to landlords and backed up by vigorous code enforcement. New York City, for example (always the first to innovate, and always the least to make any actual ingress into the slums), already has an emergency-repair operation in which city crews can make necessary repairs and charge the landlord. The city also has a receivership program, under which buildings with hazardous violations can be taken over by the Department of Real Estate, repaired to a level of code conformance and reclaimed by the landlord if he pays the costs.

A number of minor changes in regulations could multiply our tools for improving ghetto housing. For example, new public housing now costs as much as $22,500 per unit, largely because of extraordinarily high standards of construction required by federal regulations. Archaic and inflexible local building codes encumber new construction and rehabilitation and add substantially to costs. These regulations are not merely vestigial or accidental. They are promoted and protected by the organized groups in the construction and real-estate industries whose interests are served by maintaining traditional and costly methods of building. Even these minor reforms require the mobilizing of political support.

Federal mortgage and grant programs for low-income re-

habilitation are now underused, partly because of certain limiting regulations. For instance, federal low-cost mortgages have not
been fully exploited (New York City's allotment for the current
year is set at $150 million, but much of it is likely to go unused).
There are two reasons: Only nonprofit or limited-profit corporations are eligible, and modest rent supplements are needed in
addition to low-cost mortgages in order to yield low rents. Local
government could help create such corporations (drawing in
churches, settlement houses or community organizations as sponsors); it could provide rent-supplement funds from local revenues
(barring any expansion and relaxation of restrictions in the
federal rent-supplement program). But none of this is likely to
work so long as low-income housing arouses intense local opposition because it is tied to racial integration.

The new demonstration-cities bill authorizes $900 million over
two years for slum rehabilitation. The legislation is broadly
permissive, so that localities can propose a wide variety of programs. (Note that congressional opposition to the bill was only
overcome by a last-minute amendment barring use of the legislation to promote racial balance.) If liberals follow their accustomed route and force new contests over desegregation, this
bill is likely to go the way of earlier housing measures, weakened and mangled at each stage of public decision.

The point, in short, is that if reformers can be persuaded to
forfeit for a time the ideal of desegregation, there might be a
chance of mustering political support and money for low-income
housing. This would be no small achievement.

## DESEGREGATING EDUCATION

To emphasize the importance of upgrading ghetto housing is
also to accept racially homogeneous elementary schools in large
cities, at least for the foreseeable future. Integrated education
has been one of the central goals of reformers, and few seem
prepared to relinquish this objective. However, the demographic
and political realities in large cities cast grave doubts on the
feasibility of achieving anything resembling integrated education
at the early grade levels.

As a result of the housing patterns described earlier, blacks are rapidly becoming the largest group (in some cases, the majority) in the central areas of many large cities. Furthermore, they represent an even greater proportion of the school-age population because Negro families are usually younger, larger and without the resources to place their children in private schools.[12] The white youngsters with whom black children presumably are to be integrated are slowly vanishing from inner-city areas, and there is every reason to expect that these demographic trends will continue.

The issue of integrated education is also complicated by socioeconomic factors, particularly in the cities. Recent evidence suggests that diverse economic backgrounds of pupils may be more important than racial diversity in the education of the Negro student. One study of American education, for example, shows that mixing middle-class students (either black or white) with lower-class students (either black or white) usually has a decidedly beneficial effect on the achievement of the lower-class student and does not usually diminish the middle-class student's achievement.[13] By contrast, the integration of poor whites and poor blacks does not seem to yield improved achievement in either group.[14]

But the number of middle-class whites available to be mixed educationally with lower-class Negroes is rapidly declining, and of the whites left in the city with children who attend public schools, an increasing proportion is poor. (As for middle-class Negroes, their numbers are very small to begin with, and many send their children to private schools.) If mixing along class lines is to be achieved, therefore, educational arrangements in which suburban and ghetto children are brought together will be required. Such arrangements are improbable. The defense of the neighborhood school is ardent; it reflects both racial and class cleavages in American society. Efforts to bring about racial mixing, especially when coupled with the more meaningful demand for economic-class mixing, run head-on into some of the most firmly rooted and passionately defended attitudes of white families.

*Busing versus "educational parks."* Two schemes have been advocated for achieving racial integration while minimizing political resistance. One involves reshuffling children to achieve a racial balance by busing them to distant schools. Aside from the logistical problems this poses, busing usually has met violent opposition from all sides.[15] The second scheme is the development of massive "educational parks," which would centralize upper-grade facilities for children from a wide area. The superiority of these new plants, it is argued, will help to overcome the opposition of white parents to integration. However, even in such plants segregation is likely to persist on the classroom level as a result of the "tracking system," particularly because educational parks are intended only for older children, whose academic levels already reflect wide inequalities in home environment and early schooling. Equally important is the fact that the cost of such educational parks would be enormous. It is improbable that many such parks would be built, and the merits of such an investment must be weighed against alternative uses of funds for the direct improvement of program and staff in ghetto schools.

*Improving ghetto schools.* The lower-class school, particularly in the large-city ghetto, has always been an inferior institution. Recently the physical facilities in many ghetto schools have improved because of new building programs, but the lower-class black school still reflects significant inequalities when it is compared to its white middle-class counterpart. For example, the quality of the teachers has been shown to have a critical influence on the child's learning—lower-class schools, however (especially ghetto schools in large cities), have inferior teachers and are generally characterized by higher staff turnover. To overcome historic inequalities of this kind would be no small achievement.[16]

We conclude, in short, that although schools that are racially and economically heterogeneous are probably superior, removing class inequities in the quality of teachers and programs is also an important goal—and a far more realistic one. Such educational improvements in the ghetto will require public action and expenditure, and these are likely to be achieved only if massive political opposition to demands for class and racial mixing is avoided. As in the case of housing, the coupling of measures for integration of education with measures to improve existing conditions in large-city ghettos must lead to the defeat of both. The choice is between total defeat and partial victory; to many it may appear a difficult choice—but at least it is a choice.

### PRIVATE SOCIAL WELFARE:
### SEPARATIST INSTITUTIONS

In discussing housing and educational reforms for the urban ghetto, we have stressed the political futility of integration measures. It is not only the feasibility of integration that is open to question; it is also far from clear that integration is always desirable.

Liberals are inclined to take a "melting pot" view of American communities and to stress the enriching qualities of heterogeneous living. However, the history of ethnic groups in American society belies this view. There have always been ethnic institutions, and these, as has been widely observed, have served important functions in the advancement of different groups. An important precondition for the establishment of such separatist institutions—particularly when the members of the ethnic group are poor—has been the existence of substantial aggregations of people in residential proximity. The current emphasis on integrating people physically in schools and neighborhoods thus deflects attention from a fundamental problem confronting blacks—the lack of organizational vehicles to enable them to compete with whites for control of major institutions that shape the destiny of the ghetto (housing and educational systems, governmental bureaucracies, corporate economic complexes, political parties and so forth). Without separatist organizations the Negro is not likely to come to share control in these spheres, and the powerlessness of the ghetto's population will persist.

The value of separatist institutions is revealed clearly in the field of social welfare. There is, of course, considerable precedent for ethnically based social-welfare institutions, which symbolize for many the highest values of self-help. Networks of agencies have been formed by Jews and white Catholics; even Protestants—under the impact of a pluralism that has made them act like a minority as well—have formed essentially white ethnic welfare institutions to advance their interests. Throughout the country these voluntary agencies raise a huge amount of money, which is directed to the less fortunate in their respective ethnic and religious communities (and sometimes to those in other communities as well).

POLITICAL INTERESTS

The point that is not generally recognized about private agencies, however, is that they are as much political as they are social-welfare institutions; they serve as organizational vehicles for the expression of the ethnic group's viewpoints on social-welfare policy and also as the institutional means for other forms of political association and influence. Religioethnic welfare institutions—from hospitals to child-care facilities—command enormous amounts of tax money. In New York City, for example, they are now routinely paid over $100 million annually from the municipal budget (exclusively of antipoverty funds). Thus, these agencies are important political interest groups that, in acting upon their own organizational needs, serve the interests of their ethnic and religious constituencies as well.

Exerting pressure for various forms of public subsidy is only one of the political functions of private agencies. They maintain a deep interest in many forms of governmental policy and actively seek to influence the shaping of policy in ways consistent with their interests. These political activities tend to be overlooked because private agencies exert power chiefly at the municipal level—not at the more visible level of national politics. However, large areas of public service *are* controlled locally, and even when programs are initiated and supervised by federal or state authorities, it is primarily at the municipal level that services are organized and delivered to their intended consumers. Public welfare, education, urban renewal, housing-code enforcement, fair employment, law enforcement and correctional practices— all of these are, in large part, shaped by local government.

Nowhere is there a Negro federation of philanthropy—and there are few Negro private social-welfare institutions. Consequently, the Negro is not only without an important communal form but also lacks the opportunity to gain the vast public subsidies given for staff and services that flow into the institutions of white communities. In effect, to advocate separatism in this area means to insist that the Negro be given the prerogatives and benefits that other ethnic and religious communities have enjoyed for some decades.

If the Negro expects to influence the proliferating social-welfare activities of government, he will need his own organizational apparatus, including a stable cadre of technical and professional personnel who can examine the merits of alternative public policies, survey the practices of governmental agencies and activate their ethnic constituencies on behalf of needed changes.

## COMMUNAL ASSOCIATIONS

Ethnic social-welfare institutions serve another important function. This country has faced the problem of assimilating poverty-stricken minority groups into its economic bloodstream many times in the past, and religioethnic institutions of various kinds have played a significant part in that process. One of the ways by which such groups effect their rise from deprivation is to develop communal associations, ranging from fraternal and religious bodies to political machines. These communal associations provide a base from which to convert ethnic solidarity into the political force required to overcome various forms of class inequality. They are therefore an important device by which the legitimate interests of particular groups are put forward to compete with those of other groups.

The black community lacks an institutional framework in private social welfare (as well as in other institutional areas), and the separatist agencies of other ethnic and religious communities are not eager to see this deficiency overcome. Where the black is concerned, they resist the emergence of new separatist institutions on the grounds that such a "color conscious" development represents a new form of "segregation." This view has frequently been expressed or implied in behind-the-scenes struggles over the allocation of antipoverty funds. In one city after another, private agencies have either fought against the development of Negro-sponsored programs or have sat by while black groups argued in vain with municipal, county or federal officials over their right to form autonomous ethnic institutions to receive public funds.[17]

By and large, private agencies have contended that race is an irrelevant issue in deciding who should mount programs in a ghetto. Existing agencies, it is argued, have the proved professional and organizational competence to operate new programs, and many have succeeded in obtaining public funds to do so. In the end, however, this form of "desegregation" is destructive of black interests. Although coalitions of existing ethnic and religious agencies may provide services to the ghetto (especially with the financial incentives of the antipoverty program), these services do not strengthen the ghetto's capacity to deal with its own problems. Rather, they weaken it. Through the "integration" of Negroes as clients in service structures operated by others, political control by outside institutions is extended to one more aspect of ghetto life. Furthermore, the ghetto is deprived of the resources that could encourage the development of its own institutions or bolster them. Existing voluntary agencies could serve the ghetto far better if they lent political, technical and financial aid to the development of new social-welfare institutions that would be under black management and control.

Class power in the United States is intimately connected with the strength of ethnic institutions. Powerlessness and poverty are disproportionately concentrated among minority groups—Puerto Ricans, Mexicans and so forth. The success of traditional ethnic and religious social agencies in resisting the emergence of Negro institutions is a reflection of class power differentials. But it also reveals that class power is produced and maintained in part by racial and ethnic power differentials.

## NEED FOR SEPARATIST
## ORGANIZATIONS

A new system of voluntary social-welfare agencies in the ghetto can hardly be expected to produce the collective force to overcome the deep inequalities in our society. Ethnic identity, solidarity and power must be forged through a series of organized communal experiences in a variety of institutional areas. In housing, for example, energy should be directed not only toward improving ghetto conditions but also toward creating within the ghetto the organizational vehicles for renovating buildings and, more important, for managing them.[18] Similarly, educational reforms should mean not only improvements in facilities and staff but also arrangements under which the local community can participate in and influence the administration of the schools.[19]

What blacks need, in short, are the means to organize separately and a heightened awareness of the distinctive goals to which their organizations must be directed. The black poor in our society do have interests distinct from and, more often than not, in conflict with those of other groups. Unless they organize along separatist lines, it is unlikely that they will have much success in advancing these interests. Judging from the history of those ethnic groups that have succeeded in gaining a foothold in our pluralistic society, it seems clear that ethnic separatism is a precondition for eventual achievement of full economic integration. Minority groups will win acceptance from the majority by developing their own bases of power, not by submerging their unorganized and leaderless numbers in coalitions dominated by other and more solidary groups. Once they have formed separatist organizations, participation in coalitions (whether councils of social agencies or political parties) can then be a meaningful tactic in bargaining for a share of power over crucial institutional processes in the broader society.

In a recent essay David Danzig observed:

It is, to be sure, a long step from the recognition of the need for power to the building and strengthening of indigenous social and political institutions within the ghetto from which power can be drawn. The Negro as yet has few such institutions. Unlike most of the other religio-ethnic minorities, he lacks a network of unifying social traditions, and this is why he must depend on political action through color consciousness as his main instrument of solidarity. That solidarity entails a certain degree of "separatism" goes without saying, but the separatism of a strengthened and enriched Negro community need be no more absolute than that, say, of the Jewish community. There is no reason, after all, why the Negro should not be able to live, as most Americans do, in two worlds at once—one of them largely integrated and the other primarily separated.[20]

In these terms, then, physical desegregation is not only irrelevant to the ghetto but can actually prevent the eventual integration of blacks in the institutional life of this society. For integration must be understood not as the mingling of bodies in school and neighborhood but as participation in and shared control over the major institutional spheres of American life. And that is a question of developing communal associations that can be bases for power—not of dispersing a community that is powerless.

## NOTES

[1] The proportion of nonwhites living in segregated census tracts in New York City rose from forty-nine to fifty-three percent between 1940 and 1950. In 1910 sixty percent of the Negroes in that city lived in assembly districts that were less than five percent Negro. By 1960 sixty-two percent were in districts that were over fifty percent Negro. "The Program for an Open City: Summary Report" (New York: Department of City Planning, May 1965). (Mimeographed.) See also Davis McEntire, *Residence and Race: Final and Comprehensive Report to the Commission on Race and Housing* (Berkeley: University of California Press, 1960), p. 41.

[2] See *Our Nonwhite Population and Its Housing* (Washington, D.C.: Housing and Home Finance Agency, 1963), pp. 1–3. The nonwhite population in central cities reached 10.3 million in 1960 and may exceed 16 million by 1975, according to McEntire, *op. cit.,* pp. 4–5, 21–24.

[3] George Schermer, "Desegregating the Metropolitan Area." Paper presented at the National Housing Workshop, National Committee Against Discrimination in Housing, West Point, N.Y., April 1966.

[4] "More Negro Families Are Utilizing Fair Housing Law Here and in Suburbs," *New York Times,* October 23, 1966, p. 117.

[5] McEntire, *op. cit.,* pp. 135–147. In New York City, for example, there are three times as many substandard units occupied by nonwhites as whites at each income level.

[6] *Negroes in Cities: Residential Segregation and Neighborhood Change* (Chicago: Aldine Publishing Co., 1965).

[7] Criticism of urban renewal has been launched from both the right and the left. See Martin Anderson, *The Federal Bulldozer* (Cambridge, Mass.: MIT Press, 1965); Herbert J. Gans, "The Failure of

Urban Renewal," *Commentary,* Vol. 39, No. 4 (April 1965), pp. 29–37; and the replies to Gans by George M. Raymond and Malcolm D. Rivkin, "Urban Renewal," *Commentary,* Vol. 40, No. 1 (July 1965), pp. 72–80.

[8] For a review of experience with relocation see Chester Hartman, "The Housing of Relocated Families," *Journal of the American Institute of Planners,* Vol. 30, No. 4 (November 1964), pp. 266–268.

[9] James Q. Wilson analyzes the political dilemmas created by renewal programs in "Planning and Politics: Citizen Participation in Urban Renewal," *Journal of the American Institute of Planners,* Vol. 29, No. 4 (November 1963), pp. 242–249.

[10] "An Analysis of Current City-Wide Housing Needs" (New York: Department of City Planning, Community Renewal Program, December 1965), p. 67. (Mimeographed.)

[11] Michael D. Appleby, "Logue's Record in Boston: An Analysis of His Renewal and Planning Activities" (New York: Council for New York Housing and Planning Policy, May 1966), p. 43. (Mimeographed.)

[12] Blacks already comprise over fifty percent of the school-age populations in Chicago, Philadelphia and Washington, D.C. (where they comprise more than eighty percent). In other cities they are rapidly approaching the majority—Detroit, for example, has well over a forty percent population of school-age Negroes.

[13] James R. Coleman *et al., Equality of Educational Opportunity,* (Washington, D.C.: U.S. Government Printing Office, 1966).

[14] Several studies show that by no means do Negroes do uniformly better in integrated schools. They either do better or worse than in segregated schools. One intervening variable appears to be the degree of bigotry exhibited by whites: The greater the bigotry, the more likely that Negroes will achieve less than in segregated schools. Poor and working-class whites have traditionally held the most prejudiced attitudes: integrating them with poor Negroes may actually hurt Negroes. *Ibid.,* especially pp. 330–333. See also Irwin Katz, "Review of Evidence Relating to Effects of Desegregation in the Intellectual Performance of Negroes," *American Psychologist,* Vol. 19 (June 1964), pp. 381–399.

[15] There seems to be a somewhat easier acceptance when numbers of black children are assigned to white schools than when white children are assigned to ghetto schools. This has not been tried on a sufficient scale to put white tolerance to a genuine test, however. It is also true that Negro parents do not want their children to travel far, either.

[16] There have been many studies—including the work of Allison

Davis and subsequent studies by August B. Hollingshead—on class biases in the intelligence test and the differential response of the school system to children of different socio-economic backgrounds. Many other studies document the sharp differences between the low-income school and its middle-class counterpart. For a recent study of inequalities by class in a large northern urban school system, *see* Patricia Cayo Sexton, *Education and Income: Inequalities in Our Public Schools* (New York: Viking Press, 1961).

[17] Some OEO funds have been used to stimulate the growth of Negro welfare institutions. Bitter conflicts have inevitably followed—as in the case of New York's HARYOU-ACT and the Child Development Group of Mississippi. Neither of these embattled agencies has received appreciable support from established social agencies.

[18] In a tentative way, this possibility is now being explored by some groups (e.g., churches), which are receiving loans to rehabilitate ghetto buildings under the federal low-cost mortgage program. These groups form local corporations to rehabilitate and later to manage houses.

[19] Parent groups in East Harlem recently boycotted a new school (P. S. 201); they abandoned earlier demands for school integration to insist that the Board of Education cede a large measure of control to the local community. The ensuing controversy brought to the fore certain issues in professional and community control. As of this writing, a final resolution has not been reached. Without some administrative arrangement to insure greater involvement by the ghetto community, the schools will continue to be responsive to other, better-organized religious, ethnic, and class groupings that traditionally have been powerful enough to assert the superiority of their claims for educational services and resources over that of the ghetto. There is some indication that such arrangements may also bring educational benefits. A recent study showed a high correlation between the achievement of Negro children and their feeling that they can control their own destinies. *See* Coleman *et al., op. cit.*

[20] "In Defense of 'Black Power,' " *Commentary*, Vol. 42, No. 3 (September 1966), pp. 45–46.

# The Imperative of Deghettoization:
## An Answer to Piven and Cloward

CLARENCE FUNNYÉ AND RONALD SHIFFMAN

It has been observed too infrequently that the political spectrum is more circular than linear, that the ideas of the left and the right tend to merge. The language may differ, but the content is the same regarding isolationism, big government versus individual initiative, and, apparently, housing versus integration. Thus, a basic and fundamental question of human rights—a question supposedly decided in the 1954 Supreme Court decision that declared the "separate but equal" doctrine a fallacy—has been answered in the South by massive building of physical plants to demonstrate that "theirs is just as good as ours." Thus, too, the new trend among segments of the northern liberal community is to talk in terms of impacting the ghetto rather than creating a truly democratic society.

This development is demonstrated in the article by Piven and Cloward in the last issue of *Social Work*, which blamed the inadequate supply of low-income housing on integrationist pressures and advocated intensified ghettoization as a necessary price for obtaining this housing.[1]

*Clarence Funnyé, M.A., was director, Idea Plan Associates, New York, New York, an independent planning group, and was a former chairman of New York CORE. He was the author of a study, "Toward Deghettoization: A Proposal for Decisions in Housing and Planning in New York City," and a book, Deghettoization. He was consultant in housing and planning for the National Congress of Racial Equality, and was a member of the board of directors of the National Committee Against Discrimination in Housing and the Citizens' Housing and Planning Council.*

*Ronald Shiffman, M.A., was associate for design, Idea Plan Associates, and assistant director of the Pratt Center for Community Improvement, Department of City and Regional Planning, Pratt Institute, Brooklyn, New York. He wrote a study, "Strategy for a Coordinated Social and Physical Renewal Program: Bedford-Stuyvesant," member of the board of directors of the Metropolitan Council on Planning, and cochairman of the Federation of Fair Housing Committees of New York City.*

Reprinted with the permission of the authors and *Social Work*, volume 12, no. 2. (April 1967).

They appear to have been lured into an astonishingly paternalistic surrender of the American right of freedom of choice. They justify this cavalier disposition of the rights of others by establishing a false "either/or" premise: Either housing for the poor is improved or integrated housing is sought; the two are mutually exclusive.

The question is not whether the city will be integrated *or* the ghetto rebuilt. It is not whether a harmonious environment will be built for the poor *or* the rich, or for black *or* white. We can—and must—build viable cities for all our citizens. And we can—and must—adopt two complementary goals: the revitalization of the ghetto and the integration of the city.

These goals will not be realized in days, or weeks, or even years. They may take a generation or more. But every step that is taken along the way—every public-housing site chosen, every urban-renewal project undertaken, every highway built, every school designated—will either enhance or impede these goals. There is no neutrality; the choice must be made now, before unjust, inequitable and harmful urban patterns are set with which future generations will have to contend.

## ENFORCED SEGREGATION OF
## LOW-INCOME HOUSING

The authors state that, historically, low-income-housing construction in this country has been impeded because of insistence on integration. This assumption is not borne out by fact. Public-housing construction in this country has historically followed the path of least resistance, in almost every case avoiding a confrontation with the imperatives of deghettoization. While there have been isolated instances in which public housing has been opposed solely because of racial fears, these instances are balanced by support for government-aided middle-income housing, which has been substantially integrated.

Nearly all of the low-income housing units constructed since 1937 have been built on the premise that they would be segregated. Most often, this has been accomplished by location—a public-housing monolith built in the midst of a massive ghetto would be unlikely to contain a substantial portion of majority-group tenants. Overtly or covertly discriminatory rental policies have also contributed heavily to this enforced separation.

At the same time, throughout the postwar period the force of government was used actively to promote racial separation. Approximately 15 million new dwellings were built in this country from 1939 to 1950, the period when the suburban phenomenon was firmly established. Government guarantees to private enterprise were a key factor in this growth. These guarantees were not open to Negroes for a number of reasons:

1. Housing was available only to those able to pay the full economic price; this ruled out the vast majority of Negroes.

2. Federal policies were based on the concept that economic and social stability in neighborhoods was of primary importance, and that this could be achieved only by keeping their populations homogeneous.

3. Federal policies (Federal Housing Administration and Veterans Administration) excluded families that did not fit their definition of responsible; therefore, single persons, elderly couples, families with low or questionable incomes and families with female heads or with female wage earners to supplement male income were considered bad prospects and ineligible for FHA and VA guarantees.

In addition, federal policies were primarily responsible for the rapid ghettoization of our cities. FHA and VA programs did not provide liberal terms for older homes in cities or comprehensive programs for multifamily housing, thus encouraging the middle-class flight to the suburbs.

While federal policies were modified after 1950 to eliminate the more blatant pressures to reinforce separation, such as restrictive covenants, the government has actively promoted nondiscrimination in housing only in the last five years, and these efforts are still not universal in their application.

Not only was confrontation on the question of deghettoization avoided by public officials; it was also avoided by civil-rights advocates. Time after time the minority leadership has accepted reinforcement of the ghetto as the price that must be paid for improved housing conditions. While the pressure for integrated private housing has recently been increasing, the question of the location and character of low-income housing has been relatively ignored.

Thus, when urban renewal was undertaken in Newark, N.J., low-income units were included in the plan to obtain the support of a ghetto politician. But while the project produced years of wrangling over the location of other facilities, no questions were raised by any significant element of the community, Negro or white, about the fact that low-income units were to conform to established racial patterns.

Thus, in Chicago, Taylor Homes, built at a cost of $70 million to contain 27,000 Negro men, women and children, is a point of civic pride, perhaps because of the fact that the project is so comprehensive that its inhabitants need never leave the ghetto environment except to seek employment.

Thus, in New York City, the first realistic attempt to confront the problem of deghettoization related to public housing is only just now being undertaken, with an attempt to disperse vest-pocket low-income units in majority-group areas. As recently as two years ago the Housing Authority sent publicity releases to civil-rights groups, pointing with pride to the high percentage of low-income units built in ghetto areas—and yet no voices were raised in protest against this separatist policy.

Such acquiescence in the face of racial discrimination, in the name of survival, is not new. Booker T. Washington proudly proclaimed that "in all things that are purely social, we can be as separate as the fingers," in exchange for economic advancement promised by white missionary benefactors.[2] And now, almost 100 years later, other missionary benefactors urge that Negroes defer their manhood for yet another generation, in the interest of strategy.

### INCORRECT ASSERTIONS

The Piven-Cloward assertion that demands for integration have cost the poor decent housing is therefore a flight into sociological fantasy. Not only has this confrontation been avoided, but government and private enterprise have spent most of the last thirty years actively working to impede deghettoization.

The authors' assertions not only ignore historical fact, they also ignore present political realities. The first, and most important, of the facts that do not fit Piven and Cloward's thesis is the economic demands of the Vietnamese conflict and the space race. This drastic realignment of national priorities threatens not only low-income housing but also the whole range of social-welfare programs designed to aid the poor and the cities that contain such a large percentage of the poor. The second fact is that the great majority of the poor are white. How is reinforcing the ghetto to help these needy citizens? Why is the Piven-Cloward final solution designed solely for the Negro poor? The third fact is that the electorate is increasingly demonstrating a reluctance to approve public spending, and this pattern is apparently unrelated to racial considerations. Voters have slashed suburban school budgets, hampered air-pollution appropriations and vetoed a host of other bond issues for projects totally outside the racial context. What would happen to public-housing appropriations if Piven and Cloward's separated social order were to obtain? (In fact, in New York State, where the issue of dispersed low-income housing is only now being confronted, voters have consistently rejected every proposal for public-housing fund increases, despite the fact that integration was not an issue at the time of these votes. And interestingly enough, the negative vote came mainly from upstate New York, not from New York City where most of the state's Negroes are concentrated and integration is thus a more immediate threat.) Piven and Cloward assert that reinforcing the ghetto would remove voter antipathy to public housing, but in fact it would continue to have the effect of making the need for public housing virtually invisible, by isolating the most needy from the general electorate.

This pattern of statistics and misinterpreted facts runs throughout the Piven-Cloward piece. But its effect is to emasculate a very new and fragile effort to promote a democratic restructuring of our urban environment. Their talents might better have been used in examining the nature of the problem of housing for the poor against the background of the urban crisis, of which it is an integral part.


## ECONOMIC, NOT RACIAL, PREJUDICE

The striking fact that site selection for middle-income housing has never been a serious problem, while low-income housing has been relegated to slum areas, might indicate that the issue is not, basically, racial prejudice but economic prejudice. Economic status is, after all, relative rather than absolute. The middle-class individual is middle-class not because his income has reached a certain level but because it is higher than that of the poor person. This tenuous hold on superiority must be maintained in all its manifestations if status is to be maintained. Thus, while the poor are ethnically or geographically identified, the meat of prejudice lies in the fact that they are poor, and that any increase in the status of the poor brings a corresponding decrease in status for the middle class.

The prejudice against Latin Americans, ninety percent of whom are white, cannot be explained on racial grounds any more than can the hostility against southern hillbilly migrants in certain areas of the country. But it can be explained on economic grounds, and the question then becomes economic, not racial, advancement.

## CALL FOR MORE LOW-INCOME HOUSING

The basic fact that prompted the Piven-Cloward article is indisputable—that more low-income housing is desperately needed, and in great quantities. But their exegesis on this point is totally outside the realm of sound social and physical planning. Let us examine the implications of their solution, which basically calls for an impacted racial stratification based on exclusive concentration on the construction or rehabilitation of low-income housing in a ghetto structure and the acceptance by Negroes of endless confinement in ghettos and ghetto schools.

1. This solution would call for rapid expansion of the ghetto's boundaries, thus intensifying the flight to the suburbs and further eroding the city's tax base, with the resultant relentless decrease in city services and increase in environmental deterioration.

2. It would preclude construction of middle-income housing. Piven and Cloward have ignored the urgent need for middle-income housing in our cities, and fulfillment of this need would serve many purposes of benefit to the poor. Skewed rents and rent-supplement programs could open a substantial number of

these units to the poor. Attraction of middle-income families back into the city would improve the city's tax base, with the poor the major beneficiaries of improved ability to provide services. And opening up the housing market would free a substantial number of good-quality units for occupancy by the poor, in the "filtering down" process that accompanies new housing.

3. It would increase the racial and economic stratification that has intensified competition and hostility between national and economic enclaves within the metropolitan boundaries.

4. The emphasis on rehabilitation and the downgrading of the potential of urban renewal would, in many instances, mean patching up housing units that were unfit for human habitation when built and are now totally beyond any but temporary recall. This is especially true of New York City's 42,000 old-law tenements, housing more than 1 million poor people, which were built before the turn of the century and can never, because of inherent design deficiencies, provide decent living accommodations. The cost of decent temporary rehabilitation of these buildings is between $13,000 and $17,000 per unit, now far below the cost of building roomier and more habitable new housing. Construction innovations may bring these costs down to the point at which this stop-gap solution is feasible, but rehabilitation of bad buildings can never be anything but a temporary compromise. Rehabilitation of structures that are basically sound is another matter, but the number of buildings in this category in ghetto areas is not substantial. The Piven-Cloward antipathy to urban renewal is similarly shortsighted, since the current emphasis on comprehensive physical and social renewal provides the first real promise for revitalization of ghetto areas and of the city as a whole. The "bulldozer" approach to urban renewal is, happily, becoming a thing of the past, of which Piven and Cloward apparently are not aware. Rehabilitation of basically sound structures and judicious placement of compatible new buildings and facilities is increasingly combined with a host of supportive social services. As social scientists, Piven and Cloward should be the first to acknowledge that provision of four walls is only the first step to creating a healthy environment. To cheat the poor of this potential for creative action to solve their varied and interlocking problems is a cruel hoax.

### GHETTO LIFE IS DEMORALIZING

But the overriding consideration that demands repudiation of the authors' thesis is the very real and dangerous psychological damage created by the fact of ghetto existence, a consideration that they ignore. Ghetto residents recognize the implication of undesirability and inferiority that is inevitably conveyed by the fact of their forced separation from the majority community. This awareness stunts their aspirations, from their earliest schooldays to their working days. It contributes in great measure to antisocial behavioral patterns, to crime and delinquency, to environmental deterioration and to other manifestations of the ghetto pathology.

This fact of enforced separation is not lost on the majority community. It is a prime factor in the inadequacy of services that creates appallingly high infant mortality and disease rates, abysmal education, rudimentary police protection and sanitation, and other ghetto characteristics.

Piven and Cloward advance the idea that ghetto schools could be improved if integration pressures were dropped. Again, they see only the desperate need for quality education for ghetto children, ignoring the vicious impact of the ghetto's all-pervading sense of worthlessness on its children. Recent studies have shown that the quantitative dollar difference between ghetto and nonghetto schools is insignificant; the difference mainly lies in the ghetto child's lack of self-confidence, which prevents him from finding any value in education, since he can see no future for himself in conventional society.

We do not reject the hypothesis of a revitalized ghetto. But to seek to revitalize it as a compound for Negroes is self-defeating. The efforts of the body politic must be directed toward creating a wholesome, balanced community out of our cities' present ghettos. A physically and socially healthy community would combine housing and services for all income levels and all ethnic groups. With creative design and imaginative application of technical and social resources and techniques, these communities can be made attractive to all citizens. They can be brought back within the economic and social mainstream and become the focal point for a revitalized city.

## REORGANIZE RESIDENTIAL PATTERNS

Deghettoization would, as Piven and Cloward assert, mean massive movement of people and reconstruction of residential patterns. They indicate that such a large-scale reorientation is impossible. But the suburban genesis that they cite represents just such a gigantic social upheaval, a mass migration that was a direct result of government policies and actions. Government chose to encourage construction of segregated housing in the suburbs and to discourage middle-income-housing construction in the cities. The FHA even went so far as to recommend to suburban builders, in a 1938 handbook, that "if a neighborhood is to retain stability, it is necessary that properties shall continue to be occupied by the same social and racial group," and to include a sample restrictive covenant to insure this segregation.[3] When coupled with the large-scale in-migration from rural areas to the cities that accompanied this suburban social reorganization, its scope becomes truly enormous.

Even today, in a period of relative social stability, the American penchant for mobility is demonstrated by the fact that one family in six moves every year. And this mobility is not restricted to the middle class. Ghetto inhabitants, while they may be bound by the ghetto's confines, move constantly, from one street to another, from one ghetto to another, from one city to another, from one region to another. A recent poll of Harlem residents, made by John F. Kraft, Inc., indicated that nearly half the residents had lived at their present addresses for less than five years, and eighty-four percent were not born there.[4]

Furthermore, the imperatives of housing needs within the next forty years will require an even greater reorganization of residential patterns. Estimates indicate that housing stock must be more than doubled by the year 2000 in order to fill projected demand.[5] This means the creation of massive new towns, it means building within the cities on a gigantic scale, and it means a complete change in the structure of our present suburbs.

This impending social reorganization will create vast problems. But it also creates an unparalleled opportunity to accomplish deghettoization of our cities. If, as Piven and Cloward suggest, present housing patterns were to be frozen and the ghetto's walls expanded, those low-income families for which the authors express such concern would be frozen out of this new society. If, on the other hand, planning were to be done for the sensible and sensitive mixture of income levels and races in this new order, the goal of freedom of choice in a free society would be achieved.

## NEW DEVELOPMENTS

Piven and Cloward's doomful pronouncement on the future of democratic planning for our cities has in fact appeared at the very moment when new developments show, at last, some promise for a dynamic and equitable solution to urban ills. Among these developments in the last twelve months are the following:

The demonstration-cities program, the first major effort to wed social and physical planning in the urban context, was passed into law. Although its funding is grossly inadequate, this new departure sets precedents for future urban action.

The meetings of the Subcommittee on Executive Reorganization of the Senate Committee on Government Operations, popularly known as the Ribicoff hearings on the urban crisis, have focused attention, for the first time in a comprehensive and imaginative way, on the complex of urban problems, with special attention to the problems of the poor, particularly the ghetto poor.

The White House Conference "To Fulfill These Rights" developed some very bold proposals for the advancement of the Negro American in the context of deghettoization.

Senator Robert F. Kennedy issued a comprehensive blueprint for simultaneous treatment of the whole range of ghetto problems, with the express intention of revitalizing the ghetto to achieve deghettoization.[6]

The Departments of Health, Education and Welfare and Housing and Urban Development shifted focus to delineate the function of the ghetto in the destruction of the individual inhabitant, and in issuing new guidelines to inhibit use of urban-renewal funds for impacting the ghetto or for "Negro removal."

In New York City a whole range of developments has shifted the city's focus toward a commitment to deghettoization. These developments include former Borough President Constance Baker Motley's seven-point program for the revitalization of Harlem and the subsequent state decision to build a small office facility in that ghetto; Senator Robert F. Kennedy's far-reaching proposal for a collaboration of indigenous talent and initiative with private business and government in the rebuilding of Bedford-Stuyvesant; Mayor John V. Lindsay's decisions to concentrate urban-renewal activity in the city's three major ghetto areas and to scatter low-income housing in majority-group communities; and the Logue report on the city's future planning direction, which also focused on the three major ghetto areas and saw their revitalization as the key to the city's progress.[7]

Unfortunately, Piven and Cloward's opinions have been shared and enlarged upon by a group of planners and social scientists who have successfully ignored the neo-*apartheid* implications of their pronouncements. They have ignored, as well, the fact that their theories are not new; proposals for de-ghettoization were rejected by Congress in 1949 when it was considering the Housing Act, after Senator Paul Douglas advanced the thesis that these proposals would impede the building of low-income housing.[8] Those who have been concerned with urban problems on a long-term basis have realized that this thesis is not true to fact; those who have lately arrived in the urban pastures apparently seek to revive this fallacious argument with no regard to history.

The validity of Booker T. Washington's "separate fingers" theory has confronted the test of history and been found wanting. It represented, in fact, license for exploitation of Negroes. We sincerely hope that this new attempt to resurrect it is rejected before the potential for new exploitation inherent in the Piven-Cloward thesis is realized.

## NOTES

[1] Frances Fox Piven and Richard A. Cloward, "The Case Against Urban Desegregation," *Social Work,* Vol. 12, No. 1 (January 1967), pp. 12–21.

2 Speech at the opening of the Cotton State Exposition, Atlanta, Ga., September 1895.

3 *Underwriting Manual* (Washington, D.C.: Federal Housing Administration, 1938), Sect. 98 (-1).

4 "Housing Assailed in a Harlem Poll," *New York Times,* January 15, 1967.

5 *Our People and Their Cities Chartbook* (Washington, D.C.: Urban America, undated).

6 U.S., *Congressional Record,* 89th Cong., February 2, 1966.

7 "Let There Be Commitment, a Housing, Planning, Development Program for New York City," report of a study group of the Institute of Public Administration to Mayor John V. Lindsay, September 1966.

8 See Richard M. Dalfiume, Letter to the Editor, *New Republic,* January 14, 1967.

The Case for Urban Integration:
An Answer to Piven and Cloward

WHITNEY M. YOUNG, JR.

It is interesting that at this point in history, when so much has been done in so short a time, voices should be raised in support of a "temporary" abandonment of the goals of integration and a retreat into self-segregation.[1] Such proposals for future civil-rights strategy come, strangely enough, at a time when there is almost unprecedented intellectual ferment, a time when new ideas and new solutions for the enormous problems afflicting the Negro poor abound. There is no doubt that the only way Negro citizens can achieve their goal of equal opportunity is through coalition with those elements in the larger society that share a

*The late Whitney M. Young, Jr., M.S.W., was executive director, National Urban League, New York, New York.*

Reprinted with permission of *Social Work*, vol. 12, no. 3 (July 1967).

vision of an America from which discrimination has vanished, an America that apportions its wealth on an equitable basis.

The civil-rights movement has followed this general approach and, by and large, has been successful. It is hard to realize in 1967 that barely a decade ago Negroes were burdened by a vast network of legal obstacles to their progress. The accomplishments of the still-young civil-rights movement are impressive. It has effectively established equality under the law as a public policy and, through its coalition with other groups, brought about a federal commitment to improve the economic and social conditions of Negro citizens.

If the movement did nothing else, these would still be great accomplishments, laying the groundwork for future gains. But along with this, it has created a spirit within the Negro community itself that has led to a new self-respect and a determination to overcome the crippling limits set by racism. It has also laid bare the latent prejudices of the nation, bringing them to the surface where they can be fought and placing the United States in its most profound moral crisis since the question of slavery split the nation a century ago.

But this record of accomplishment is offset by the deep entrenchment of forces prejudicial to Negro advancement. For many Negroes, too, the limited achievements of the movement have resulted in rising expectations that cannot be fulfilled, and the resultant bitterness has fed the flames of separatism and disillusionment.

But are not the goals of the separatist essentially the same as those of the backlasher? The white suburbanite who says, "I don't want Negroes living here," and the separatist who says, "All right, I won't move to your nice neighborhood; I'll try to make my own a bit more livable," are in substantial agreement. Both implicitly agree that some areas shall be white, some Negro. Both agree that there shall be limits placed on the Negro's opportunities solely because of his race.

The white bigot thinks as he does because his goal is to exclude the Negro from the mainstream of society, but the separatist endorses self-segregation as a means of strengthening the Negro community so that, in some vague manner, it can "negotiate" on an equal basis with whites at some indeterminate future date and thus achieve integration.

## SEGREGATION BREEDS SEGREGATION

It will not work. All that comes from segregation is more segregation. The problems faced by Negroes today stem from segregation. Whether imposed from outside or sought from within, segregation leads to disadvantage in competing for the rewards of society.

Countless studies have confirmed the disabilities that derive from segregation. In education, for example, the recent report by the U.S. Civil Rights Commission convincingly documents the benefits of integration. The report states:

> Negro children who attend predominantly Negro schools do not achieve as well as other children, Negro and white. Their aspirations are more restricted than those of other children and they do not have as much confidence that they can influence their own futures. When they become adults, they are less likely to participate in the mainstream of American society. . . .[2]

The report found that schools with Negro enrollments in the majority are regarded by the community as segregated and inferior, a view that is shared by students, teachers and parents alike. It was also found that compensatory efforts by the schools often failed because the students' problems stemmed from the racial isolation that pervades our cities.

Contradicting a hallowed myth of the separatists, the commission found:

> Disadvantaged Negro students in school with a majority of equally disadvantaged white students achieve better than Negro students in school with a majority of equally disadvantaged Negro students.[3]

Integration in and of itself is therefore a major factor in improving the achievement of Negro youngsters.

The same hard facts apply to housing and economic areas. So long as Negroes are a separate, isolated minority, living, working and studying apart from the white majority that considers them inferior, they will suffer a disproportionate share of deprivations and limitations. Integration is no distant goal to be reached after conditions of solidarity and isolated self-improvement are met; it is a precondition to such improvement of status and living conditions. To deflect from the straight and narrow path of pursuing integration is to condemn future generations to poverty and discrimination.

## NEGRO PROGRESS IS URBAN PROGRESS

Increasingly, the problems of Negro citizens are seen as being those of urban civilization itself. The large-scale migrations of southern Negroes to the urban North and West have resulted in fiscal and social pressures on those areas and in turn have led to a national concern with the future of the American city.

A recent Ford Foundation study looks ahead to the year 2000 and predicts that seventy-seven percent of the nation's population will live in three gigantic urban regions—California, Florida and an urban belt stretching from the Atlantic seaboard to the Middle West and Great Lakes region—and in nineteen smaller regions and metropolises.[4] The extent to which the nation has already urbanized is seen by the increase in standard metropolitan regions from 176 to 214 in the six short years between 1960 and 1966.

So when we think of the future face of the nation, we must realize that today's segregated suburbs are about to become tomorrow's urban centers, linked in great chains of cities, large and small. The present fiscal and social problems of the American city, traceable in large part to massive migrations from the South by relatively unskilled and uneducated Negroes, must be solved if the nation is to be able to live with the population patterns now being set.

The old days of piecemeal attacks on the problems of the ghetto are waning. The success of the Defense Department's systems-engineering approach—the technique of organizing and directing team efforts on an interdisciplinary, multi-industrial basis in an effort to deal with all the aspects of a problem simultaneously—has encouraged planners to use this method in the ghetto. This approach has been used for a wide range of programs, from the development of the atom bomb to space exploration. The model-cities legislation is an example of how it can be used for concrete attacks on social dislocation. Proposals have been made to try a similar approach to housing and other urban needs.

The whole focus on urban problems has shifted to include an overview of total metropolitan problems. Just as local inadequacies gave rise to regional health, transportation and economic agencies, so, too, the weakness of localities in dealing with the problems of housing and education has led to revived interest in metropolitan and regional government and plans for federal-government incentives to encourage this.

Edward J. Logue, development administrator, Boston Development Authority, has proposed use of the tax structure to effect changes in ghetto housing.[5] He has suggested that depreciation write-offs for slum housing be tied to conformity with local building codes, and has proposed accelerated write-offs for housing and business investment in the ghetto and other changes in the tax laws to encourage private interests to help make the ghetto livable. Educational parks, "turnkey" housing, plans for apartment ownership in the ghetto, experiments in education and in training are all taking place. This innovative thrust is one of the most promising developments in recent years, for it embodies the traditional preconditions for meaningful social change. Out of this welter of ideas and experimental projects will come added opportunity for the man in the ghetto.

As the problems facing the Negro are seen to be ones that the larger society must deal with and solve if it is itself to survive, they will be solved. So long as the Negro was confined to a small part of the city he could be ignored and left to his own devices, but as the ghetto has grown, so, too, have the problems facing the city and metropolitan region at large. The tremendous fiscal pressures faced by cities in trying to cope with educational and welfare expenditures make it mandatory for the nation to bring the Negro back into the mainstream of its economic life.

## FEDERAL ROLE

The federal government is firmly committed to policies of integration and expanded social welfare. Federal power has exerted pressures that have affected whole areas of the South. Despite some laxness in enforcement of existing statutes, significant changes have been made. The federal judiciary, too, has consistently upheld and applied civil-rights legislation. The recent decision upholding the U.S. Office of Education's guidelines for southern school integration is an example of how both the executive and the judicial branches are working to force swifter changes.

While many have criticized such programs as the War on Poverty, rent supplements, Model Cities and others as being underfinanced and less than adequate to meet the crying needs of the ghetto, it must be acknowledged that they represent significant advances. An examination of the federal budget shows that since 1961 expenditures for housing and community development, health, labor, welfare and education have tripled.

Such an increase in social-welfare funds is significant for two reasons: (1) It indicates an awareness of the federal government's responsibility to end poverty and assist people and communities to their rightful share in the nation's prosperity. (2) The precedent set by these programs makes it even more likely that they will be expanded or improved. The history of social reform in the United States shows that programs of social welfare start modestly, win acceptance and are eventually expanded. The lesson is clear that even programs considered paltry will result in large changes.

## CHANGES IN THE NEGRO COMMUNITY

Despite the obvious inequalities that still exist, changes have occurred within the Negro community that will enable Negroes to make more progress in the years ahead. Although Negro income remains only fifty-six percent that of whites, the figure hides the improved economic position of many Negro citizens. In 1959 only one Negro family in ten had an annual income between $7000 and $15,000. In 1965 more than one in five reached that middle-class level. A decade ago only about twelve percent of Negro workers held white-collar jobs, including professional and managerial jobs. Now about twenty percent of Negro workers hold such jobs, and conservative estimates place the figure for 1975 at about thirty percent.[6]

Three conclusions can be drawn from this: (1) Negro families are moving out of poverty to an unprecedented degree (they are crossing the poverty line at a faster rate than white families). (2) The statistics reflect the great increase in college-trained Negroes. (3) This growing middle class comes out of the ghetto and represents an articulate, responsible group conversant with the frustrations and angers of the ghetto and capable of providing the leadership and power to effect change.

The great migrations to the city also changed the picture for Negro aspirations. When the Negro was an isolated minority in a hostile South he had little hope for integration, full citizenship rights or improved education, housing or jobs. With his concentration in the urban areas of the largest states comes the political power that goes with the right to vote. Negroes are in the majority in such cities as Washington, D.C., and Newark, N.J. Before too long, many of the largest cities in the country will have Negro majorities. In all large cities today Negro votes are influential, often spelling the balance of power for candidates. Increasing sophistication on the part of the Negro voter means that the vote will be used for advancement of the Negro's interests, while the strategic location of Negro voters in the most populous states means they will have increased leverage in influencing candidates for national office. Even in the South the startling gain in Negro voting—double what it was in 1960 and brought about largely through the efforts of the coalition that fashioned the Voting Rights Act of 1965—has been a moderating influence on many southern officials. The power of the ballot has resulted in hundreds of Negro officeholders at the federal, state and local levels after the 1966 elections.

## THE JOB REVOLUTION

Patterns of employment have changed drastically. Manufacturing employment has leveled off and the 13 million new jobs that have been created since 1950 are in wholesale and retail trade, banking, insurance, government employment and other service industries. In addition, new fields are coming into being. Dr. William Haber of the University of Michigan points out:

> There are over 40,000 listings in the 1965 Dictionary of Occupational Titles. Since the second edition 6,500 were added. One in every four of those employed 25 years from now will be on jobs that do not even exist today.[7]

Business publications report that the growth of the computer industry is limited only by the drastic shortage of programmers.

What does all this mean for the Negro? It means that it is in the economic interests of this country to integrate him into its economic mainstream. When this nation needed the Negro for manual labor it evolved social systems and patterns to keep him in that role. Slavery and—later—segregation were devised as economic means of ensuring cheap labor to do the hard and unwanted dirty jobs that had to be done.

Now, however, the nation's business has no use for strong backs and arms. It needs brainpower and skilled employees who can deal with the increasingly complex machinery and paper work of a technologically advanced society. Because business and government alike have an insatiable need for such workers, the social and economic patterns suited to an earlier era have become outmoded and new ones will have to be evolved. Because most of these new jobs are in the very urban areas in which there are large concentrations of Negroes, this means that discrimination must end and that schools and other aspects of society must change to meet the new needs of business. The very system that once oppressed the Negro will need him again, this time on a basis of equality and opportunity. And this situation has led otherwise conservative businessmen and administrators to support civil-rights causes.

## COALITION

Coalition has usually meant the liberal-labor-Negro coalition, and it has been attacked on the grounds that the basic interests of the participants are not the same. While some strains are bound to show—defection of liberals to the peace movement, antagonism toward Negro membership by some unions—these

groups share essentially the same vision of the future. No interaction between groups is entirely immune to stresses, but even
when the greatest degree of conflict exists there is basic agreement on ultimate goals. The white construction worker competing for scarce jobs may fear widescale introduction of Negroes
into his union, but both he and the Negro are in favor of a
massive building program that would create enough work for all
and would fill the need for decent low-cost housing.

But the view that the civil-rights groups are locked into a
coalition exclusively with labor and liberal groups is false. The
coalition is wider than that, and it is broadening into a general
consensus of the major power groups of the nation. Religious
organizations of all faiths are a major component of the coalition. They are speaking out, organizing programs in the ghetto
and beginning to use their financial power to open jobs for Negroes in industries that are slow to respond to the need. Foundations and other nonprofit organizations are part of this coalition.
Many of the largest ones support not only traditional social
welfare and educational programs but also community organization in the ghetto and experimental projects. Federal pressures
for fair employment practices, the problems of urban areas and
the need for skilled workers are all contributing to make business
a partner in the coalition too.

Perhaps most important, there is a feeling among the youth of
America that discrimination is wrong. Those in their twenties
who have lived through the current civil-rights movement have
a sense of identification with the movement and a fervent belief
in its ultimate victory. Most areas of American life have been
touched by the civil-rights movement, and elements in all these
areas are part of the broad coalition supporting the Negro's
efforts to enter the mainstream of American life.

## CONCLUSION

All these factors ensure that the Negro will not be a powerless
junior partner in a coalition with liberals and labor and other
elements of society but will have an important voice. No attempt
has been made here to paint a picture of a thriving, happy situation for Negro citizens. It is far from that. But the positives must

be stated, accepted and built upon if there is to be further progress. Despite the ills that afflict the ghetto, it must be realized
that the past several years have seen substantial changes in the
total society and its efforts to integrate the Negro, and within the
Negro community itself. There have also been less obvious but
equally important changes in the way people are beginning to
see the problems of the Negro and the degree to which the Negro's problems and those of the larger society are now inter-
twined. It has become clear to an increasing number of people
and institutions that the Negro's demand for integration is right
and just and that it is in the self-interest of American society to
heed it. The present condition of the Negro is a threat both to
the nation internally and to its position with respect to the rest
of the world. Conditions now exist that will make it possible for
Negro citizens to achieve their goal of equal opportunity and
close the gap in their life chances.

Certainly Negroes should strengthen their own organizational
structures and devote their resources and energies to self-improvement, but this is not the same as self-segregation. To abandon
integration now is to play into the hands of racists and ensure
ultimate defeat, because segregation by definition means exclusion from any chance to influence society and advance self-
interest.

Many of the encouraging developments of the present day
would fade away if the Negro ghettos were to chart a course of
separatism and self-imposed *apartheid*. Pressing the claims of
integration, while it may arouse backlash and bring latent prejudices to the fore, is the only practical method for achieving equal
rights. The shortest distance between two points is still a straight
line.

## NOTES

[1] Frances Fox Piven and Richard A. Cloward, "The Case Against
Urban Desegregation," *Social Work*, Vol. 12, No. 1 (January 1967),
pp. 12–21.

[2] U.S. Commission on Civil Rights, *Racial Isolation in the Public
Schools*, Vol. 1 (Washington, D.C.: U.S. Government Printing Office,
1967), p. 193.

[3] *Ibid.*, p. 204.

4 Jerome P. Pickard, "Future Growth of Major United States Cities," *Urban Land News and Trends,* Vol. 26, No. 2 (February 1967).

5 Edward J. Logue, "Let's Make Rebuilding American Cities Simple," address before General Alumni Association and American Management and Civilization Program, George Washington University, March 1967 (Boston: Boston Development Institute, 1967). (Mimeographed.)

6 Dan Cordtz, "The Negro Middle Class Is Right in the Middle," *Fortune* (November 1966), p. 179.

7 William Haber, "The Economy—Where Is It Going?" Herbert R. Abeles Memorial Address, Thirty-fifth General Assembly, Councils of Jewish Federations and Welfare Funds, Los Angeles, California, November 1966 (New York: Councils of Jewish Federations and Welfare Funds, 1966), (Mimeographed.)

## Separatism Versus Integration: A Rejoinder

FRANCES FOX PIVEN
AND RICHARD A. CLOWARD

The reiteration of integrationist principles by Funnyé and Shiffman in the April issue of *Social Work* and by Whitney M. Young, Jr., in the present issue is hardly an answer to an analysis of the political consequences of integrationist policies. It behooves us to look at what integrationist ideals have given (and will give) the Negro poor in our time. We tried to provide such an analysis by calling attention to the hard facts of urban population trends, the continuing failure of housing programs to provide either low-income or integrated housing, and the role of American racism in creating, maintaining and exacerbating these problems. Funnyé, Shiffman and Young, by ignoring that analysis, invite us to repeat the mistakes of the past, but with our integrationist banners held even higher.

They fault us mainly on two points. First, we have presumably failed to recognize the role of federal policies in promoting hous-

Reprinted with the permission of *Social Work,* vol. 12, no. 3 (July 1967).

ing segregation—policies, they add, in which Negro leaders have acquiesced. Second, they suggest that the prospects for desegregation have brightened because urban areas are to be rebuilt and Negro and white can be shuffled about in that process.

As to the first point, we agree that federal policies have promoted segregation, and we said so. But we said something else as well: that when efforts have been made to use federal housing to promote integration, housing appropriations have been cut and localities have rejected the programs. The result is virtually no new housing for the poor of whatever color. As if to underscore our argument, Funnyé and Shiffman cite our example of Newark, N.J., where public housing projects were *not* used to promote integration, with the result that a great deal of low-rental housing was built.

Funnyé and Shiffman think that federal policies have promoted segregation because integrationists have not been ardent enough in pressing their cause. Whatever their ardor, it should be recognized that integrationists are in the minority. Whether or not to integrate big cities is not a politically real choice; had Negro leaders resisted segregated-housing policies in Newark, for example, the program would have been stalled by controversy and probably killed.

What, then, of the massive rebuilding programs predicted for our future and of the possibility of exploiting them to desegregate the great urban ghettos? The only concrete program that can be pointed to is the Model Cities Act—a poor case from which to take heart, since its funding seems likely to be all but eliminated by Congress. Otherwise they cite mere rhetoric: the Ribicoff hearings, which "focused attention . . . in a comprehensive and imaginative way" on urban problems; the "comprehensive blueprint" issued by Senator Robert F. Kennedy; and the White House Conference on Civil Rights, which "developed some very bold proposals" for housing reform. Nor does the new emphasis in urban-renewal programs on "comprehensive physical and social renewal" hold real promise that the poor will get more housing, segregated or not. What it really means is that government will be less brutal about dislodging the poor to make way for more white-middle-class facilities.

Even if huge rebuilding programs were to be undertaken in the next several decades, does it follow that desegregation will result? Even the most cursory examination of urban political trends dictates precisely the opposite conclusion. The white suburbs now contain more people than the cities, and reapportionment has given them electoral power commensurate with their numbers. These suburban majorities, in alliance with inner-city whites, will dominate the shaping of future governmental programs for the urban community. Nor is it difficult to imagine what the priorities will be—such as long-term, government-insured mortgage programs to proliferate the single-family suburban dwellings that Funnyé and Shiffman blame for current segregation. Desegregation will hardly top the list.

The real question confronting Negro leaders in the central city is whether the Negro poor will get anything from this white urban coalition except more "human renewal" programs—programs that appease, guide and control the recipients of service but do not alter their environment.

We too have been reading the portents for the future. Our predictions, however, are based not on proposals advanced at conferences and hearings but on the political realities of population shifts. Negroes and whites are now being distributed along firm city-suburban jurisdictional lines, and this is likely to accentuate racist policies. In the suburban-dominated constituencies that will shape future governmental policies, the Negro will simply be shunted aside if he insists on integrated housing and education. On the other hand, by consolidating his power within the central city the Negro might have some impact on the environment of the ghetto itself. To exact even these concessions from the white urban coalition, however, the Negro must organize as a bloc—that is, he must organize separately. And the route to effective separatist power does not begin with proclamations that the ghetto must be dispersed.

One final point. Funnyé, Shiffman and Young attack us for failing to comprehend the depersonalization and demoralization of life in the ghetto. In this they join a distinguished body of intellectual and integrationist leaders who have engulfed us with reports and studies purporting to show that the Negro community is a tangle of pathology, that the Negro family has deteriorated beyond precedent and that the Negro personality is deformed by profound feelings of inferiority. And what is the solution to these problems? Integration. Not reallocation of gov-

ernmental subsidies and other community wealth to make the
Negro ghetto as suitable a place to live as the many white ethnic
communities, not the building of black power to give the Negro
some measure of control over his destiny, but submergence of
the Negro in the white majority.

What is it that we whites are implying about the Negro and
the Negro about himself by this integrationist strategy? To say
that Negro children are not learning for lack of pride and
motivation is one thing; to insist that they cannot find pride
and motivation unless surrounded by whites in the classroom is
quite another. For this precisely has been the tragedy of the
Negro: that he has seen himself through our eyes and has made
his own feeling of personal and collective worth dependent on
our feelings toward him. Thus, the Negro has waited helplessly
for us to proffer brotherhood. And he has waited in vain. One day
an interpretation of American racism will be written, and it will
say that White supremacy ultimately succeeded because the Negro
was led to believe that he could have no reality, no identity, except as a reflection of whites.

There is another solution to the Negro's predicament, and some
Negroes are struggling toward it. That solution seeks to protect
the Negro from the devastating effects of American racism by
building black pride, black solidarity and black power. Funnyé,
Shiffman and Young chose to ignore this part of our argument.
But if any lesson is to be drawn from the experience of other
minorities in America, it is that the strength to resist majority
prejudices, to advance in spite of them and ultimately to overcome them must be found within a countervailing ethnic community.

# Militant
# Civil Servants

FRANCES FOX PIVEN

Not long ago, thousands of people massed in front of New York's City Hall and sang "Solidarity Forever." The image was of workers marching against Pinkertons. But the ranks were middle-class civil servants, and their solidarity was directed against the black and Puerto Rican poor. The issue on this occasion was school decentralization, but that is only one of a host of issues currently galvanizing white civil servants and dividing them from the enlarging minorities in the cities.

The rising militancy of public employees needs no documenting here. New York's 60,000 school teachers have been shutting down the school system regularly; this fall it was the Day Care Center workers; slowdowns by police and firemen are becoming commonplace. And if public employees are more militant in New York, where they are the most numerous and best organized, public unions across the country are catching up. Teachers prevented schools from opening this fall in Illinois, Ohio, Indiana, Massachusetts, Pennsylvania, Connecticut, Rhode Island, Wisconsin, Minnesota, Utah and Tennessee. Last year Detroit's police were hit by the "blue flu"; while Cleveland's police threatened outright rebellion against Mayor Carl B. Stokes. In Atlanta the firemen went on strike; in Newark the police and firemen simultaneously called in sick.

These events are not, as they are sometimes described, simply contests between unions and the "general public." The keenest struggle is with residents of the central-city ghettos (who in any

Published with permission of *Transaction*, vol. 7. No. 1 (November 1969).

case now form a substantial segment of the "general public" in most big cities). Police, firemen, teachers and public-welfare workers increasingly complain about "harassment" in the ghettos. For their part, growing numbers of the black poor view police, firemen, teachers, public-welfare workers and other city employees as their oppressors.

The emerging conflict is not difficult to explain. Whites and blacks are pitted against each other in a struggle for the occupational and political benefits attached to public employment. Whites now have the bulk of these benefits, and blacks want a greater share of them. Nor is it only jobs that are at stake. Organized public employees have become a powerful force shaping the policies of municipal agencies, but the policies that suit employees often run counter to ghetto interests. We may be entering another phase in the long and tragic history of antagonism between the black poor and the white working class in America.

## THE ETHNIC STAKEOUT

Municipal jobs have always been an important resource in the cultivation of political power. As successive waves of immigrants settled in the cities, their votes were exchanged for jobs and other favors, permitting established party leaders to develop and maintain control despite the disruptive potential of new and unaffiliated populations. The exchange also facilitated the integration of immigrant groups into the economic and political structures of the city, yielding them both a measure of influence and some occupational rewards. Public employment was a major channel of mobility for the Italian, the Irish and the Jew, each of whom, by successively taking over whole sectors of the public services, gave various municipal agencies their distinctly ethnic coloration. Now blacks are the newcomers. But they come at a time when public employment has been preempted by older groups and is held fast through civil-service provisions and collective-bargaining contracts. Most public jobs are no longer allocated in exchange for political allegiance but through a "merit" system based on formal qualifications.

The development of the civil-service merit system in municipalities at the turn of the century (the federal government adopted it in 1883) is usually credited to the efforts of reformers who sought to improve the quality of municipal services, to eliminate graft and to dislodge machine leaders. At least some of the employees in all cities with more than 500,000 inhabitants are now under civil service; in about half of these cities, virtually all employees have such protections.

Although the civil service originated in the struggle between the party leaders and reformers for control of public employment, it launched municipal employees as an independent force. As municipal services expanded, the enlarging numbers of public employees began to form associations. Often these originated as benevolent societies, such as New York's Patrolmen's Benevolent Association which formed in the 1890s. Protected by the merit system, these organizations of public employees gradually gained some influence in their own right, and they exerted that influence at both the municipal and the state level to shape legislation and to monitor personnel policies so as to protect and advance their occupational interests.

Shortly after World War I, when the trade-union movement was growing rapidly, public employees made their first major thrust toward unionization in the famous Boston police strike. About 1100 of the 1400-man force struck, goaded by the refusal of city officials to grant pay raises despite rapid inflation and despite the favorable recommendations of a commission appointed to appraise police demands. The strike precipitated widespread disorder in the streets of Boston. Official reactions were swift and savage. Calvin Coolidge, then governor, became a national hero as he moved to break the strike under the banner "There is no right to strike against the public safety by anybody, anywhere, anytime." Virtually the entire police force was fired (and the few loyal men were granted pay raises). More important, the numerous police unions that had sprouted up in other cities, many of them affiliated with the American Federation of Labor, were scuttled. Public unionism did not recover its impetus until well after World War II.

In the meantime, civil-service associations relied mainly on lobbying to press their interests, and as their membership grew they became an effective force in party politics. Although the mode of their involvement in party politics varied from place to place and from time to time, the sheer numbers of organized public employees made political leaders loath to ignore them. One measure of their impact is the number of major party leaders who rose from their ranks. In New York City, for example, Mayor William O'Dwyer was a former policeman; Abe Beame, the Democratic candidate for mayor in 1965, was a former school-teacher, and Paul Screvane, his competitor for the Democratic mayoralty nomination in that same year, began as a sanitation worker.

## PUBLIC UNIONISM

Now unionism is on the rise gain, signaling a new phase in the political development of public-employee groups. It is even spreading rapidly to the more professional services, such as education and welfare, whose employees have traditionally resisted the working-class connotation of unionism. The American Federation of Teachers has organized so many teachers as to force the National Educational Association, which considers itself a professional association, into a militant stance (including endorsing boycotts and strikes by its members). In New York, firemen last year successfully wrested the right to strike from their parent International Association of Firefighters, and the Patrolmen's Benevolent Association is exploring the possibility of an affiliation with the AFL-CIO. The American Federation of State, County, and Municipal Employees—half of whose members work for municipalities—is one of the fastest-growing affiliates of the AFL-CIO, having increased its membership by seventy percent in the last four years. Overall, unions of public employees are adding 1000 new members every working day, according to a member of the National Labor Relations Board.

By becoming part of the labor movement, public employees are augmenting their influence in two ways. First, they can call for support from other unions, and that support can be a substantial force. New York's teachers were backed in the struggle against school decentralization by the Central Labor Council, which represents 1.2 million workers. (The Central Labor Council, headed by a top official from the electricians' union, and with an overwhelmingly white membership, also had its own interest in the school issue: The Board of Education disperses over $1 billion annually for maintenance and construction. Under a system of community control, contracts might be awarded to black businesses or to contractors who hire black workers. Some black labor officials, seeing themselves allied against their own communities, broke ranks with the Central Labor Council over the decentralization issue.)

Unionism also means that public employees feel justified in using the disruptive leverage of the strike. Transit workers bring a metropolis to a standstill; teachers close down the schools; sanitation men bury a city under mounds of garbage. With each such crisis the cry goes up for new legislative controls. But it is hard to see how laws will prevent strikes, unless the political climate becomes much more repressive. So far political leaders have been reluctant to invoke the full penalties permitted by existing law for fear of alienating organized labor. Thus, New York State's Condon-Wadlin Law, enacted in 1947, was not used and was finally replaced by the "model" Taylor Law which, as the experience of the last three years shows, works no better. Theodore Kheel, one of the nation's most noted labor arbitrators, in pronouncing the failure of the new law, pointed out that the state Public Employment Relations Board, established under the Taylor Law to arbitrate disputes, took no action on either of the New York City teacher strikes. The *New York Times* concluded with alarm that "The virus of irresponsibility is racing through New York's unionized civil service," and "There is no end, short of draining the municipal treasury and turning taxpayers into refugees or relief recipients. . . ."

Public unions must be controlled, so the argument goes, because they are uniquely capable of paralyzing the cities and gouging the public as the price of restoring services. In a recent decision, New York's highest court held that a legislative classification differentiating between public and private industry was reasonable and constitutional, thus justifying prohibitions on the right of public employees to strike. The courts unanimously held that public employees could "by the exercise of naked power" obtain gains "wholly disproportionate to the services rendered by them."

As a practical matter, however, these distinctions between pub-

lic and private employees do not hold up. Strikes in the public
and private sectors rely on the same forms of leverage, though in
varying degrees. Private-sector strikes result in economic losses,
but so do strikes in the municipal services (for example, transit
stoppages). Even teachers and welfare workers exert some economic pressure, although they rely more heavily on another form
of leverage—the cries of a severely inconvenienced and dis-
comfited populace—to force government to settle their grievances.
But private strikes of milk or fuel deliveries, of steel workers or
transportation workers, also discomfit large sectors of the population and generate pressure for government to intervene and force
a settlement.

Nor is it true that the coercive power of municipal unions en-
ables them to obtain more favorable settlements than private
unions. If, under the pressure of a strike in municipal services, the
public is often unmindful of the impact of settlements on taxes,
the public is equally unmindful of the eventual costs to consumers of settlements in the private sector. Industrial strikes are
by no means necessarily less disruptive than public strikes or less
coercive in pressing for a greater share of the public's dollar.


## BLANKET SECURITY

Despite the continuing controversy over the right to strike, it is
not the root of the trouble over municipal employment. Rather
it is that the gains won by employees after long years of struggle
now seem to be in jeopardy.

In fact, some groups of public employees had managed to secure
substantial control over their working conditions long before they
began to unionize, and in many cases long before comparable
gains had been secured by workers in the private sector. These
victories were won by intensive lobbying and by the assiduous
cultivation of influence in the political parties at the municipal
and state levels.

In the past, except where wages were concerned, other groups
in the cities rarely became sufficiently aroused to block efforts by
public employees to advance their interests. On issues such as
tenure or working conditions or career advancement, and even

retirement (which does not involve immediate costs) the civil-services associations were able to make substantial strides by using conventional means of political influence.

First, with their jobs secured by the merit system, public workers in many agencies went on to win the principle of "promotion from within." This principle, together with promotion criteria that favored longevity, assured the career advancement of those already employed. But such a system of promotion, because it has the consequence of restricting outsiders to the bottom rank of public employment, is being opposed by new groups. When proponents of school decentralization insist that these requirements be waived to place black people in supervisory or administrative positions, spokesmen for the New York school supervisors' association answer that it will "turn the clock back 100 years and reinstate the spoils system."

In some municipal agencies, moreover, newcomers are even barred from lower-level jobs. Building inspectors in New York City are required to have five years' experience in the building trades. Police associations oppose any "lowering" of hiring standards, proposed as a way of facilitating entrance by minority groups, arguing that the complexity of modern law enforcement calls for even higher educational standards. (Police have even objected to lowering the physical-height requirement, which now excludes many Puerto Ricans.) When New York City recently announced that impoverished people would be granted up to twelve extra points on civil-service tests for fifty low-paying jobs in antipoverty agencies, the very meagerness of the concession cast in relief the system of exclusion it was to modify.

Public employees have also been successful in preempting some of the future resources of the city. Demands for improved retirement and pension plans, for example, are prominent: New York's transit workers recently settled for a contract that awarded pension pay on the basis of a time-and-a-half provision during their last year of employment and the police are demanding the right to retire after fifteen years. Such benefits are often won more easily than wage demands, for it is less onerous for a mayor to make concessions payable under a later administration.

Obviously, elaborate entrance and promotion requirements now limit access by blacks to municipal jobs. Indeed, one can almost measure the strength of public-employee associations in different cities by their success in securing such requirements, and in keeping minority members out. In New York, where municipal workers are numerous and well organized, ninety percent of the teachers are white; in Detroit, Philadelphia and Chicago, where municipal employees are not as well organized, twenty-five to forty percent of the teachers are black.

## MORTGAGED TREASURIES

The number of jobs at stake is vast, and black demands are mounting. New York City employs 325,000 people, and personnel costs naturally account for the lion's share (about sixty percent) of a municipal budget topping $6 billion. And the share is growing: The number of public employees continues to rise (up sixty percent in New York City since the end of World War II), and wages and benefits are also rising. The question is not whether these costs are legitimate—but who will benefit by them. For as blacks become more numerous in cities, they will come to power only to find the treasuries mortgaged to earlier groups.

Unionization has been important mainly (but not exclusively) in the area of wages, where public employees often lagged behind organized private workers. Relying as they did on political influence, they were blocked by taxpayer groups who usually opposed higher municipal salaries. However, with unionization and strike power, public employees are no longer dependent on the vicissitudes of interest-group politics to get higher wages, and so, as the *New York Times* notes with horror, they have begun to "leapfrog" each other in salary demands.

Unionization is also enabling large numbers of municipal workers who hold less coveted jobs to move forward. By and large, hospital workers, clerks and janitors, for example, were left behind in the process of advancement through the civil services and through party politics. In New York City many of these workers have now been organized by District 37 of the State, County and Municipal Employees Union. Furthermore, because these are low-paid, low-prestige jobs, they are often held by blacks, who constitute about twenty-five percent of District 37's membership. (This helps to explain why Victor Gotbaum, the outspoken head of District Council 37, bucked the Central Labor Council in the school-decentralization fight.) And following the path of earlier public-employee groups, District 37 is beginning to press for a series of civil-service reforms to enable its members to move up the municipal career ladder. The much-publicized struggles of the garbage workers in Memphis and the hospital workers in Charlotte are efforts by low-paid blacks who, by using militant union tactics, are making their first advances.

Competition for jobs and money is by no means the worst of the struggle between the ghetto and public employees. In the course of securing their occupational interests, some groups of public employees have come to exercise substantial control over their agencies, and that control is now being challenged, too. The struggle over school decentralization in a number of cities is a prime example.

Public employees have been able to win considerable influence over the tasks they perform and other conditions of work. Many civil-service positions are now enshrined in codified descriptions which make both the jobholder and the work he performs relatively invulnerable to outside interference, even by political leaders. Furthermore, substantial discretion is inherent in many civil-service tasks, partly because legislative mandates are obscure, and partly because many civil-service positions require the occupants to be "professionals," enabling them to resist interference on the ground that they are "experts."

Public employees often use both the codified protection of their jobs and their powers of discretion to resist policy changes that alter the nature of their work. When former Mayor Robert Wagner asked the police department to patrol housing projects, the police refused and were supported by the police commissioner. School personnel effectively defeated desegregation policies by simply failing to inform ghetto parents of their right to enroll their children in white schools, and by discouraging those parents who tried to do so. The combined effect of procedural safeguards and professional discretion is suggested by the often-noted dilemma of a board of education that is simultaneously too centralized and too decentralized: It is hamstrung by regulations that seem to limit policy options, while its personnel retain the license to undermine central directives.

If some public employees have always had the ability to undermine policies, they now want the right to set policies, usually on the ground that as professionals they know what's best. Thus, teachers recently demanded that the New York City Board of Education expand the "More Effective Schools" program, and that they be granted the right to remove "disruptive" children from their classrooms. Threatened by the efforts of ghetto parents to free their children from an unresponsive educational system, the union became the major force opposing school decentralization. Similarly, New York's striking welfare workers bargained for (but have not yet won) the right to join the commissioner in formulating agency policies, arguing that 8000 case workers ought to have a say in policy decisions. The Patrolmen's Benevolent Association has begun issuing its own instructions to policemen on how the law should be enforced, to countermand Mayor John Lindsay's presumed indulgence of looters and demonstrators. And only through a full-scale public campaign was the mayor able to override the PBA's stubborn resistance to a "fourth platoon" permitting heavier scheduling of policemen during high-crime hours. All of these ventures by the unions represent incursions on matters of municipal policy. That they are made under the banner of professional commitment to public service should not obscure the fact that they will entrench and enhance the position of the public employees involved.

In part, demands in the policy area are being provoked by the feeling among public employees that they must defend their agencies against black assailants. The black masses are very dependent on public services, but these services have been conspicuously unresponsive to them and have even become instruments of white antagonism, as when police services take on the character of an army of occupation in the ghetto. The fierce fight waged by the New York Patrolmen's Benevolent Association against a civilian review board reveals the intensity of the conflict over the control of municipal agencies. In education and public welfare the effects of cleavage between white staff and black recipients are even more pervasive and tragic, for by blocking and distorting the delivery of these services white staffs virtually fix the life chances of the black poor.

Jobs and services have always been the grist of urban politics. By entrenching and enlarging control over municipal agencies, white-controlled public-employee unions are also blocking a traditional avenue by which newcomers become assimilated into the urban political and economic system. Politicians who depend on the black vote have not been oblivious to this obstruction. One response has been to generate new systems of services to be staffed by blacks. By establishing these services under separate administrative auspices and by calling them "experimental," political leaders have tried to avoid aggravating white public employees. Thus, the national Democratic administration which took office in 1960 created a series of new programs for the inner city in the fields of delinquency, mental health, poverty, education and the like. Federal guidelines required that blacks have a large share of the new jobs and policy positions (e.g., "maximum feasible participation of the poor"). In general these "demonstration" programs have been more responsive than traditional municipal agencies to black interests. Of course, the white-dominated city bureaucracies fought for control of the new programs and sometimes won: At the least, they obtained a substantial share of the new funds as compensation. But regardless of who has control, the new programs are minuscule compared with existing municipal programs. If anything, the antipoverty program has made more visible just how little blacks do control, thus precipitating some of the current wrangles over control of traditional municipal programs.

## IRONIES OF HISTORY

There are ironies in these developments. Reformers struggled to free municipal services from the vicissitudes of party politics; now some politicians are struggling to free municipal services from the vicissitudes of employee control. The advent and (at this writing) likely defeat of the Lindsay administration in New York City is a good illustration, for it exposed and escalated the conflict between blacks and whites. Lindsay campaigned against the old Democratic regime to which the unions were tied. His election was made possible by the defection of almost half of the black voters from Democratic ranks, and by middle- and upper-class support. It was to these groups that he appealed in his campaign and to which he is now trying to respond through his public posture and policies. To the black voter he has been a politician who walked in the ghetto streets, who allowed the welfare rolls to rise, who attempted to assert control over the police force and to decentralize the school system; to the middle and upper classes he has been a reformer and innovator who revamped the city's bureaucratic structures and appointed prestigious outsiders to high administrative posts. Appeals to both constituencies led him to do battle with the public unions regularly, for these moves threaten the control exerted by employee groups over municipal services. These battles have activated race and ethnic loyalties so fierce as to seem to rupture the city; and the possibility that Lindsay has even alienated the largely liberal Jewish vote exposes the intensity of the struggles for control of municipal benefits. Similar alliances between the black poor and affluent whites are also appearing in other cities (Cleveland, Detroit, Gary) with similar reactions from public employees, and white ethnic groups generally.

There is still another irony, for the militancy and radical rhetoric of the rapidly growing public unions have led some observers to define them as the vanguard of a reawakened labor movement. Bayard Rustin and A. Philip Randolph were recently moved to applaud the New York teachers' union for "having clearly demonstrated that trade unionism can play a useful part in obtaining needed facilities for . . . radically improving the quality of education for all children." One could wish the applause were justified; one could wish that white workers were allies of the black masses. But it is turning out that most advances by the public unions are being made at the expense of the black masses. As it now stands, there is only so much in the way of jobs, services and control over policy to be divided up. As one black spokesman said of the struggle between the UFT and the Ocean Hill–Brownsville governing board, "The name of the game is money and power for blacks!" Or, he might have added, for whites.

But the bitterest irony of all is that the struggle between whites and blacks is being played out within the narrow limits of the resources available in municipalities. There is nothing unreasonable in white employees' pressing to hold and expand the gains they have won, which in any case are not so munificent. What is unreasonable is that their gains are being made at the expense of blacks, not at the expense of affluent and powerful sectors of the society. How to shift the struggle from the arena of municipal jobs and services to the arena in which national and corporate wealth are divvied up is hardly clear. But one thing is clear: The burden of shifting the struggle should not fall on blacks, for they are only now getting their first chance at a share of what the city has to offer. Confined to the municipal sphere, blacks will oppose the advances of the white unions and fight for what others got before them. And they may have cause to worry— not only that the stakes of municipal politics are limited, but that all of the stakes may be claimed before they have joined the game.

# Black Control of Cities: Heading It Off by Metropolitan Government

FRANCES FOX PIVEN
AND RICHARD A. CLOWARD

Metropolitan government is a recurrent theme of civic reform. The spread of urban blight cannot be prevented or services provided efficiently, it is said, until municipal boundaries are made coterminous with expanding areas of settlement. It is even said that metropolitan government can overcome *de facto* segregation by breaking down city-suburban lines.

Yet proposals by cities to annex adjacent areas have been consistently defeated by the voters. Functional districts (for education, transportation, etc.) are mushrooming, up by half in the last decade alone. The United States has 91,000 local governmental districts, an average of 87 for each of the 225 standard metropolitan areas defined by the Bureau of the Census. The Chicago metropolitan area has 1060 governmental units of one kind or another; New York has 1400.

In our judgment, voters will probably continue to reject referenda for consolidation; nevertheless, local autonomy is being overcome. For what cannot be done electorally is being done administratively, as a result of federal intervention. The federal government is beginning to force localities to subordinate themselves to new areawide planning bureaucracies. Localities which do not come together to establish cross-jurisdictional agencies will soon find it difficult to obtain federal grants-in-aid. In this way a new domain of government is emerging.

The autonomy of local government will not be the only casu-

Originally published in two parts in the *New Republic*, September 30 and October 7, 1967. Copyright by the authors.

alty of administrative metropolitanism; Negroes will be the losers, too. The black masses are now building to electoral majorities in the larger American cities, but the promise of urban political power will be frustrated, for the new administrative government will be responsive to a majority coalition of suburban and inner-city whites. As blacks rise to power in the city, the city will lose power to the metropolis.

## THE METRO FRAMEWORK

Last January, the president summed up the move toward metropolitanism in a special message to Congress: "Over the past five years the Congress has authorized federal grants for urban transportation, open space, and sewer and water facilities. The Congress has required that such projects be consistent with comprehensive planning for an entire urban or metropolitan area. The federal government has thus stimulated cooperation and joint planning among neighboring jurisdictions. . . ." The president went on to propose that additional federal benefits be awarded to localities when they "show that they are ready to be guided by their own plans . . . and where they establish the joint institutional arrangements to carry out those plans."

The legislative framework is still skeletal. Nevertheless, under the impetus of the National Housing Act of 1954 and subsequent measures providing funds for areawide planning, three-fourths of the nation's metropolitan areas now have some form of areawide agency. The Department of Housing and Urban Development gives priority in granting its "planning assistance" funds to agencies in populous urban areas with jurisdiction over wide geographic areas and with cooperative planning relationships with other units and levels of governmental planning. Since federal agencies usually entertain applications for moneys far in excess of appropriations, they can reward localities which respond to their guidelines.

The Housing Act of 1961 is an early example of legislation specifying that a metropolitan plan must be submitted before federal funds would be released. By 1964, according to the Advisory Commission on Intergovernmental Relations, fourteen of

the forty-three federal urban programs required areawide planning. Localities have frequently met this stipulation by forming
an *ad hoc* metropolitan body to prepare a single proposal. But
*ad hoc* arrangements will not do much longer. The Federal
Highway Act of 1962 foreshadows the future pattern: To get
money, localities must submit a comprehensive metropolitan-
transportation plan and establish a permanent planning agency.

Until recently the federal requirement for areawide planning
was confined to particular functions, such as highway development or water resources. This was the natural outcome of
legislation produced by functional congressional committees,
administered by functional federal bureaucracies and promoted
by functionally oriented interest groups. Now the federal government is moving to require *multifunctional* plans as a condition of
aid for any single project. The Transit Act of 1964, for example,
says that an area seeking funds for highway construction will need
to prepare a comprehensive plan (including plans for housing,
water supply, etc.) of which transportation is but one component.
Finally, metropolitan agencies will be asked to preempt decisions
on future action. Thus, a comprehensive planning-and-coordina-
tion bill now before Congress would provide special financial
incentives to localities which develop comprehensive four-year
plans.

Whatever the scope of metropolitan planning, it is vitiated
when the local community can opt out at will; therefore federal
power is being conferred upon metropolitan agencies. The Model
Cities and Metropolitan Development Act of 1967 stipulates
that requests for funds for "metropolitan development projects"
must first be reviewed by an agency designated as the metropolitan planning body. And to smooth the way with incentives
instead of sanctions, local projects deemed consistent with "coordinated planned metropolitan development" will become eligible for supplemental federal grants of up to twenty percent.

The metropolitan planning apparatus will also draw on the
power of state government, a point which should be underlined
because the states have the authority to override local decisions.
Although federal grants for localities have traditionally been
channeled through the states, funds for many newer programs are
being funneled directly to urban areas. The states will not be

granted preeminence in metropolitanism, at least not by a national Democratic administration. The federal government will, however, link them to the new system by making federal grants to state agencies conditional on their cooperation with metropolitan planning agencies. When the New York State Office of Planning Coordination recently requested federal funds for planning which would include the Long Island area, it was directed by HUD to submit its proposal to the Nassau-Suffolk Regional Planning Commission for prior review. Grant by grant the states will be brought into the metropolitan apparatus, and metropolitan preeminence over local government will be reinforced by drawing on the authority of collaborating state agencies.

If the federal government is to control metropolitan decisions, its myriad grant-in-aid decisions must be dovetailed to exert a consistent force. Legislation which created HUD directed that it "mesh together all our social and physical efforts to improve urban living." But HUD lacked power over its peer departments. Consequently the president assigned coordinating responsibilities to the Bureau of the Budget in the fall of 1966. This agency, probably the most powerful in the executive branch and surely the most sensitive to the White House, now reviews all proposals for grants-in-aid in order to promote, in the president's words, "comprehensive planning covering wide areas."

It is not easy to describe the formal structure of the evolving metro agencies, since some of the legislation is so recent. A new agency may be established or an ongoing one assigned expanded functions, as when a transportation-planning body is designated to do comprehensive planning. Professional staff usually report either to a lay board or to a "metropolitan council of governments" (a device first formed in 1954 which now exists in about seventy-five places).

In any case, the metro agency will be the hub of a network of administrative relationships linking the federal government to a host of local and state agencies. Each of these agencies will have to produce a plan conforming to federal guidelines in order to receive federal money, and the metro agency will be authorized to assess the plans. The metro agency will be the control point in an all-embracing bureaucratic system.

## URBAN PROBLEMS:
## TECHNICAL OR POLITICAL?

The classic rib to buttress the federal case that urban problems—whether pollution, congestion or blight—can't be solved without areawide planning is the four-lane highway that turns into a cowpath at the county line. Transportation needs are, to be sure, generated by regional social and economic interrelations, and services should be designed from a regional perspective. Water-resources management, already generally administered on a regional basis, cannot be local. (Private economic investment decisions also have repercussions throughout a region. However, government has rarely intruded into this area, contenting itself largely with providing the services and facilities required by industry and commerce, or trying to cope with the worst social effects of their investment decisions. Neither of these responses requires an areawide purview.)

As a practical matter, local governments could make considerable progress on many problems without waiting to act in concert. Air pollution would be reduced if each jurisdiction were willing to regulate industry, utilities and automobile owners. With federal aid, open space and such amenities could be provided if local governments were willing to preempt land from private developers. Central-city congestion, although created in part by people driving from dispersed suburbs, could be eased by banning cars from congested places and developing more-efficient internal circulating systems. Similarly, localities can act within their own boundaries to restore blighted neighborhoods, drawing on the federal subsidies for low-rental housing which they now often ignore. *Communities fail to deal with many of these problems, not for lack of areawide planning and coordination, but for lack of political will.* In any event, whatever the technical advantages of planning, these are not necessarily political advantages; by themselves they do not explain the national Democratic administration's push for metropolitan consolidation.

What, then, does explain it? The key, we believe, is in some well-known demographic trends. Standard metropolitan statistical areas now include two-thirds of the population and eighty percent of manufacturing payrolls—that is, most voters and most corporate economic power. The Democratic leadership wants to build firm majorities from this electorate by reaching out for the allegiance of the burgeoning white suburbs while holding the support of the racially divided cities.

The central cities have been Democratic for more than three decades, but recent population shifts are undermining these strongholds. Rising numbers of blacks in the city arouse the antagonism of whites in the old Democratic coalition, especially working-class ethnic groups. The result is party splits and voter defections in New York, Cleveland, Philadelphia, Detroit, Baltimore, Gary and other cities.

As internal conflict weakens the old city coalition, suburban support has become critical in national politics. The growing suburbs overshadow the central cities; and reapportionment has given them electoral power commensurate with their numbers. As a result of reapportionment, the suburbs sent twenty additional representatives to the House in the 90th Congress. And although suburban Republicanism is tempered by the influx of Democratic voters, so are Democratic affiliations tempered by movement into the middle class and a prestigious Republican milieu; eighteen of the twenty new suburban congressmen are Republicans.

The Democratic administration must also contend with a deepening rift between core city and suburbs. Fierce hostility greets demands for open occupancy and educational arrangements that would disperse the ghetto. The political repercussions are evident in Senator Charles Percy's landslide majorities in Chicago's suburbs, and in Governor Ronald Reagan's victory, especially in suburban Los Angeles. The more the city becomes poor black, the more the suburbs may be expected to withhold allegiance from a national party which speaks for the city. Class and racial cleavages in metropolitan areas thus foreshadow the next axis of antagonism in American politics: Major alignments of the future will not be North *vs* South or rural *vs* urban, but city *vs* suburb. To retain its majorities, a national Democratic administration must find a way to hold together the conflict-ridden cities, to garner support in the suburbs and somehow to avert the political expression of the schism between core and suburb. And that promises to be no small feat.

To shore up its coalition, the national Democratic administra-

tion has employed the time-honored strategy of fashioning programs to meet the interests of different groups. There are now
several hundred grant-in-aid programs; federal expenditures to
states and localities rose from $1 billion in 1946 to $15 billion in
1966 and will probably reach $60 billion by 1975.

Within the central city, groups profit variously from this
strategy. The black poor get a little public housing, a modest
antipoverty program and may gain a bit of relief from the model-
cities program; middle-income whites get rather generous housing
subsidies; and business and real-estate interests receive substantial urban-renewal funds.

Some of the larger federal programs are partly or wholly
suburban oriented: highways, airports, sewage and water facilities,
mortgage insurance and tax write-offs for homeowners. With these
subsidies, the national Democratic leadership is moving to win
and hold the suburban electorate. It is also moving in response
to powerful corporate interests which are rapidly decentralizing
and want subsidized facilities and services.

In light of the fact that urban localities, especially big cities,
suffer from limited taxing powers and a declining tax base (local
debt per capita has quadrupled since 1946 while the per-capita
federal debt has declined substantially), the inducement of federal
money should ease conflict and encourage Democratic adherence.
But it does not. There are few federal programs to which some
local group does not take sharp exception. In the central city,
urban renewal for the affluent arouses bitter protest from uprooted slum businesses and residents; public housing generates
fierce opposition from the neighborhoods selected. The federal
highway program is stymied despite ninety-percent financing:
held up for years in New Orleans and Baltimore, rejected in
midconstruction by San Francisco and regretted on completion
in Boston. To avoid politically bruising battles, big-city mayors
turn down some federal programs, stall on others in the hope
that local tension will eventually subside, or simply ignore those
which seem irrelevant to their concern with managing an
increasingly volatile electorate. Thus public-housing and rent-
supplement allotments are often not used, and many urban-
renewal proposals never emerge from bureaucratic mazes.

Nor are federal programs faring well in the suburbs. Although suburbanites want such federally subsidized facilities and

services as highways, commuter railroads, bridges and jetports, each community is determined to keep out congestion, traffic and noise. Rumors about the proposed location of these facilities elicit howls of protest from one town hall after another. As a result, suburban communities also avoid federal programs, or implement them amid such acute controversy that victors and losers alike are embittered.

Two features of local government help to account for these difficulties. First, the historic mark of local government has been its vulnerability to a wide range of interest groups, and thus its inability to act on divisive issues. Local government is physically proximate to the electorate and hence more accessible than other levels of government; the constituency as a whole is smaller, so that a dissenting group is more likely to be prominent and influential; and since local government is less bureaucratized, decisions are more susceptible to influence. Furthermore, local conflict has been sharpened in recent years by racial cleavage. The result is open controversy on virtually every public issue.

The second feature of local government which works to thwart federal programs is that it does not reflect the interests of its newer constituents. The central cities are still dominated by white ethnic groups which resist federal programs intended for the growing ghettos. Suburban governments are similarly dominated by longtime residents who try to keep out newcomers by upgrading zoning, and who oppose the intrusion of decentralizing corporate enterprises which would reduce tax burdens and thus make it possible for the less affluent to move in. For instance, wealthy residents in the suburban township of Harrison (Westchester County) furiously resented a plan to locate the headquarters of Pepsico there. Older suburban towns spurn urban renewal and public-housing funds for their growing enclaves of minority poor. Local government, in brief, reflects the influence of traditionally dominant groups. From a national perspective, these groups are declining in political importance and they block federal programs designed for those whose national influence is on the ascendancy—the Negro and the new suburbanite.

Local controversy not only stymies federal programs in the field but reverberates on the floors of Congress, spelling trouble for an antipoverty program, a model-cities bill or an education act, and thus jeopardizing the legislation required to forge a new

urban coalition. In these ways, local government hinders the
Democratic strategy for building a metropolitan constituency.

## POLITICAL USES OF PLANNING

To circumvent local resistance, the federal government is developing new mechanisms to field its programs. Bit by bit, as we
noted earlier, a metropolitan administrative apparatus is being
empowered to see that localities comply with a comprehensive
plan drawn up in accord with federal guidelines. "The plan"
will have extraordinary utility in securing local acquiescence.
First, insisting that adjacent localities submit to areawide planning as a condition for federal aid will bind them to a cooperative program. This is no mere window dressing. HUD recently
indicated that it not only would require localities to join together to produce plans for "orderly metropolitan growth" but
would enforce conformity to such plans by withholding project-
development funds from recalcitrant areas. It canceled a large
grant for the construction of various facilities in suburban Washington because one of the participating counties had quietly re-
zoned without conforming to the areawide "master plan."

Second, to get money for what it does want, each locality will
have to undertake programs it does not want. Until now, localities
have had considerable freedom to maneuver among federal
agencies, picking and choosing among assorted offerings. Fort Lauderdale, for example, after accepting federal money for water-
supply and sewage-disposal projects, abandoned plans to rebuild
a Negro ghetto following widespread protests from white groups.
And Fort Lauderdale is only one of about eighty localities that
have turned down renewal funds in the last few years. By coordinating its various funding decisions—that is, by insisting on
multifunctional planning and making each grant conditional
upon the acceptance of other grants—the federal government has
a better chance of inducing such localities to accept modest
urban-renewal programs for their ghettos.

Third, "the plan" preempts future decisions; it requires long-
range commitments at the time any grant is negotiated. Nor can
such commitments be overturned easily, for they soon come to be
reinforced by a network of related actions. If a bridge is projected,

it will be linked to other substantial investments—highways, jet-ports, industrial parks—made in anticipation of it. To re-nounce the bridge decision at the point of final implementation means disruption of this network. Moreover, the long-range decision builds its own special constituency. The decision to build the bridge at a future date alerts builders and construction unions, business and real-estate interests. But affected residents are not likely to respond to remote events. And when the event is upon them, they may be powerless to overcome corporate interests which have developed extensive stakes in the venture in the interim.

Finally, metropolitan planning arrangements will help to obviate local controversy by screening local decisions from public scrutiny. Embedding individual decisions in a complex, multi-functional, areawide, long-range plan obscures them from view, and the obscurity is deepened by the technical and scientific procedures which are a natural corollary to the emphasis on planning—a process said to require consideration of a vast array of factors, calculation of their interrelations and so forth. All of this may improve administrative competence, but it will also vest greater power in planners and administrators. As the busi-ness of government comes to be carried on by a coalition of federal, metropolitan and local bureaucracies in the language of expertise, local groups and elected officials will become puzzled outsiders, lacking the specialized knowledge to perceive and artic-ulate their interests.

If planning removes government decisions from popular pur-view, the rationale given is that the problem at hand is merely technical. Political issues are redefined as matters for experts to deal with, requiring the application of knowledge, not power. Planning thus brings with it a way of looking at issues which denies divergent group interests; as a result, groups are less likely to be alerted and less likely to align themselves against one another.

Even if the uninitiated could comprehend the intricacies of planning, it is another matter to watch over and influence plan-ning agencies. Public bureaucracies thrive by getting things done. Because public exposure entails the risk of political impasse, they avoid scrutiny. Moreover, as planning becomes more complex and information more limited, local public officials and other affected groups will even fail to recognize and exploit their formal prerogative to review technical decisions. In sum, the language and strategy of planning are serving to centralize power for political ends.

We are describing an emerging pattern of metropolitan government: We do not contend that political leaders are conspiring to produce it. No secret blueprint exists. As each election reveals strains within a constituency, one or another palliative is put forward. When these programs in turn run aground on local reefs, new devices are sought to set them afloat. Sometimes the new devices don't work. Thus, direct funding of ghetto anti-poverty programs to placate ghetto leadership antagonized the white ethnic party apparatus in the cities. Attempts to implement programs through metropolitan mechanisms have seemed to work better, and so they are repeated and extended. In this pragmatic way, then, the apparatus of metropolitan government is emerging.

## HOW THE BLACK WILL LOSE

Whether these developments should be applauded or deplored is not easy to say. On the one hand, centralization removes government from popular control; on the other hand, local populism has generally yielded much harsher policies toward the poor and minorities than those of the federal government. But when oppressed groups obtain hegemony over local government, populism works to their advantage. This opportunity now looms before Negroes, whose numbers are swelling to majorities in many American cities. From the perspective of the national Democratic administration, this is cause for little but apprehension, since black control can only deepen racial cleavages in the urban area. However, metropolitan reorganization, by limiting the traditional powers of the city, will mute the political effects of black ascendancy. Consider what might otherwise happen.

Perhaps most obvious, black control of city government will endanger major interests which depend on the city core. Until now city government has tried to hold back the spread of the densely packed ghetto and to reclaim the city center for business and for higher-income groups. A municipality controlled by blacks is far less likely to protect these property interests, and surely not if to do so entails "Negro removal."

Black majorities also mean the alienation of urban whites. The frequent assertion that in time all whites will simply flee to the suburbs ignores the logistics of finding space for so many people, most of them not wealthy, in the already developed suburban ring. Millions of whites, unable or unwilling to leave, will remain in the core cities, a fact of key political importance, since they will fiercely resist the exploitation of municipal power for black interests. Moreover, whites have the organizational vehicles with which to fight on all levels of government, for they control the labor unions and professional associations and the host of nongovernmental institutions of the city. What this spells for national Democratic leaders is the inevitable deepening of conflict in the cities.

Perhaps the most dangerous possibility is that blacks will emerge as a separatist bloc in national politics. The experience of political incumbency, and control of municipal resources, will work to consolidate a black electorate, and city government will become the vehicle for black interests in the arenas of state and national politics. The impact on existing electoral coalitions can only be disruptive. How is the national Democratic party to placate alienated white working-class groups and garner the suburban support it needs to build a new urban coalition when it must also answer to a black bloc? In short, the articulation of Negro interests threatens to have far-reaching and disruptive effects on national political alignments.

If the federal government is to prevent the exacerbation of racial conflict in urban areas, the political repercussions of impending black control of the cities must be averted. Metropolitan government will help to achieve that end by usurping many powers of the city. We can expect, as a consequence, that urban redevelopment will suit the substantial commercial enterprises in the central city and the middle-class professionals who choose to live near the cultural center. But clearly there will be no concerted efforts to disperse ghetto populations to the suburbs, as some liberal critics have hopefully predicted.

There will, of course, be programs for the black minority: some housing rehabilitation, expanded educational programs and a host of social services of the "human renewal" variety—

programs which appease, guide and control the recipients of service and which exact no visible toll from dominant groups. Local resistance, which until now has stymied even these programs, will be overcome, and that is what Negroes can expect to gain as the minority constituency in metropolitan consolidation.

The metropolitan planners will be especially sensitive to private and public corporate groups which have the resources and the foresight to spot their interests in the planning process and the know-how to make their way through bureaucratic labyrinths. The recently inaugurated Nassau-Suffolk Regional Planning Commission has a lay board of six, five of whom are executives in prominent private corporations. The board of the new Metropolitan Commuter Transit Authority in New York, which will control policy and planning for all transportation agencies in the New York metropolitan area, includes representatives of powerful public agencies, such as the Triborough Bridge and Tunnel Authority and the New York City Transit Authority, as well as previously quasi-public corporations, like the New Haven Railroad and the Long Island Railroad. This empire was created by negotiations among existing transportation agencies and with business and labor, trading in commitments to build the highways, bridges and other facilities needed by corporate enterprises in and outside the city, and by suburban whites. It is not so likely, however, to build the cheap, efficient mass-transit networks required to get Negroes from the inner-city ghettos out to jobs in the new suburban industrial complexes.

As for programs the Negroes will get, private corporate interests will play an increasingly active role. Witness the potpourri of recent proposals and the convocations of an "urban coalition" to induce private enterprise to invest in ghetto redevelopment (with government guarantees of profit). These corporations will work with the federal bureaucracies and their metropolitan offspring; together they will obtain hegemony over the ghetto and the city.

*What, then, are Negroes to do? Were they a cohesive and disciplined political force, they might use their great numbers in the city to impede metropolitan reorganization. Although metropolitanism is probably inevitable, its growth can be slowed and its form modified. As the price for their cooperation, blacks could demand their share of space in the cities, massive investments in housing and education, and programs to guarantee em-*

*ployment and income. Of more long-run importance, they could
bargain to retain substantial power for the municipal government to which they will soon fall heir. They could insist on the
right to veto major metropolitan decisions, resisting arrangements
in which the central cities are granted one vote along with each
suburban township—as is typical in "metropolitan councils of
governments."*

However, even if black leaders were persuaded that an ob-
structionist strategy would yield benefits, the Negro community
cannot be mobilized. It is not laced together by the institutional
systems which are required to convert ethnic solidarity into
economic and political power. If blacks already controlled the
cities, they could exploit municipal powers to compensate for
the institutional weakness of their community. But they do not
yet control the cities, and metropolitan consolidation may be well
advanced before they do.

Far from seeking to undermine metropolitan government,
traditional Negro leadership will probably become its agent.
Much Negro leadership exists largely by the grace of white institutions: white political parties and government agencies, white
unions and businesses and professions, even white civil-rights
organizations. Everything in the environment of the Negro
politician, civil servant or professional makes him attentive to
white interests and perspectives. If black leadership were based
in separatist institutions—particularly economic ones, such as
black labor unions—it might be capable of some independence,
but those separatist systems do not now exist. Moreover, metropolitan government will provide many new opportunities for
the advancement of a Negro elite, and leadership will easily be
absorbed. By abetting metropolitanism, in short, Negro leaders
will forfeit much of the political power that impending black
majorities in the cities might produce.

## CREATIVE FEDERALISM?

It is the custom of American political commentators to interpret
major government actions as—by and large—responses to electoral preferences, and sometimes to the preferences of special

interests. But the urban electorate is surely showing no signs that it wishes state and local government to be emasculated. Indeed, according to a recent Gallup poll, seventy percent of the electorate thinks that the states spend money more wisely than the federal government.

Some policies are, of course, formed in response to well-organized interests which know what they want from government and how to get it. But policy is also used by political incumbents to activate special interests and to shape the preferences of an amorphous electorate. The legislation of the New Deal, for example, was not simply the reflexive response of Democratic leadership either to the sentiments of the electorate or to pressure from organized interests. Much New Deal legislation can be understood, rather, as the entrepreneurial use of government policy to cement the working class into a new Democratic coalition. Not so very long ago, urban problems were the special domain of the civil reformer and of the professional. Presumably urban conditions have worsened substantially, but it must also be recognized that government can cultivate public demand for programs, and then offer those programs in order to establish a constituency. This is especially true in the metropolis, where there is neither a tradition of federal responsibility to shape public expectations nor a unified constituency to speak for a "metropolitan" interest. And it is most true in the suburbs, where the electorate, left to itself, might demand little from a national administration other than that the black poor of the cities be contained.

Similarly, the intricacies of electoral districting and of allocations of power to various units of government in the federal system are neither accidental nor simply reflections of popular will. These structural arrangements are the object of continuous maneuvering by political incumbents to divide, aggregate and weight the plebiscite so as to form the electoral majorities which keep them in power. Through its expanding role in local affairs, the national administration is reshaping the federal system, pre-empting local powers and aggregating white majorities in order to rebuild a Democratic urban coalition.

Summing up this approach, Vice President Humphrey said: "Federal policy has moved to meet the realities of an urbanizing nation . . . programs for urban mass transportation, open space land, public facilities vital to the community's life, stimulation of homebuilding for the low- and moderate-income market.

"By the 1960s, we recognized that we were not dealing with a collection of separate problems in our urban areas—but with one total, interrelated urban problem with many special aspects and needs.

"We began then to bring our lines of action together, to enact legislation to deal with urban planning and development on a coordinated basis, and to fashion the administrative organization that could weld these varied operations into a common policy and approach."

This is called "creative federalism" and hailed as fresh evidence of the adaptability of a system in which local, state and national governments are partners, sharing a fluid and shifting power, and thus maintaining the conditions for a democratic pluralism. But the federal government now collects two-thirds of total tax revenues, while the municipal share has fallen from fifty-two percent in 1932 to less than seven percent today. The national administration does not enter the jousts as just another contender in local affairs. It possesses unparalleled resources, and it can employ them to subordinate local jurisdictions to metropolitan systems.

It appears that consolidation and centralization are inevitable, impelled by the technical demands of a complex corporate society, the expansionist tendencies of governmental bureaucracies and, not least, the political needs of the national administration. Were the national administration to become Republican, the trend toward consolidation would not be reversed, although its direction would probably shift. Since Republicans must build their coalition from suburban and rural areas, federal agencies might join with the states to mark out "substate regions" as the focus for centralization instead of metropolitan areas. In any event, the end result of this process is likely to be not "creative federalism" but the submergence of the minority which now stands to gain most from localism—the black.

# What Chance for Black Power?

Frances Fox Piven
and Richard A. Cloward

If there is a lesson in America's pluralistic history, it is that the ability of an outcast minority to advance in the face of majority prejudices partly depends on its ability to develop countervailing power. It is extraordinary that so conventional an idea has evoked so bitter a controversy in the civil-rights community. For, stripped of rhetoric, the idea of "black power" merely emphasizes the need to augment Negro influence by developing separatist institutions, ranging from economic enterprise to political organization.

Older civil-rights organizations take umbrage at the separatist impulse because it appears to repudiate the principle of integration. Considering that ethnic labor unions, ethnic political machines and other ethnic institutions have been essential to the rise of various minorities, it is puzzling to hear it said that Negroes must restrain themselves from following the same course. Indeed, those institutions in the black community which are "integrated"—whether political organizations, the rackets or social-welfare agencies—actually contribute to black impotence, for they are integrated only in the sense that they are dominated by whites and serve white interests.

Those who are dismayed by the separatist position also fear that it will alienate liberal and labor allies. Blacks are a minority, to be sure, and cannot go it alone. But neither will they ever be more than a nominal participant in coalitions unless

Originally published in the *New Republic*, March 30, 1968. Copyright by the authors.

they are better organized; rather, their leaders will serve mostly
to legitimize programs from which others benefit. An organized
group need not sit about debating the pros and cons of seeking
allies; it will be sought out by others, and offered genuine concessions because it has strength to bring to any alliance. Those
who now urge color-blind coalition are unable to show why
the black poor would have more effective leverage in future
alliances than they have had in the past.

Before damning black power for its principles or dooming it
for its strategy, one should look at what the Negro has so far
achieved without power, and what the future holds if his powerlessness persists.

The upheavals which are sometimes called "the Negro revolution"—the civil-rights protests, the spreading violence in the
cities and the controversy over black power—are reflections of
economic changes. When old patterns are rapidly undermined,
dislocating masses of people, disorder often follows.

No group has been more acutely affected by technological
change than the Negro, although the middle class and the poor
have been affected quite differently. Educated Negroes are in demand in professional, scientific and technical occupations because
of the growing need for skilled manpower. Since the end of World
War II the proportion of Negro families earning between $5000
and $7000 (in 1965 dollars adjusted for price changes) almost
trebled and now approximates the proportion of whites in that
income class. The proportion earning between $7000 and $10,-
000 did treble and is now about two-thirds of the proportion of
whites in that income group.

It was this rising class that launched the civil-rights movement, especially the young of a newly arriving southern bour-
geoisie. As is often the case, ascending economic fortunes had
themselves generated expectations which outpaced the actual
rate of advance. Thus Negro colleges, once training grounds for
a segregated elite, suddenly disgorged cadres to lead boycotts,
freedom rides and sit-ins. Nor was this economic discrepancy the
only source of discontent. A segregated society also deprived
them of the symbols of prestige which normally accompany
higher economic status. Spurred by these status discrepancies,
the movement focused much of its energy on desegregating

lunch counters and public accommodations, and on gaining the vote.

Much of what was aspired to has been achieved—the legal and symbolic representations that American institutions were made "for whites only" are crumbling. That these features of our social life are collapsing so quickly (as these things go) is a mark of the extent to which they had become outmoded as a result of economic changes.

For the mass of black poor, however, the technological revolution has had less happy consequences. Although the proportion of poor families has dropped considerably in the past two decades, more than half of the black families in America still have incomes of less than $5000, and one in four subsists on less than $3000. Furthermore, apparent increases in income are often offset by the forced migration to the cities, where it costs more to live. Most ominous, the technological advances which made old patterns of segregation obsolete are also making a substantial segment of the black poor obsolete. Southern Negro sharecroppers, driven off the land by machines, can now eat at a desegregated lunch counter, take a desegregated interstate bus North and arrive in a city with a fair-employment ordinance —but no jobs. The mechanization of the farms they left is matched in the cities by the automation and decentralization of industry. Wherever black people are concentrated, North or South, true rates of unemployment (both those looking for work and those who have given up) range from twenty to fifty percent.

In the rural South the more fortunate among the unemployed barely subsist on federal surplus commodities; the less fortunate starve. If they could get on the welfare rolls, people would have a bit of money, but they are kept off by a tangle of exclusionary laws, bureaucratic obstacles and just plain illegal rejections. Feared at the polls and no longer needed in the fields, they are told to go North. As it happens, the women and children are more likely to get on the welfare rolls in the North, provided that their men "desert" them first. And so unemployed husbands and fathers stand about "in hiding" on every ghetto street corner. Meanwhile, welfare administrators and politicians curry public favor by promoting job training for welfare mothers—but not for their men. At that, the women are trained for jobs that don't exist, or won't for long. The work they do get is in low-paid, dead-end jobs: In 1966 Negroes composed forty-two percent of the private household work force and twenty-five percent of nonfarm laborers. Poor blacks, in brief, are being shut out of the economic system. They have progressed from slave labor to cheap labor to no labor at all.

The violence in the cities is the response of the black poor to their new social and economic condition, just as the civil-rights protests were the response of the black middle class to their changing condition. It is not that poverty or unemployment produces mass discontent and violence, for if this were so no society could be stable. Rather, massive economic displacement may have a reverberative effect on other institutions, weakening their capacity to regulate sentiments and behavior, and culminating finally in violence.

The most obvious reverberation is the shift of populations from rural to urban areas. Blacks have become an urban people in just two or three decades, and this has set them loose from existing structures of social control. Although a repressive, feudalistic system persists in the South, a great many Negroes have been liberated from it just by no longer being there. Nor have they been absorbed by the main regulatory institutions of the city, especially the economic system. Ghetto institutions, such as churches and political machines, have also not incorporated them. Furthermore, the press of numbers is disrupting traditional accommodations upon which racial peace depends: The boundaries of previously sacrosanct white neighborhoods and schools are being breached, and white political power in city halls is threatened. When tensions rise as institutional controls weaken, the eruption of violence should not be surprising.

The splintering off of a segment of the civil-rights movement—symbolized by the raised black fist and the cry of "black power"—is also a response to these upheavals. New conditions of life, by altering mass attitudes, undercut old patterns of leadership. Traditional Negro elites who have maintained their hegemony by serving as the agents of white power and resources are being challenged by new aspirants to leadership whose insistent nationalism reflects the current mood of discontent. And

whatever else may be said of its rhetoric—the language of violence and the allusions to revolution—black power, by calling
on people to be, feel, think and act black, is fostering a new
sense of community in the ghetto, especially among the young.
This is a hopeful trend, for solidarity is one prerequisite to the
political power without which the mass of black poor cannot
advance economically.

There is no doubt that major governmental action will be
taken to deal with disruptions in the cities. Corporation executives and mayors, union officials and presidential aspirants—
men whose interests are in one way or another threatened by
urban disorder—are agreed in demanding federal programs to
stem rising municipal costs, "crime in the streets" and riots. But
while this "urban coalition" wants to ease urban trouble, the
groups it includes have interests quite at odds with those of the
black poor. And experience shows that the poor have good reason to be apprehensive about programs formed in their name
by the powerful.

To appreciate the grounds for apprehension, look at the differences between government programs for the organized and
unorganized poor. In response to the crisis in the thirties, the
federal government proclaimed its responsibility for the poor
but promulgated legislation favoring those of the urban poor
who, already partly organized in unions and political machines,
were important to the newly formed Democratic coalition. Political leaders pressed through a series of social-welfare measures
designed to protect the urban worker—unemployment compensation, old-age and survivors insurance, and housing loans for
those with moderate incomes. More important, workers got concessions that nourished their organizations, especially the Wagner Act, which gave them the right to bargain collectively and
thus made the growth and stabilization of unions possible—
membership expanded from 3 million in 1930 to 14 million in
1945. In this way the working classes were able to make gains
in the economic system, and to guard governmental programs
designed for them.

The poor who lacked political power were left behind. The
worst poverty still exists among those who did not win collective-bargaining rights by legislation, such as agricultural la-

borers. In the cities the still unorganized black masses continue
to be victimized by programs ostensibly intended for their
benefit. Consider for example the public-welfare programs enacted in 1935 which promised decent subsistence for everyone;
three decades later the average family of four on ADC (Aid to
Dependent Children) gets only $1800 a year. The Public Hous-
ing Act of 1937 proclaimed the goal of providing decent housing
for the poor; today there are about 10 million substandard
dwelling units in the country, for only 600,000 units of public
housing have been constructed. Our national policy of full employment, enunciated by legislation in 1946, has proved to be
meaningless rhetoric.

Worse yet, manifestly egalitarian measures have been turned
against the poor. Federal agricultural subsidies, established to
aid all farmers, actually helped to bankrupt small ones and enrich large ones. The Housing Act of 1949 asserted the right of
every American to "a decent and standard dwelling unit," but
initiated the Urban Renewal Program that destroyed 350,000
low-rental housing units in the course of reclaiming slum neighborhoods for commercial facilities and better-off residents. Several hundred thousand more low-rental homes were demolished
during the same period by public works and federal highway
construction. . . . Indeed, government has destroyed more low-
rental units than it has constructed since the Public Housing
Act was passed.

Finally, what concessions the unorganized poor did get actually inhibited their capacity for political action. This is especially true of public-welfare and public-housing programs in
which benefits are made conditional on compliant behavior by
recipients. The poor, dealt with as supplicants by functionaries
who can evict them or cut off their checks at will, are rendered
more helpless in exchange for the benefits they receive.

New proclamations about action to help the poor are now
being made, and new programs discussed. But what reason is
there to suppose that these measures will not also be tokenistic,
or turned to serve the interests of other groups, or designed to
intimidate the recipients still more? For the simple truth is
that governmental action has not worked for the unorganized
poor and is not likely to work for them in the future unless
they become a political force in initiating and shaping it.

How, then, are the black poor to develop greater political influence? Some observers point to the fact that the growing concentration of blacks in the central cities is making them a substantial electoral force. Earlier groups of the poor, it is noted, exploited the resources and powers of municipal government to aid their rise in the economic order; why not blacks as well? The parallel is far from exact, as we shall show. For the moment, however, let us assume that the black community is not weaker than earlier ethnic communities, and that city government is as important in the federal system as it once was.

First, as majorities in the cities, or even as large voting blocs, blacks would have the means to prevent the recurrent incursions on the ghetto by urban renewal, highway construction and public-works programs. At the same time, funds now being spent on others could be directed to improving ghetto services and facilities. Municipal power might also be used to force private enterprise and unions to admit Negroes. Public officials have numerous sources of leverage: They fix budget allocations for services and projects, approve private construction plans and decide whether to pass on requests for state and federal grants. Each of these decisions is an occasion to exact concessions from other groups. Employers who want city contracts can be induced to hire and promote blacks. Similarly, unions can be opened to Negroes by blocking approvals for new construction or by threatening to reform archaic building codes on which their jobs partly depend.

These powers also offer a way for blacks to gain access to the more desirable neighborhoods now occupied by the white working and middle classes. Black government can override resistance to public housing in white areas and enforce bans on discrimination in the rental and sale of housing. Where public officials are elected on a precinct basis, the spread of blacks would entrench their political control by assuring majorities in each district.

Acquiring access to white institutions is one way to advance; developing black institutional relationships to the society is another and more important way. Separatist institutional development will not take place quickly, but in the long run its effects could be profound, for nothing about the Negro community is more conspicuous than the absence of its own institutions. In part this condition is a heritage of slavery and of laws passed in the wake of Reconstruction which prohibited free assembly and the formation of associations among Negroes. The traditional isolation of most blacks in rural and feudalistic settings has also inhibited the formation of institutions, especially of a kind that would be viable in the city.

The need for communal institutions is one of the major themes of black-power advocates. And municipal control could be the key. Where else is the money to come from to foster such a development? The black poor are very poor indeed, and they confront an economy dominated by large-scale corporations, in which the would-be entrepreneur has far less likelihood of success than in the more open economy of the past. Nor can much be expected of efforts to unionize blacks, for many of them, if they work at all, are in occupations too marginal and dispersed to be organized effectively (e.g., domestic service). Moreover, the black middle classes will not lead a separatist development; they have been absorbed into white institutions and cannot be enticed back unless substantial occupational rewards are available. To overcome these obstacles, blacks need the resources controlled by municipal officials—contracts for all manner of projects and services to nurture new enterprises, as well as the leverage over white economic interests to induce them to deal with black enterprises. In these ways urban power might in time enable the black community to develop the infrastructure which has served other groups so well, especially black economic enterprise and black labor unions to organize the workers in the resulting jobs.

Finally, greater black influence in national politics depends on strong local organization capable of promoting electoral participation and assuring discipline. To build organization, black leaders need the platform of municipal office to articulate black interests, and the resources of public office to reward their followers. For all these reasons, many now see the city as the hope for the Negro.

But the prospects for black urban power, as we have just defined them, rest on the erroneous assumption that American politics are formed by voting numbers alone. The conventions of electoral politics are regularly subverted in many ways. Those already holding power will not yield the spoils of office quickly or easily to new majorities. Even when official representation is achieved, responsiveness by government requires a constituency capable of watching over and pressuring officials. To be sure, blacks will assume nominal power in the cities because of the sheer weight of their numbers; but compared to earlier groups, blacks have few organizational ropes to keep rein on their leaders. Black officials will find themselves confronted by a variety of well-organized white groups—such as unions of public employees and corporate interests—who have the power to obstruct the business of government. They will be pressed to defer to these white interests, and an unorganized black constituency will give them the slack to do it.

Moreover, local government has been greatly weakened since the heyday of the ethnic urban machine. Localities now collect a mere seven percent of tax revenues, while the federal government collects two-thirds. This fiscal weakness underlies the great vulnerability of local government to national centralized power as reflected, for example, in new encroachments by the federal government under the guise of metropolitan planning. As we have said elsewhere, the national government is beginning to use its multitude of existing programs for localities to form a new system of metropolitanwide bureaucracies. This new level of government will impose federal policies on localities in the course of channeling grants-in-aid to them.

The need for metro administration is commonly justified on the ground that the concentration of people in sprawling urban areas has produced a host of problems—transportation, water supply, pollution control—which transcend narrow municipal boundaries. The solution of these problems is said to require programs planned and implemented on a metropolitan basis. For some problems, perhaps so; however, many urban problems remain unsolved, not for lack of areawide planning but for lack of political will. That communities do not apply for federal funds to build public housing needs no explanation beyond local reluctance to house the poor and black. Nevertheless, metro bureaucracies are emerging, and they will supersede the cities just as blacks come to power.

Whose interests will the federal metro agencies reflect? It takes no special acumen to see the answer. Their policies will be formed in deference to the inner-city and suburban whites who are an overwhelming majority in the metro region. Thus, programs for the inner city will be designed to protect and ease the ethnic working classes, the residual middle class, and corporate groups with heavy property investments in the core. And there will be suburban services and facilities to meet the needs of decentralizing industry and white residents, whose electoral power now exceeds that of inner-city populations. Judging from the past, programs for blacks will be designed to treat their presumed deficiencies—to engender "good work habits and incentives," strengthen family life, improve mental health.

The black poor, then, have few prospects for political or economic advancement. Because of the current disruptions they will get a few concessions to restore tranquility. But once the cities are tranquilized, what then? As we have said, the main chance for black power is in the cities, but the odds are lengthening.

# PART FOUR

## The Great Society:
## Moderating Disorder
## in the Ghettos

Introduction

The 1960s brought an enormous expansion of the welfare state; federal expenditures for domestic programs grew by tens of billions. Many of the new programs were directed to the big cities, and some of the most publicized were directed to the ghettos, first under the banner of the "New Frontier" and then of the "Great Society." The official rationales were familiar ones: The federal government was acting to deal with a variety of social problems that plagued the cities, from juvenile delinquency and crime, to poverty, to urban blight.

But official rationales did not go far toward explaining this pattern of federal action. Why, for example, were funds for the "war on poverty" concentrated in the big-city ghettos when the incidence of poverty was much higher among rural whites? Furthermore, many of the new federal programs were distinguished from earlier grants-in-aid by a curious administrative feature which was eventually to cause an uproar in local government, and which official rationales did little to illuminate: Federal funds were channeled to ghetto areas by mechanisms that tended to bypass the state and local agencies that traditionally operated federal programs. And even when these agencies were not bypassed, their discretion in administering the programs was sharply curbed by federal guidelines.

Several analysts were quick to offer explanations. One of the first is contained in the book *Dilemmas of Social Reform* by Peter Marris and Martin Rein. The authors are generally sympathetic to the programs and interpret their distinctive administrative features as an effort to "shake-up" the old line local bureaucracies—such as the schools—whose obsolete policies and practices were thwarting the assimilation of the black poor and thus contributing to pressures toward social disorganization

267

and deviant behavior in the cities. They trace the genesis of the new programs to the efforts of reformers in the professions, the universities, the foundations and the federal agencies, all of whom wanted to promote "experimentation" and "innovation" in the offering of local services, hoping to make these services more "responsive" to the needs of blacks. A short time later, Daniel Patrick Moynihan offered a not dissimilar explanation in his book *Maximum Feasible Misunderstanding;* he also attributed the federal programs to the efforts of a handful of would-be reformers, although in this case the most influential of the reformers were said to be social scientists. Moynihan, however, thought the programs a disastrous mistake because the reformers organized the black poor against the white-dominated bureaucracies of local government and thus precipitated intense political conflict and racial polarization. Accordingly, he judged the social scientists to have been both presumptuous and wrong.

Either way, this type of explanation was idiosyncratic, attributing large-scale change and sustained activities by government to the good or mischief that could be wrought by a handful of not very powerful people. To accept such an explanation was to believe that major political developments occur virtually by chance, according to the whim of particular personalities and without reference to broader political forces in a society.

We proposed a different analysis. The scale of federal action, and its distinctive administrative features, could best be understood as a response to major political disturbances in the United States. The movement of blacks from the rural South to the ghettos of the big cities, followed by the eruption of disorder and protest, had come to pose unique problems for the presidential wing of the national Democratic party. The programs for the ghettos were, we thought, a groping effort to cope with those problems, in part by drawing the black poor into the urban political process itself through requirements that they (and not just white political leaders and bureaucrats) "participate" in the development and operation of programs.

This conclusion was based on our analysis of the circumstances of the national Democratic party. Black migration to the cities meant that blacks acquired the vote, and their votes were concentrated in the industrial states that figured so largely in presidential contests. The first major repercussion of this development was felt in the presidential election of 1948 when Henry A. Wallace, who led left-wing elements of the Democratic party in a third-party effort, made a concerted bid for black support, thus forcing Harry S. Truman to take a strong position on civil rights to forestall black defections from the Democratic column. From the outset, however, such gestures by Democrats to assure the loyalty of black voters and their liberal allies generated defections within the powerful southern wing of the party. These defections were no small matter; they threatened to tear apart the regional alliance on which the Democratic party had relied. And so, once the left-wing insurgents had been defeated in the election of 1948, national Democratic leaders tended to avoid civil-rights commitments, hoping thereby to straddle the widening regional divisions within the party.

However, the civil-rights movement which emerged in the midfifties made it increasingly difficult to conciliate the South. Dramatic confrontations staged by the movement in southern communities antagonized and hardened white resistance, accelerating defections despite the placating efforts of national party leaders. At the same time, the civil-rights movement, and the violent reactions it provoked throughout the South, inflamed the northern ghettos and produced defections from the party whose presidential nominee in 1956 would only commit himself to "slow but deliberate" speed on desegregation. And it was not black voting behavior alone that was becoming volatile. Discontents born of uprooting and unemployment were activated by the civil-rights movement and increasingly took form in street protests, mass marches, sit-ins and riots. In an article entitled "Politics and Poverty," we argued that this chain of disturbances ultimately led the White House to inaugurate a series of new programs for the ghettos. The New Frontier and the Great Society were an effort to restore order to the cities, and to solidify black-voter allegiance.

The federal approach was to initiate a series of new "social welfare" programs, some to be channeled through traditional municipal agencies, with the proviso that services be provided to blacks; others to bypass the local service structures and to create new agencies in ghetto neighborhoods. To proceed in either fashion meant that the national government was entering a terrain thickly populated with local vested interests that were certain to oppose one or another feature of the new programs. The stratagems by which the federal government attempted to minimize local opposition were analyzed in "Federal Intervention in the Cities."

As it turned out, most of the gains made by the black poor as a result of federal intervention were in public welfare. This was partly a reflection of the fact that when desperately poor people began turning to the new federal agencies for help, it was money they needed, and quickly. Welfare was the place to get it.

Black people also needed housing, health care, jobs, education and relief from police coercion. But efforts to achieve these goals turned out to be far less successful than efforts to obtain welfare, for other organized groups began mounting new claims of their own. Black demands made against school systems, or hospitals, or police departments triggered a spiral of demands by schoolteachers, health personnel and policemen for larger salaries, or reduced work loads, or more secure tenure. These groups were well organized and well respected; they enjoyed broad popular support. Moreover, entrenched as they were in the urban bureaucracies, they had the power to cause chaos (by strikes, for example) in the delivery of services. Mayors were thus in no position to resist their demands. The result was spiraling municipal costs and what has come to be called the "urban fiscal crisis." The changes these several developments signified in the nature and character of the urban political system were analyzed in "The Urban Crisis: Who Got What, and Why?"

# The Great Society as Political Strategy

FRANCES FOX PIVEN

So far, the Nixon administration has not made precipitous changes in social-welfare policy, but it has shown an inclination to shift federal attention from the cities to the states, and from the North to the South. Whereas the Democrats' Great Society poured money into the urban ghettos, and yielded a measure of control over the funds to slum residents, President Nixon's New Federalism is intended to give federal revenues to the states and to enlarge state control over antipoverty, model cities and other Great Society programs. It should be obvious that the Nixon administration is making these changes for political reasons. Similarly, although it has been anything but obvious to commentators and critics, the Kennedy-Johnson administrations of the sixties launched the New Frontier/Great Society programs for political reasons. Now that that era is virtually over, it may be instructive to examine the forces that prompted the creation of these programs, and thereby, perhaps, put in clearer perspective the rash of criticisms currently directed against them.

By 1960 the Democrats felt that the black vote, especially in the cities, had become crucial in presidential elections. (The story of how Kennedy captured Illinois by a mere 8000 votes, the result of landslide majorities in the black South Side wards of Chicago, quickly became fixed in Democratic lore.) Yet blacks had not become integrated into urban political parties, nor were the agencies of city governments giving blacks a share of pa-

Reprinted with permission of the *Columbia Forum*, Volume XIII, number 2 (Summer 1970).

tronage, power and services commensurate with their voting numbers. To remedy this imbalance, the Kennedy-Johnson administrations gradually evolved a two-pronged approach: First, they developed a series of novel programs directed to slums and ghettos, bypassing both state and local governments; second, they encouraged various tactics to pressure city agencies into giving more services to blacks.

The best-known of the new federal programs—no doubt because it created such a furor—is the "war on poverty," declared in 1964 and subsequently attacked as inviting every abuse, from fiscal mismanagement and embezzlement to demonstrations and even riots. Contrary to popular view, the new federal approach neither began nor ended with the war on poverty. From 1961 to 1967 the federal government sponsored a wide range of programs in the ghettos. They included youth-development projects (to prevent and combat juvenile delinquency), mental-health centers, community-action programs, remedial educational services, model neighborhoods (housing renovation, block-renewal schemes) and neighborhood service centers (offering legal aid, medical clinics, housing advice, etc.). The money authorized for these projects gradually increased from $10 million for the first venture to several billions for later ones.

Neither the defenders nor the critics have cast much light on this eruption of legislation for the cities. It is often said in its defense, for example, that new programs were needed to deal with one or another "urban problem"—whether crime, mental illness, poverty or blighted housing—because the city government lacked not only the money but also the competence to cope with them. But while there was much to complain of in housing, education, health and law enforcement, few of these problems were new, and in any case there were traditional federal programs that provided the vehicles, if not the funds, to help the cities. Legislation and agencies existed to relieve poverty (public welfare, social security), to build housing (public housing, federal mortgage insurance) and to redevelop slum neighborhoods (urban renewal).

The critics point out that crime, mental illness, poverty and bad housing remain despite the new programs, and that they have been worsened by disorder and rebellion; opinions vary as to who is to blame for the Great Society fiasco. Daniel Patrick

Moynihan, for one, seems persuaded that the antipoverty programs failed largely because of the inept counsel given by social scientists—"those liberal, policy-oriented intellectuals who gathered in Washington, and in a significant sense came to power, in the early 1960s"—who promoted "diverse and contradictory goals" and otherwise did "inexcusably sloppy work." (Moynihan's various criticisms have been published in many places, but are more or less pulled together in *Maximum Feasible Misunderstanding*, The Free Press, 1969.) On the other hand, Peter Marris and Martin Rein (*The Dilemmas of Social Reform*, Atherton Press, 1967), blame local public officials, especially bureaucrats, for resisting or corrupting the reforms.

Merely to define such critiques is to reveal their inadequacy, for local political leaders of the sixties were not more "political" than their predecessors, nor were national political leaders peculiarly susceptible to the counsel of social scientists. What accounts for the initiation of anti-poverty and other programs ostensibly designed to deal with the "urban crisis," and the subsequent troubles that beset them, was not the stupidity or cupidity of particular leaders (or their "idea men") but the profound political realignments that had been taking place in the United States over the preceding two decades. To be precise, the Great Society programs, far from being rash blunders by foolish men, represented a coherent political response that was slowly elaborated, corrected and enlarged over the years. To answer the question, then—why existing programs that channeled money through state and municipal agencies were superseded by programs that channeled funds directly into inner-city neighborhoods (allowing the new money to be used to agitate *against* city halls)—one must examine the political context in which the new programs were launched.

Probably the single most important fact underlying domestic politics of the last decade was the massive movement of disfranchised blacks from the rural South to the urban North where they became at least nominal participants in electoral politics. In 1940 seventy-seven percent of the nation's blacks lived in the South; only half are there now. By 1960, ninety percent of all northern blacks were concentrated in ten of the most populous northern states (California, New York, Pennsylvania, Ohio, New Jersey, Michigan, Massachusetts, Indiana and Missouri). One in five residents of the fifty largest cities was a black, and some of these cities (Newark, Cleveland, Detroit and Philadelphia, for example) were well on their way toward black majorities. Agricultural modernization, by driving blacks into the cities, also brought them into the electoral system. But what marks the history of this period is the resistance of the urban political apparatus to the newcomers. Despite growing electoral leverage, blacks got little for their votes. Indeed, in some respects their circumstances worsened precisely because their numbers expanded.

As the swollen ghettos began to encroach on white neighborhoods, schools, parks and hospitals, sharp conflicts were set off with the older inhabitants. The trouble was publicly attributed to deteriorated housing or inadequate schools, but its main source was the tension between whites and blacks. Thus, the long battle for school integration, culminating in demonstrations by blacks and counterdemonstrations by whites, helped produce "the education problem"; and the struggle for open housing had a great deal to do with the "housing problem." Even the city's fiscal troubles, although real enough, aroused intense political conflict because rising costs were linked to the influx of destitute black migrants.

That these conflicts were so bitter, and that the political parties remained so rigid in the face of them, was partly a result of changes in the style of urban politics. In the era of the machine, a degree of consensus was maintained by converting public goods into private favors divided among various groups. What one group got did not directly or obviously infringe upon the interests of other groups. Gradually, however, municipal services replaced personal favors as the grist of city politics. But such services— whether in education, housing or law enforcement—cannot be easily divided. If new schools or housing are provided for one group, it is usually at the expense of another—and it is usually obvious that that is the case.

Confronted by seemingly irreconcilable group demands, mayors generally favored their older white constituents at the expense of the black newcomers. Federal funds for public housing, for example, went unused because the projects were fiercely opposed by whites who feared the invasion of the black poor. By 1960 a huge reservoir of southern black migrants eligible for public assistance had built up in the cities, but fewer than half of them received aid. Urban-renewal projects emphasized "slum clearance"—the policy was evict the poor, reclaim the land and restore it to "higher economic uses" (i.e., to uses that would keep better-off whites and their businesses in the central city). Seventy percent of the families uprooted were black. City government, in short, was not delivering to black voters.

Worse yet, there were signs that the urban political machinery was grinding to a halt under the impact of racial conflict. Political leaders in some cities were so threatened by cleavages in their constituencies that, to avoid further trouble, they simply ignored more controversial national candidates such as Adlai Stevenson (an "egghead" who found little favor among the urban working classes), and concentrated instead on winning local contests. Nor did local white politicians work to get out the black vote or to stimulate participation by blacks in party politics.

From the perspective of the Democratic administration taking office in 1960, these urban troubles were cause for great concern. The old New Deal coalition of southern states and northern cities was crumbling, and as the once solid South gave way, the northern cities became more important. This shift cast in sharp relief the weaknesses in the liberal-labor-ethnic alliances on which Democratic power in the cities had been based since the thirties. Kennedy owed his narrow victory to the heavy Democratic vote in key northern cities, and especially to the black vote. But Kennedy's good showing in the northern ghettos was not simply a reflection of black party loyalty to well-oiled municipal machinery. Urban blacks had been Democrats for almost four decades, yet as their numbers in the North grew, they began to defect: seventy-nine percent voted Democratic in 1952, but only sixty-one percent in 1956, indicating that the black vote could not be taken for granted. By taking a strong stand on civil rights (as Stevenson had refused to do in either 1952 or 1956), Kennedy won back some of the blacks (sixty-nine percent in 1960). The political lesson seemed clear: The urban black vote had not only become critical, it had become volatile as well. The new Democratic administration began to look for ways to strengthen the allegiance of urban blacks.

The search entailed large political risks. For one thing, to call for new civil-rights legislation would jeopardize the support of the powerful southern bloc in Congress on many New Frontier programs. And so Kennedy avoided the civil-rights issue until

after the unprecedented Democratic victory in the midterm congressional elections. In the meantime, he sought other ways to
reach and reward the urban black voter—ways that would not
unduly antagonize urban whites, since white ethnic blocs still
constituted the major Democratic base in the cities. By 1960 their
hostility to the burgeoning ghettos was apparent; indeed, in some
big cities, whites were threatening to defect from the party, especially from national candidates who appeared to champion black
interests. In short, the party had to find an approach to the cities
that would consolidate the allegiance of black voters without
alienating white voters. Moreover, a way had to be found to
prod the local Democratic parties to perform their traditional
function of cultivating and integrating new groups by making
concessions to them. It was no small problem.

What emerged, gropingly at first and then in rapid-fire order,
was a series of service programs for the "inner city," a euphemism for the ghetto neighborhoods that the programs were designed to reach. The tactics recalled those of the old political
machine. Local agencies were created, many of them in storefronts. They were staffed by professionals who offered residents
help in finding jobs, in obtaining welfare or in securing a host
of other public services. Neighborhood leaders were sought out
and hired as "community workers" (close kin to the old ward
heelers) to distribute patronage. The neighborhood leaders, in
turn, drew larger numbers of people into the new programs, and
in that way spread the federal spoils. It made little difference
whether the funds were appropriated under delinquency-prevention, mental-health, antipoverty or model-cities legislation; in
the ghettos the programs looked very much alike.

New citywide coordinating structures—such as antipoverty
councils and manpower-development agencies—were also created
for blacks. Because of federal requirements that the poor "participate," blacks came to staff and control many of these agencies,
much as Italians or Irish or Jews had come to control other
municipal departments. Thus, the national administration was
revivifying the traditional strategy of urban politics: offering
jobs and services to build party loyalty.

But it was not altogether as simple as that. The federal government had to take a unique initiative. It had to establish a
direct relationship between the national government and the

ghettos, a relationship in which both state and local governments were bypassed. It was this shift in relations among levels of government that caused much of the controversy. That state governments were ignored by national Democratic administrations hardly requires explanation. A number of northern states were controlled by Republicans, and in the South the controlling Democrats could hardly be expected to cooperate in new programs for blacks. But many of the big northern cities, traditional Democratic strongholds, were also bypassed, at least in the early years of the Great Society, a clear mark of the concern felt by national leaders over the rising number of blacks in the cities, and the failure of urban political organizations to deal with them.

This was not the first time that shifting political alignments in the United States prompted federal action to undercut established relationships among levels of government. The New Deal Democratic administration, for example, bypassed recalcitrant state governments in order to channel grants-in-aid directly to the party's urban strongholds.

But by the sixties it was city government that had become recalcitrant, and from the outset federal officials viewed city government as a major impediment, an obstacle to be hurdled or circumvented if the new funds were to reach blacks. Therefore, the money was given to a host of other intermediaries, including new agencies created in the ghetto (seventy-five percent of the antipoverty programs were conducted by private agencies, according to the Advisory Commission on Intergovernmental Relations). And even when funds were funneled into regular city agencies, specific guidelines were imposed on their use. As William F. Haddad, one of the early architects of the antipoverty schemes, remarked: "We were trying to set up competing institutions for the traditional services of government."

Much of the controversy over the Great Society programs grew out of this feature, for local officials were hardly happy to have the substantial patronage and publicity of new programs escape their control. Still, the risk of antagonizing local politicians had to be run; if the funds were channeled through local white ethnic political leaders, they would probably never reach the ghettos.

But it was the second part of the federal approach—forcing city agencies to respond to blacks—that made the fur fly. If local white politicians were agitated because so much patronage was eluding them, they became virtually hysterical when the new agencies began to put pressure on the municipal services themselves. Local political leaders depended on the distribution of these services to traditional white constituents in order to maintain power. By pressing for changes in who got what, the Great Society programs shook established relations among constituent groups in the city. That urban politicians reacted with indignation is hardly startling.

But the federal government had to bring municipal agencies into line if it was to cultivate political allegiance among the newcomers to the city. The new ghetto agencies were relatively small and impermanent compared to ongoing programs in education, housing or health. For blacks to obtain more substantial and lasting concessions, the existing service structures of local government, which controlled the bulk of federal, state and local appropriations, had to be reoriented.

Various tactics to produce municipal reform were tried, at first under the guise of experiments in "institutional change." With that slogan the Washington officials who administered the juvenile-delinquency program (under Robert Kennedy's direction) required as a condition of granting funds that local governments submit "comprehensive plans" for their own reform (i.e., for giving blacks something). But the mere existence of such plans did not turn out to be very compelling when the time came to implement programs. Therefore, as turbulence spread in the northern ghettos, the federal officials began to try another way to promote institutional change—"maximum feasible participation of residents of the areas and members of the groups served."

Some deference to "citizen participation" has always been important in legitimizing governmental action in America. But the Great Society programs went beyond token representation. They gave money to ghetto organizations that then used the money to harass city agencies. Community workers were hired to badger housing inspectors and to pry loose welfare payments. Later the new community agencies began to organize the poor to picket the welfare department or to boycott the school system. Local officials were flabbergasted; one level of government and party was financing the harassment of another level of government and party!

At least as disturbing to some white politicians, "nonpartisan" voter-registration drives were launched in the ghettos with Great Society funds. More black voters meant larger pluralities for the national Democratic party, but they presented local white incumbent politicians with a new and threatening constituency. To such local leaders, voter registration in the ghettos seemed an incredible way to deal with juvenile delinquency or mental illness or poverty, and they were quick to say so. But as a device to promote a modest shift in the political balance between voting constituencies, it was not incredible at all.

Little of this was mapped out in advance, but it was not accidental either. Federal officials were feeling their way, step by step, casting about for a way to deal with political problems in the cities. When controversies flared, the federal government withdrew a step or two and attempted to conciliate local officials, especially where white ethnic political organizations were still firmly entrenched. Most of the juvenile-delinquency projects, for example, were allowed to collapse when they ran afoul of city governments, but they were replaced by antipoverty agencies and on a much larger scale. When mayors and local bureaucrats rose up in even greater indignation, the national administration retreated again, terminating a few of the most abrasive projects and conceding more control by local politicians over others. (By then, however, there were signs that federal intervention was taking effect; chastened by controversy, the mayors and other local officials had reached accommodations with the projects, and only a handful of cities made use of the option to enlarge their control of the new agencies.) Subsequently, when the model-cities program was designed, some of this bruising struggle was avoided by funneling federal benefits to the ghetto via city government. Even so, local officials were subjected to the federal-funding requirement that they negotiate agreements with ghetto residents. Thus modified and adapted, the Great Society went forward.

The approach being described was a precarious one for a Democratic administration to undertake in its own local strongholds; there was every reason to fear a backlash from white politicians and their traditional constituents who were, after all, the stalwarts of the Democratic party. However, various tactics evolved that served to avert that danger, at least for a time. It was probably only because of these tactics that the Great Society programs were able to do as much as they did do for the black poor (however little that may have been in the larger scheme of things), and that the backlash, when it came, seemed to catch federal officials by surprise.

One tactic was the emphasis on "community development," a reassuring concept to whites because it suggested that the "pathology of the ghetto" would be attacked, not white stakes in neighborhoods, schools, jobs or public services. The creation of separate citywide coordinating structures (e.g., antipoverty councils) also deflected white antagonism; it suggested that blacks were to be conciliated with a measure of influence over entirely new structures, rather than with greater control over traditional municipal agencies dominated by whites.

Perhaps most reassuring of all were the rationales put forward for the new activities. Juvenile delinquency, mental illness, family deterioration, poor work habits and welfare dependency among the black poor were, after all, precisely what many whites thought the "urban crisis" was all about. By promising to solve these problems, and to do so within the confines of the ghettos themselves—that is, without interfering with the interests of other groups in the cities—the programs would not only conciliate blacks but also appeal to whites, easing the way for federal intervention in the face of growing political divisiveness in the cities.

There were other reasons why the political interests at stake were not widely recognized, at least at the beginning. One is the larger role played by social scientists and other professionals, who provided the theoretical justifications for the Great Society. Each new measure was presented at the outset as a politically neutral "scientific cure" for a disturbing social malady, thus obscuring the fact that the federal government was trying to give something to blacks. Furthermore, as concrete programs evolved they were cloaked in a web of esoteric terminology that concealed the class and racial interests at stake, so that few groups could decipher who would gain from the new programs, or who would lose. Finally, the professionals lent an aura of scientific authority to what might otherwise have been perceived as mere political rhetoric.

Indeed, the neatness of the mesh that developed between professional perspectives and political concerns deserves to be wondered about. Ordinarily the variety of professionals who specialize in "social problems" offer a wide range of opinions as to the causes of these ills, and what must be done to remedy them. Clinical psychologists, for example, might stress the treatment of individuals as a way of dealing with delinquency or educational retardation or "economic dependency." But the particular professionals selected to advise the Great Society emphasized *institutional* disorders and so stressed the need for "institutional change." The way to deal with crime or illiteracy or poverty, they argued, was to reform the courts, the schools and the job market. Moreover, these professionals seemed to promise that the necessary "institutional reform" could be "engineered" solely by the application of "scientific techniques." The perspective was disarming, and it nicely matched the political needs of the national Democratic administration, for what was being called "institutional change" was in fact part of a general strategy to produce change in urban politics.

As the Great Society evolved from "institutional change" to "citizen participation," professional perspectives adjusted accordingly. Professional journals began to feature articles that prescribed political participation (if not outright agitation) as a "therapy" for delinquency and drug addiction. Indeed, the professionals hired by the program were often more aggressive than the "citizen participants." Hundreds of lawyers, for example, defended the poor in dealings with bureaucracies, coached them in tactics such as rent strikes and took public agencies to court—whether over eviction procedures in public housing, the termination of welfare payments or disciplinary suspensions in the schools. With such developments, the war on poverty became a war in fact.

To be sure, some groups were wary from the beginning, especially the local agencies, both public and private, on whose terrain the federal government was venturing. But professional explanations helped to assuage their fears, too. The new federally funded projects were called "experiments" or "demonstrations" or "scientific inquiries." Traditional agencies were led to believe that there was no cause to worry that new policy precedents were being established. Once the viability of a new policy or practice had been "demonstrated," it would be up to the regular agencies to make appropriate changes in their own programs, and the threatening "pilot" projects would wither away.

Established agencies were all the more ready to be assured because they were also given a piece of the action, a stake in the Great Society. What some have criticized as the incredibly intricate networks of Great Society agencies, held together by multitudes of subcontracting arrangements that brought tears of frustration to the eyes of auditors, were merely the structural reflections of political concessions. The new programs were being launched in a crowded terrain, and many interested parties had to be wrapped in—municipal agencies, private social agencies, universities, new ghetto organizations, business corporations and so on. To justify such arrangements, professionals devised curiously murky definitions of social problems, calling them "multifaceted," for instance, and therefore in need of "comprehensive" and "coordinated" solutions. As for the professionals themselves, they served the Great Society fully and they served it gladly, for the new federal approach also afforded boundless opportunities for the expansion of their own professional interests.

In other words, far from causing trouble by their muddleheadedness—by what Moynihan calls their "diverse and contradictory goals"—professionals helped to muffle and delay the conflicts inherent in the Great Society programs. That controversies were nevertheless detonated by these programs is understandable, for the stakes were high. At bottom, they were struggles over existing services. Billions of government dollars were flowing through municipal welfare agencies, housing agencies, health agencies and school systems. But city governments controlled these services —and managed them in the interests of whites. The relatively modest funds expended through the new federal measures acted as a lever in redirecting and enlarging some of the money already flowing through municipal agencies. Between 1960 and 1968, for example, welfare expenditures nearly tripled, and most of that increase occurred in the 121 most urbanized counties (counties containing cities of at least 100,000 persons), with blacks getting a disproportionate share. The Great Society programs, in brief, were an effort to force modest changes in city politics by changing city policies. A little federal money was going a long way—it was beginning to put the apparatus of city services to work for the national party by turning some of the benefits of city services to blacks.

To be sure, the national Democratic party appears to have been badly bruised in the last election [of 1968]. But it remained as strong as ever in the cities, partly because of the Great Society. According to the postelection Harris poll, the Democrats managed to hold the allegiance of most urban whites, and won an astonishing ninety percent of the black vote as well.

It was the wreckage of their regional coalition that defeated the Democrats, and on which the widely publicized "southern strategy" of the Republican party is founded. Republican domestic programs will be designed accordingly, as we can already see in Nixon's proposal for a federal $1600 minimum income for a family of four. Such a minimum would be a bonanza for many people in southern states, but would benefit few in the North where grant levels are already much higher. These and other moves—such as proposals to give the Republican state-houses control over programs for the cities—are not being made because Republican policy is based on a clearer formulation of the nature of our domestic problems, as Moynihan and other critics would have it, but simply because Republican proposals are designed to deal with different political imperatives.

# The New Urban Programs: The Strategy of Federal Intervention

FRANCES FOX PIVEN

During the early 1960s, under the Kennedy-Johnson regime, a new pattern of federal-local relations took form, entailing direct intervention by the federal government in services to local neighborhoods, especially ghetto neighborhoods. Several major pieces of legislation were enacted, each enlarging the scope of federal intervention.

In 1961 the Juvenile Delinquency and Youth Offenses Control Act was passed, authorizing the expenditure of $10 million for grants to "youth development" projects for the prevention and treatment of juvenile delinquency. In 1963 the Communtiy Mental Health Centers Act authorized $150 million to finance community centers which would serve as the nucleus for what President Kennedy called a "bold new approach" to the prevention and treatment of mental illness. In 1964 Title II of the Economic Opportunity Act allocated $350 million to community-action programs which, in President Johnson's words, would "strike at poverty at its source—in the streets of our cities and on the farms of our countryside . . . calling on all resources available to the community—federal and state, local and private, human and material." In 1965, under Title I of the Elementary and Secondary Education Act, $1 billion was allocated for a variety of projects and services to disadvantaged children. And in 1966 Title I of the Demonstration Cities and Metropolitan

Originally published in Erwin O. Smigel, editor, *Handbook on the Study of Social Problems*, New York, Rand McNally and Company, 1972. Reprinted with the permission of the editor and publisher.

Development Act called for a "comprehensive attack on social, economic and physical problems in selected slum and blighted areas through the most effective and economical concentration and coordination of federal, state and local public and private efforts . . . to develop 'model' neighborhoods."

Each of these measures was proposed as a way of dealing with a distinctive social problem, presumably requiring a distinctive strategy of amelioration. Yet despite the variety of advertised social problems and legislative titles—delinquency, mental health, poverty, model cities—the major programs for the cities had remarkable similarities. First, all provided a wide variety of services, from unemployment programs to family counseling. Second, under the broad umbrella of "community development," all carved out local neighborhoods in the urban ghettos as service areas. Most important, all these enactments represented a new pattern of federal-local relations which worked to circumvent or undermine traditional municipal control of service programs.

Underlying the elaborations about "social problems" were certain pressing political realities that the new Democratic administration confronted in 1960. The victory had been a narrow one, and it seemed to bring to the forefront important changes in the party constituency. The South had once more defected, confirming what had been becoming clear throughout the 1950s— that the South could no longer be counted as "solid." (Mississippi and Alabama went States Rights; Florida, Tennessee, Kentucky and Virginia voted Republican.) Kennedy owed his victory to the heavy Democratic vote in key cities, and especially to the black vote in those cities.

The ghettos were responding to the fact that Kennedy had campaigned on a strong civil-rights platform, as Stevenson had not done in either 1952 or 1956. It was with these experiences in clear view that the new administration began to explore ways to cement the allegiance of the black vote in the cities.

Although it was important to hold and increase those black votes, the Kennedy administration faced severe problems in following through on its civil-rights promises. Civil-rights legislation was sure to meet fierce resistance from southerners in the Congress (where a coalition of southern Democrats and Republicans was in any case to make trouble for the president's overall legislative program), and civil-rights legislation was likely also to

fan the racism of the white working classes, which were already
becoming a divisive factor in Democratic urban constituencies.[1]
Alternative ways of placating the urban ghetto vote were needed.
The new administration turned to a series of service programs
for the inner city, where blacks were concentrated.

To implement this strategy of ghetto "community development," the administration had to contend with the apparatus of
city government, which in most places was likely to resist directing
any services to blacks. Merely to increase grants-in-aid intended
for the ghetto would not do, for the cities were likely to use such
funds to serve the groups to whom they were already tied—often
at the expense of blacks, as experience with public housing and
urban renewal had already shown (Anderson, 1964; Hartman,
1964; Gans, 1965). If the ghetto voters were to be reached by
new federal programs, city government had somehow to be
dealt with; the existing methods of giving grants-in-aid had to
be changed.[2] But while local agencies had to be redirected or
circumvented, their collaboration was also essential; without it,
federal programs were likely to be obstructed and federal strategy
would backfire. There was no point in cultivating the support
of blacks only to alienate municipal agencies—and their white
constituencies.[3] This delicate political problem of somehow intervening in the pattern of services to ghetto communities while
maintaining the collaboration of local agencies shaped much of
the federal activity for the urban ghetto during the sixties.

The first of the new federal programs to be launched by the
Kennedy administration was in delinquency prevention, and the
first local project created under it, Mobilization for Youth, was
located on the Lower East Side of New York City. The remainder
of this article will describe the process of federal intervention
in municipal service patterns which underlay the Mobilization
project. Some of the problems involved in such intervention, and
the outlines of a strategy to deal with them, were already apparent
in this early venture.

## EARLY DESIGN

The new administration began gropingly; all that was clear at
first was that there should be some kind of program for the inner

city. But the emergence of delinquency as a primary focus was not accidental. According to federal reports, the national rate of reported juvenile-court delinquency had doubled in the previous decade (Children's Bureau, 1960: 5). Mounting crime rates in the city were widely reported in the press and featured as a problem by an array of civic groups. More important, "crime in the streets" was becoming the focus of tension between major urban voting blocks, particularly between white ethnic groups and black newcomers. Indeed, conflict between blacks and whites was growing so intense that programs designed to placate one or the other of these contending groups were being mangled. For example, public housing, because it was associated with the black poor, had aroused so much opposition from whites (particularly when projects made incursions into white neighborhoods) that it had come to a virtual standstill in many cities.

By contrast, the delinquency problem seemed an especially fortunate issue around which to frame a federal program. It held out the promise of new services to blacks and, simultaneously, the promise of law and order to whites. The very services which would appeal to the swelling numbers in the ghettos would also assuage the whites who feared the ghettos.

The administration began its venture in delinquency by calling together a group of experts and professional leaders, among them a representative from the Ford Foundation, which was already associated with activities for the inner city. In this way the federal effort was connected with the various ideas and programs already in the field.

The Ford Foundation played a uniquely entrepreneurial role in these events (see Marris and Rein, 1967).[4] Because the foundation had money to give, it attracted proposals from a wide variety of groups and became a kind of clearinghouse for ideas about ambitious new ventures. And because they saw themselves as innovators and promoters, Ford personnel used these ideas widely and actively in the course of dispersing—or not dispersing—their money.

During the 1950s the Ford Foundation had initiated a variety of projects in metropolitan government, urban renewal, education, delinquency, criminal jutsice—in short, all of the current "urban problems"—under its public-affairs division. Foundation staff saw the deterioration of the inner cities as a potentially explosive problem, compounded of a failure in civic leadership and of institutional obstructions to the assimilation of new urban groups. The proper role for the foundation, they thought, was to stimulate reform among the various people and organizations whose activities somehow affected these urban problems. As one staff member said in retrospect, "There was no ideology in all this."[5]

During the next few years foundation staff began to talk more with sociologists. Although they tended to regard divergencies among sociologists as "twists of theory," still, as one staff member said, "We were very much interested by the conception of opportunity systems, value systems, cultures and subcultures." Among these theorists, Ford personnel were apparently particularly struck with Columbia University proponents of what came to be known as "opportunity theory" (see Cloward and Ohlin, 1960), which presumably was being developed into an action program on the Lower East Side of New York. Ford people began to talk the opportunity-theory point of view at various meetings and to refer to it in reviewing their different projects. It was these ideas that Ford staff brought, along with the promise of Ford money, to the meeting of experts called by the new administration.

According to opportunity theory, subcultural or group delinquency is a result of the discrepancy between aspirations and opportunities in the poor community. Thus, while material success is widely aspired to in our society, opportunities for success are not widely or equally distributed. Lower-class youth are impeded by the institutions of the poor community (e.g., inferior schools and scarce occupational opportunities). Blocked from legitimate routes to success, they seek alternate routes to achievement in the delinquent subcultures of the community. It follows from this analysis that if legitimate routes to success are opened to slum youth, delinquency will be reduced. These views, while far from specific, did suggest that an antidelinquency program should be concerned with providing educational and employment opportunities in the slum community. In this way the problem of delinquency, interpreted as the problem of enlarging opportunities by reducing institutional barriers to the minority poor, provided a rationale for a federal move to reach into black communities with some of the services and economic benefits that blacks, spurred by the civil-rights movement, were beginning to demand.

## INITIATING COLLABORATION

In order to implement the new strategy for the cities, a collaborative network had to be established among a wide range of agencies, federal and local, public and private. The diverse service resources of these agencies were needed to make the service approach effective, and, in any case, their political support was necessary if the strategy was not to be obstructed.

### COLLABORATION ON THE FEDERAL LEVEL

Shortly after the 1960 election, the President's Committee on Juvenile Delinquency and Youth Crime was established by executive order and directed to "coordinate" the various federal activities in delinquency. As an initial instrument of federal action, the committee was structured to assure it several advantages. It was headed by Attorney General Robert Kennedy, and so would be responsive to the White House. It also included the secretary of the Department of Health, Education and Welfare and the secretary of the Department of Labor, and so could hope to draw on a range of existing agencies that controlled funds and programs which presumably could be redirected to the new inner-city ventures. The committee device also made possible at least a liaison relationship with the agencies that had come to think of delinquency as their own terrain.

The first task of the committee was to draft new legislation and oversee its passage through the Congress. Traditionally, the federal agencies directly concerned with delinquency legislation were the Children's Bureau and the National Institute of Mental Health (NIMH), both divisions of the Department of Health, Education and Welfare. The Children's Bureau had a juvenile-delinquency branch, established in 1952, whose main activities were to hold conferences, issue publications and send consultants around the country. The staff was small and had legislative authority only to provide technical services.

Once delinquency became a public issue in the 1950s, the bureau stepped up its public-relations activities, hoping to promote federal legislation to support its constituent social agencies throughout the country with more staff, facilities and research. Implicit in this activity, at least for some of those on the Children's Bureau staff, was the view that the compelling problem of juvenile delinquency might be exploited by the bureau to regain some of the stature it had lost since its founding in 1912. However, their programmatic ideas on delinquency were loose, formed to accommodate the competing agencies with which they dealt in child welfare, public welfare and corrections. And so they continued to make recommendations for diverse services for delinquent children, calling for federal legislation to provide matching grants to state and local agencies (Children's Bureau, 1960; Beck, 1965).

NIMH, for its part, had begun to sponsor research and demonstration projects in delinquency as early as 1954. Initially it had conceived of delinquency research as focusing largely on individual mental health, but, reflecting changes in the dominant professional ideas of the day, it later expanded its perspective to include studies based on a broader sociological view of the causes of delinquency. NIMH justified itself to the Congress by emphasizing the practical benefits of research as well as, in the case of delinquency, the promising prospects of new treatment methods. It had been exploring the possibility of sponsoring a community-wide experiment in order to test treatment methods consistent with a sociological perspective.[6]

For six years during the 1950s, prodded by the federal agencies with stakes in delinquency activity, the Congress held hearings on delinquency legislation. As one observer remarked:

Delinquency was like sin, always good for a hearing. . . . Mayor Wagner would bring down his suitcase full of knives and other weapons taken from gang members—I think he just left the suitcase here each year and opened it up at the hearing.

But while the Congress was becoming alert to the delinquency problem, the proposed legislation had little spark and acquired no important political support. It called for federal aid to state and local communities to support increased facilities and staffs —that is, for more funds to be expended through traditional agencies on various ongoing and parochial activities.

The first signs of congressional stirring in response to the rising delinquency rates came from a subcommittee of the House Appropriations Committee, headed by Representative John Fogarty (D–R.I.). Representative Fogarty called on the Children's Bureau and NIMH to prepare reports on the delinquency problem. The committee responded with some new appropriations, the larger part of which went to the more prestigious NIMH (Congress, and especially Representative Fogarty, was said to be somewhat disdainful of the female social workers of the Children's Bureau).

The real political push, however, came with the new administration of 1960. With the attorney general taking the lead in mobilizing congressional support, legislation in the form of the Juvenile Delinquency and Youth Offenses Control Act of 1961 was soon enacted permitting the federal funding of sixteen pilot delinquency programs in local communities. The first of these, as we have noted, was Mobilization for Youth on New York's Lower East Side.

## COLLABORATION AMONG LOCAL AGENCIES

The new federal program found a vast array of local organizations, in a sense, ready and waiting. The mounting rates of delinquency during the 1950s were coming into focus in the city governments, the universities and the local neighborhoods. To hundreds of agencies in scores of cities the delinquency problem seemed an opportunity for the expansion of their organizational activities. It was these organizations with which the federal government would have to deal in pursuing its strategy of intervention and collaboration, and the innumerable accommodations with these agencies helped to shape the youth-development projects that finally emerged. The Mobilization for Youth venture was not a simple act of the new administration; rather, it was the culmination of negotiations and accommodations among an array of federal and local groups whose mutual concerns with the delinquency problem could be traced back to the early 1950s.

During the fifties, local social agencies on the Lower East Side, particularly the settlement houses, had become increasingly concerned about the fighting gangs that roamed the neighborhood. The settlements and churches had attempted to deal with the problem by sponsoring recreation and counseling projects and by organizing a "community alert" to warn of gang trouble. One evening in 1957, local agency people met at the Henry Street Settlement House to discuss these various efforts. A Henry Street board member was apparently sufficiently impressed by the urgency of the problem to offer a small grant to explore "what it would take," as one participant put it, "to really do the job."

What it would take, the local agency people decided, was enough money to launch a community-wide program that would "make use of everything we knew to help children and families." Local efforts thus far had been hampered, they felt, by inadequate resources. "The problem now is not so much how to do it, since the methods are known; the problem is to find sufficient means to meet the whole problem."[7] What no one said (but everyone knew) was that the local agencies needed money. Contributions had been falling off as a result of the shifting population of the Lower East Side. The earlier Jewish poor, who had drawn contributions from Jewish philanthropies, were being replaced by Puerto Ricans and Negroes, who did not attract philanthropic contributions.

But if the local agencies felt they needed money, it was to continue the services they had been providing and to expand them to a scale commensurate with what they considered to be community needs. As one of the group said later, "We were well aware of many little and often meaningful experiences, but these were too small. No one had tried to build everything into a project that people needed." Or, as another local leader said in an early interview with the press, "We must be allowed to do everything we know how to do, at one time, in one place." In other words, the cooperating local agencies comprising the

Henry Street group proposed to saturate the community with their kinds of services.

As for the program specifics, an early prospectus described such services as recreational activities, casework and group work, family counseling and community organization. These services would be provided by the settlements, which were said to be "at the core of the neighborhood" and thus in the best position to bring services to children and their families and also to improve the neighborhood climate by "helping people to help each other."

The Henry Street group began to solicit funds from several sources. It received some encouragement from the National Institute of Mental Health, which had been looking for a "community laboratory" to serve as a testing ground for its new sociological perspective on delinquency. A long period of negotiation ensued between NIMH and the local groups, during which several proposals were submitted and turned down before the project was finally given planning funds. Throughout this process, various themes were reiterated by members of the NIMH committee. The local agencies should be united in support of the proposals. Relationships should be established with "outside centers of power"—especially with such public institutions as the schools—so as to ensure some "transfer of power" in the improvement of the community. The proposal should provide a means of bringing about innovations in the practices of existing agencies, since innovation was essential if agencies were once again to serve the community. The services introduced by the proposed program should have the potential of becoming indigenous. And something should be done for the Lower East Side, a neighborhood that had contributed so much to America's cultural heritage.

Consistent with NIMH's own organizational perspective, two conditions were especially stressed. As an agency of government, NIMH was anxious to avoid the political repercussions of the interagency squabbling that had long characterized the Lower East Side, a territory densely settled with social agencies. The community would have to demonstrate its readiness by establishing a firm collaborative structure to receive the money. The Henry Street Settlement had already begun to try to develop "cooperative working relationships" with other local institutions on whose territorial prerogatives the Henry Street program infringed. The evolution of a structure for local collaboration was marked by internecine dealings, themselves an elaborate story, revolving around local struggles for dominance. It was clear to the local agency leaders, however, that a cooperative arrangement was necessary if funds were to be granted, and they did in time submit to a collaborative structure, which they named Mobilization for Youth.

More important, NIMH was a research-oriented agency, so it required that the new project include a research-and-evaluation component, which would have to be based at a university. While the local practitioners held no particular brief for academic research, NIMH requirements were clear. After initial negotiations with a group at New York University were disrupted by internal struggles among the local agencies, the Columbia University School of Social Work was approached and agreed to prepare a research proposal.

This new linkage, in shifting the center of influence to the university, seemed also to shift the goals and ideas for the program. The university researchers were, as they said themselves, "the ones who could get the money." They shared the NIMH interest in scientific research, and not accidentally, for they were close professional associates of the NIMH advisory committee, which was composed of nationally known academicians and professionals, including one of the Columbia University researchers.[8]

The stress on research meant that whatever action programs were developed should lend themselves to research evaluation; research and action, as one of the review-committee members said, "should test each other." Service programs should be derived from the theoretical underpinnings of research, and the success of these services should be susceptible to research evaluation.[9] In concrete terms this meant that the local Mobilization group would have to undergo an extended research-and-planning period during which suitable new proposals would be developed, and during which the university researchers would have a great deal to say about the formulation of service programs.

The resulting proposal, prepared with an NIMH planning grant (and later funded by the President's Committee on Juve-

nile Delinquency and Youth Crime, the Ford Foundation and
the City of New York), was put forward in terms of the de-
linquency-and-opportunity perspective, and stressed the importance of programs to improve educational and work
opportunities in the neighborhood. The initial Henry Street
group had taken quite another view and stressed quite different
programs. The improvement of behavior, they said, "calls for
the skilled use of personal contact through face-to-face methods"
—that is, for the direct services in counseling and recreation
that settlements have traditionally provided. But other of their
views were not inconsistent with the opportunity-theory perspective. They had described their neighborhood as one in
which "the horizon is limited . . . where there are poor prospects for social or economic advancement." Such notions eased
for them the shift that was demanded by NIMH and to which
they acceded, for services of any kind would bring them funds.


## COLLABORATION AMONG
## MUNICIPAL AGENCIES

Various other groups and organizations were also moving
in response to the opportunities presented by the delinquency
problem. The Youth Board had been founded in the late 1940s
to do "street work" with delinquency-prone youth, as well as
to provide the usual assortment of services in group work, family counseling and community organization. The Youth Board
had also been charged with the coordination of all other youth
services in the city. This, however, was a formal prerogative
which the board had no capacity to implement in the face of
the vast array of existing organizations providing services to
youth, each of which was anxious to protect its jurisdiction
against any "coordinator," and some of which indeed claimed
the role of coordinator for their own.

At the same time, the city administrator's office, also formally
charged with coordination and also without the resources and
authority to coordinate, was searching for a public issue and
program around which to make a bid for increased powers. Delinquency might be such an issue, and services to children and
youth might be such a program. Still, the kinds of recommen-

dations then being put forward by different agencies, each merely stressing the expansion of its own parochial services, did not seem to provide the rationale for the comprehensive jurisdiction the city administrator's office was seeking to develop.

As gang delinquency mounted in the 1950s, various civic groups began to express concern, and fastened on the apparent lack of coordination of services for children and youth, an issue which was in part created for them by the two city agencies involved. Mayor Wagner responded by commissioning a study (as mayors are inclined to do when competing claims create a political dilemma). The findings of that study also called for coordination, but questioned the claim of the Youth Board to this role on the ground that it was administratively unsound to expect an operating agency to coordinate the activities of other agencies. Still, study reports are suffered easily, especially in New York City, and no action seemed imminent.

A protest from a group of Harlem leaders, however, precipitated a decision among the competing claims of the Youth Board, the city administrator's office and other youth-serving agencies. In 1961 the Youth Board, together with the Jewish Board of Guardians and the Community Mental Health Board, had initiated a psychiatric street-work project in Harlem. Bolstered by the new concern for Negro rights, the Harlem group took affront at this fresh display of "social-welfare colonialism." No Harlem leaders had been consulted; no Harlem agencies had been included. The group took its protest to the mayor a week before the election. Squirming to evade this new assault, the mayor turned to the city administrator's office and charged it to begin forthwith the coordination of youth services.

The city administrator's office, of course, welcomed this unexpected reinforcement of its jurisdictional claims. Still, more was needed than the mayor's mandate to make these claims good. The city administrator was therefore alert to prospects for new funds and programs being talked about by the Ford Foundation (which had been tapping various city agencies for reactions to its project ideas) and the new President's Committee on Juvenile Delinquency and Youth Crime. Thus, in 1961 the city was ripe for a bid from the federal government. There was political pressure on the mayor for a "new approach," there was an agency in the city government whose own interest would nicely complement the federal endeavor, and there was "community readiness" in the group eagerly seeking funds on the Lower East Side.

## MECHANISMS TO FACILITATE COLLABORATION

In 1962 the Mobilization for Youth project was officially launched with an announcement by the White House of a $13.5-million grant. The project's jurisdiction was a sixty-seven-block area carved out of the Lower East Side; its arsenal for "delinquency prevention" included an elaborate battery of programs in education and youth employment, as well as assorted services to groups, individuals and families in the community. Some of these programs were to be staffed and managed by the new project, some were to be run in partnership with municipal agencies, and some were to be contracted out to existing local agencies. Several federal agencies, the city government and the Ford Foundation were funding it. Columbia University was tied to the project as a research partner. Representatives from Columbia, several city agencies and local groups sat on its seventy-five-member board. Thus, the organizations involved in this early version of "creative federalism" reached from the federal government to the local neighborhood, and swept in both public and private groups. A beginning had been made in the new federal strategy of intervention and collaboration in patterns of service to the ghetto.

The key ingredient in forging a coalition from among groups with ordinarily diverse interests and outlooks was the incentive of new federal money, matched by the eagerness of local agencies for new funds. But the national government moved gingerly. It had neither the authority nor the resources to enact a strategy for the inner city unilaterally. At the outset, different organizations in different places, already alerted by the attention given the delinquency problem in the press and by civic groups and political leaders, made their separatist and competitive bids for public funds. These agencies had strong commitments to their existing approaches, commitments held fast by tradition and constituency. And so federal money was dangled before local groups and meted out through an elaborate process of accommodation in which programs were broadened, diffused and altered to meet the terms of political trading.

Still, the various parties to the dealing were obviously not equal partners. As each grant was negotiated, federal conditions were imposed, and although these conditions were often compromised subsequently, the federal agencies continued to exert the dominant influence. Moreover, the national administration dispersed its money through mechanisms that promoted collaboration, while easing the way for federal intervention.

## STRUCTURAL MECHANISMS

To ensure their cooperation, the federal government required that a structure be formed which actually incorporated the groups whose support was needed. The Mobilization project consisted of a structure that included national, citywide and neighborhood groups—as multiple sponsors, as representatives on the seventy-five-member board or as partners in various program activities. The city's support meant not only the mayor's office and the city administrator but also a number of city agencies which had to be propitiated either because the new programs impinged on their jurisdictions or because the programs required their positive cooperation. In the local neighborhood, support was needed from the settlement houses, churches and local political leaders whose territorial and functional jurisdictions were directly affected. All of these groups were structurally tied into the new venture.

The narrow jurisdiction of the project was another structural feature which paved the way for cooperation. The diverse groups from which commitments had to be secured were likely to be wary of intrusions on their domains. To smooth the way, the new project was set up with narrowly designated limits. As a community-development venture, it was to cover only a small area on the Lower East Side. Furthermore, it was defined as a "demonstration," and so would run for only a restricted period of time. Existing organizations were in this way reassured; any infringement on their jurisdictions were to be limited in scope and would continue for only a limited time.

## PROFESSIONALISM AS A MECHANISM

The federal agencies were the nexus for a new scientifically oriented professionalism which has become as important in social welfare as in other fields of national life (Piven, 1967a). This sort of professionalism played a key role in promoting federal intervention and collaboration through the Mobilization project. For one thing, organizational links had to be established, and changing ideas communicated. In this process the professionals associated with the university, the foundation and the federal bureaucracy were important agents. They gave advice as consultants, they served on advisory committees, they set fashions in ideas through the influence of their writings. These were the cosmopolitan professionals, moving easily from one organizational context to another, receiving grants even while they advised the granting agencies.

More important, these professionals formed a consensus of experts buttressing a political strategy. They lent to the new endeavor the prestige of their university associations, the authority of science and the promise of progress through scientific investigation. They were persuasive and articulate advocates of the "advanced" program ideas that were to take precedence over local and parochial agency practice. At the same time, the expertise employed by professionals swathed the project in an obscurity which, by preventing close scrutiny of the implications of various program activities, minimized dissension among the diverse groups in the collaboration (Piven, 1967b). In short, the professional experts associated with the Mobilization effort provided important political resources for the federal venture into the cities.

## RATIONALES AS MECHANISMS

The Mobilization for Youth project was to be an example of a comprehensive and coordinated approach to social welfare, a social-planning approach to community development, an experiment in social engineering, and so forth. Whatever one might think of the substance of these rationales, they provided several advantages in promoting collaboration.[10] Where concrete plans might have precipitated conflict among groups with diverse interests and perspectives, these generalities could be more easily accepted, accommodating the diverse interests and perspectives of the collaborators. Perhaps the most useful rationale in this regard was the stress on experimentation and innovation, which served to relax the logic of any set of ideas, permitting an almost startling flexibility (as evidenced by a Ford Foundation official's comment that "Poverty with spirit can do tremendous things"). To call for innovation was to call for action, but precisely what kind of action seemed unimportant.

One thing that could be said of these general ideas is that they were all-embracing, and this was useful in still another way. A multifaceted and comprehensive project meant, in effect, a variety of program activities designed to entice the different agencies whose collaboration was needed, each according to its own orientation and interest. And, all talk of comprehensiveness aside, as each group focused on the aspects of the project that were germane to its own interests, it showed little desire to examine the total set of actions contemplated by the project or to contend with the ideas that inspired those actions. For example, the staff of the city administrator's office saw in Mobilization for Youth an opportunity to expand their own planning functions and were quite indifferent to the youth-recreation programs included as a concession to the local voluntary agencies. Ideas like "comprehensive and coordinated social planning" seemed able to sweep together these diverse activities, lending them coherence and distinction.


## PROCEEDING BY TRIAL AND ERROR

The federal problem of intervention and collaboration in the cities was not solved all at once. Mobilization for Youth was only the beginning of a strategy that was developed through a continuing process of trial and error. Programs were fumbled, overreaching themselves only to be withdrawn and then put forward again with new and conciliatory elaborations. The

executive directors of the early juvenile-delinquency projects
suffered startling occupational mortality—including, in time,
the executive staff of Mobilization—as one after another ran
afoul of city government. In the end, only a few projects survived.

Conflict stemmed primarily from jurisdictional squabbles between new neighborhood agencies, established with federal funds,
and traditional municipal departments. The fact that these new
agencies tried to serve ghetto groups by pressuring municipal
agencies also did not help; and, of course, local political leaders
soon realized that the new funds being channeled directly to
neighborhoods could not be exploited by them for patronage
and publicity. When the antipoverty program generated a similar
system of neighborhood agencies, but on a much larger scale,
mayors and local bureaucrats throughout the land were outraged.
The national administration subsequently retreated, conceding
new administrative guidelines providing for more city control.
The model cities program was subsequently designed to avoid
some of this conflict by funneling federal benefits to the ghetto
by way of city government. Thus it embraced local politicians,
but nevertheless subjected them to the federal requirement that
they negotiate and reach accommodations with ghetto residents
and leaders before funds would be allocated.

The originators of Mobilization for Youth often noted proudly
that Mobilization was a model for the early delinquency-prevention programs and, subsequently, for other community-action
programs. They attributed this influence to the power of the
new ideas of service being developed on the Lower East Side.
Mobilization was indeed influential, but not as a programmatic
model. It was influential because it had been an opportune
context in which the federal agencies could explore new modes of
intervention and collaboration in the cities. It was this political
strategy which became the "model" for later programs.[11]

## SUBORDINATION OF
## SOCIAL PLANNING

Most welfare-oriented professionals espouse a comprehensive,
rationalistic approach to policy-making; that is to say, public de-

cisions should be made in terms of first principles of knowledge and value and should take account of all the conditions pertinent to these first principles. Advocates of social planning extend this ideal, believing that the diverse activities of various agencies can presumably be coordinated in terms of coherent and consistent interpretations of public-policy issues.

But, as this history reveals, organizations enter into collaboration in quite another way. The bases for cooperation are the interests of the different parties rather than a comprehensive and rationalized scheme of action. "Public policy" is a conglomerate, bits and pieces of which are divided and shifted about to secure the support necessary for collective action.

In its first *Report to the President,* the President's Committee described the new Mobilization for Youth project as

> the most advanced program yet devised to combat delinquency on a broad scale. Never before have neighborhood workers, the city government, the federal government, private agencies, and a great university of the stature of Columbia University joined together for a planned coordinated attack on the sources of a delinquency. Mobilization for Youth is the first concrete example of the comprehensive local action we believe necessary to meet the complex problems facing today's youth (President's Committee on Juvenile Delinquency and Youth Crime, 1962: 20).[12]

The Mobilization for Youth project was indeed comprehensive, in the sense that an array of neighborhood, city and federal agencies had been brought into collaboration. In the process, however, a range of goals had been promulgated for the project, and a variety of programs and structures had been incorporated. Most of the goals were very general and possibly even contradictory. Moreover, the relationship of goals to concrete programs and structures was at best unclear.[13]

## SCIENTIFIC INVESTIGATION OF SOCIAL POLICY

From the perspective of its original NIMH sponsors, the Mobilization project was a scientific investigation of delinquency-prevention techniques. Indeed, some of the early publicity de-

scribed the project as a new venture in "social engineering."
According to this view the project area was, in effect, a sixty-seven-
block laboratory in which the service programs would be carried
out as a series of scientific experiments.

A scientific investigation entailed several requirements, none
easy to meet. It meant that the programs would be designed with
reference to research surveys conducted during the earlier planning period. It also meant that the results of the action programs
would be carefully evaluated by scientific research. Finally, a
scientific investigation meant that the overall framework for the
service programs was derived from basic theoretical formulations
regarding delinquency. Little of this was in fact realizable.

For research data to be useful in formulating programs, an extended wait would be required to permit an interchange between
data and program designs. But most of the local organizational
backers of Mobilization, as well as the practitioners hired as staff,
wanted visible services, and quickly. As a result, the scheduling
of research and the planning of action were contemporaneous;
otherwise, the action programs (and presumably the goal of reducing delinquency) would have been considerably delayed.

Even if such a delay had been acceptable, the research could
be useful in designing programs suggested by the opportunity-
theory perspective only if the data gathered were pertinent to
that perspective. One of the major devices used by the research
team was the attitude survey, through which adolescents and
adults in the community were questioned about their opinions
and perceptions on a range of items, particularly their attitudes
toward delinquency and their perceptions of opportunities. Such
surveys have become very popular in sociology, and survey
methodology has become highly refined. But the information
suggested as relevant by the opportunity-theory perspective—the
distribution of employment opportunities, for example, or the
existence of institutional barriers to educational achievement or
to occupational mobility—could not be gathered by com-
munity-attitude surveys. Although research techniques were well
suited to conducting surveys, pertinent research on institutional
structures was difficult to develop. No less important (as became
evident when such studies were suggested), these institutions
were not willing to lend themselves to research scrutiny, and the
project had no means of coercing them.

Several studies were designed with the intent of evaluating program outcomes; however, the rigid requirements of that kind of experimental research were in continual tension with the imperatives of providing services, and only a few of the studies were successfully completed. For example, experimental research required that control groups be set up, meaning that some people would arbitrarily be denied services and others would arbitrarily be selected for services. An experimental design also required that each program and its service population remain discrete— that is, that the diverse program activities not overlap and contaminate each other. Such restrictions seemed intolerable to practitioners who saw services as filling human needs, and who also believed in the multifaceted approach. Moreover, practitioners, particularly in a neighborhood-based project, had to concern themselves with maintaining the goodwill of their clientele, who could scarcely be expected to appreciate the scientific investigation of social policy as grounds for denying or limiting services.

If program outcomes were to be evaluated by research, program activities would also have to be clearly structured and stable so that the research studies would be evaluating some definable method and not a fluid and changing process of uncertain character. But practitioners could not be bound in advance, trusting as they did to their experience and art in dealing with situations that could not be fully appreciated at the outset and which, in any case, were always changing. Finally, evaluation of programs required that the intended outcomes be defined by researchable indices, preferably subject to quantifiable measurement. Most social-welfare services, however, are associated with valued outcomes of a very diffuse and qualitative nature. A process of specification and quantification was likely to limit the focus to outcomes that could be clearly described and measured, and these were likely to be both different from and fewer than the outcomes considered pertinent by the practitioners.

In short, neither research interests nor research personnel were so authoritative as to structure the service programs or to force definition of their intended outcomes. Mobilization for Youth was a collaborative endeavor, backed by groups with research interests and groups with social-welfare interests. Accordingly, the project undertook both research and social-welfare operations,

blending and compromising both research and service imperatives.

Quite apart from the limitations imposed by a project in
which practitioners—and not academics—had considerable say,
the goal of a scientific experiment in social policy was formidable, even in the abstract. The basic theory of delinquency and
opportunity was far too broad and abstract to be "tested" by
researching concrete programs. Such an extension of the theory
would have been an overwhelming intellectual task. In any case,
the kinds of evaluation that would be made possible by such an
extension of the theory would not test theory but only specific
propositions describing the action strategies. This inherent gap
between basic theory and concrete action did not seem to be
recognized by the federal agencies responsible, which were only
too willing to borrow the authority of science to support their
endeavors.


INSTITUTIONAL CHANGE

To the Congress, the administration and those in the wider
public who paid attention, Mobilization for Youth was a delinquency-prevention project, funded principally from delinquency appropriations designated by the Congress.[14] According
to the project's own statements, reducing delinquency depended
on "community development," involving far-reaching changes in
the occupational structure, in the schools and in a range of other
institutions that shaped life opportunities in the poor community.
Of these, change in the occupational structure to increase employment opportunities for lower-class youth was considered
most important.

But as the planners scrutinized the strategies available to a
neighborhood-based endeavor with no jurisdiction over other
public agencies, it became apparent that a local project could
affect employment only in rather insignificant ways: by providing
work-training slots for out-of-school youth and by putting some
on the project's own payroll. The schools, as it turned out, were
also largely inaccessible to the project. At most, school personnel
could be induced to join in programs auxiliary to the regular

school curriculum. Community development had been conceived
as requiring radical changes in a number of major institutions,
but the project did not control these institutions and so was
thrown back upon the small and peripheral programs it could
generate out of its own resources.

If Mobilization did not control other institutions, it might still
be able to stimulate them to change, at least in the view of the
sponsoring federal agencies. The principal strategy to promote
institutional change, whether in the local voluntary agencies or
the public services, was to be co-optation.[15] The agencies to be
affected, such as the Board of Education and the Department of
Welfare, should be involved in the project; in this way they
would be influenced by the new program ideas. Thus, its early
concern for change in local social-agency practice led NIMH to
require the collaboration of the voluntary agencies within
Mobilization's jurisdiction. Subsequently, the President's Committee on Juvenile Delinquency and Youth Crime, concentrating
on the public services, required the involvement of the city government. In the end, the project had multiple ties to outside
agencies, both public and private, which helped fund the project,
sat on its board and shared in the administration of many of
the programs.[16]

Federal funds were, of course, the principal incentive for inducing collaboration. Once they were collaborators, the agencies
would be exposed to the merits of the innovative programs and
also to continuing persuasion by the project staff. But as it turned
out, once the funds were granted there was no way of ensuring
subsequent adoption of pilot programs. Moreover, the strategy
of inducing change through co-optation was pursued on all levels
of the project; the city and local agencies, which were the targets
of change, were also on the governing board of the project and
so were often more influential than influenced.

Institutional change meant different things to different participants in the project. To the President's Committee on
Juvenile Delinquency and Youth Crime it meant especially that
the Mobilization project should be used to stimulate the reorganization of the public agencies in the direction of rationally
planned coordination of services. This view was also prominent
in the city administrator's office, which saw planning as its own
proper function and Mobilization for Youth as a way to begin

to implement it. According to these views, Mobilization was an administrative experiment which would mark the path for future reorganization of the public services. The Mobilization project would thus initiate "comprehensive" and "coordinated" services by the liaisons it formed with the major public social-welfare agencies. For Mobilization to be instrumental in developing public planning, however, it would need considerable influence over the public services, which, as experience showed, it did not have.

Alternatively, it was also thought that Mobilization might *demonstrate* "comprehensive" and "coordinated" programming within the boundaries of its own activities. However, the project was not structured to do even this, for each of the programs within the project had considerable latitude. Each was staffed by professionals who thought of themselves as dealing with quite distinctive problems to which they brought quite distinctive techniques. Program divisions within the project even formed their own external organizational liaisons. In any case, if Mobilization for Youth were to demonstrate comprehensive and coordinated planning only within its own boundaries, it would fall far short of addressing the social conditions believed to underlie delinquency.

## CONTRADICTIONS AND ACCOMMODATIONS

These contradictions never overwhelmed the project planners, perhaps because they were wise enough not to make too strenuous an attempt to derive program activities from statements about the goals of the project. The battery of programs was formed in quite another way—through innumerable accommodations with the different organizational partners. Even the local agencies, which were in the end only minor partners, still got their share of funds for counseling and recreational activities. But while statements about goals did not dictate this process of accommodation, they were still useful. All of the agencies could share not only in the benefits of the programs but also in the prestige attending these lofty purposes. The local agencies, by making an early bid for funds, had brought the federal strategy for the inner city to the Lower East Side. In this way they not only had gotten new program money but also had transformed their jurisdictional terrain into a sixty-seven-block laboratory in community development to prevent delinquency— and poverty—by strategies of innovation and experimentation, and by comprehensive and coordinated reorganization of social services.

## CONCLUSION

As the proposals of the Great Society fade into history, liberals are becoming skeptical of government social-welfare programs. Somehow the new measures proliferated without much impact on the conditions that were presumably to be dealt with: Housing legislation did not produce much housing, at least for the groups who needed it most; employment measures reached minuscule numbers; public welfare has seemed to perpetuate the misery it was supposed to alleviate.

The critics who analyze these failures often view government social-welfare programs as hamstrung by a kind of persistent incompetence, an incompetence amplified by the complexity of our contemporary social problems. Goals are said to be hazy and ill defined; implementing structures and programs are designed carefully or inexpertly; and day-to-day bureaucratic operations are allowed to proceed as if by their own volition, disconnected from program and goals.

Thus, Daniel P. Moynihan (1966), writing about the community-action component of the poverty program, says that the difficulties encountered resulted from the diverse and contradictory goals with which the program was saddled. He points out "at least four distinct—and, generally speaking, incompatible— understandings of what constituted 'community action.' " To some, it was a "device for coordinating such programs so as to have maximum effect. The guiding principle [was] efficiency." To others, the goal was to mobilize the poor, to give them "a sense of power by means of community organization. This was to be achieved by inducing conflict: 'to rub raw the sores of discontent.' " To still others, the "guiding principle was neither efficiency nor conflict, but simply the provision of services [which would] enhance local capacities for self-help." Finally, some viewed community action as simple political pragmatism. The programs could "pass the Congress, help win the presidential election, and eliminate poverty, in perhaps that order" (Moynihan, 1966:5–6).

Moynihan is no doubt right in saying that these and other goals were associated with community action. However, by resting his criticism there he draws quite the wrong conclusion.[17] This was no failure of official and professional competence, as he implies. What appears as a government apparatus mired in confusion and ineptness is in fact a reflection of the political underpinnings of social-welfare measures—measures spawned in the first place to maintain a political leadership, and then continuously adapted to a changing political environment. In that process of adaptation, public goals come to be regarded less as a set of first principles guiding action and more as a political resource. Goals can be formulated, broadened, diffused and multiplied to suit political needs.

Similarly, the concrete programs and structures launched under the banner of lofty public goals are in fact formed to deal with the various political circumstances of any agency and to suit the political leadership on which the agency depends. The resulting cumbersomeness of government programs may be unintelligible to the critic who scrutinizes goals and programs to discern the paradigm for rational action. But the motivating force in government action, the force that shapes public goals and the programs and structures created in their name, reflects another sort of rationalism—the adaptive rationalism through which a political system and its member parts are maintained.

## NOTES

[1] The Civil Rights Act of 1964 was not submitted until February 1963, after Kennedy's position had been strengthened by an unprecedented midterm victory. Until then, he did very little aside from

signing an executive order banning discrimination in federally subsidized housing (which he did nothing to implement) and backing a
bill to ease voter literacy requirements.

2 For a description of the emergence of direct federal-city funding relations during the thirties and forties in the context of prevailing federal-state granting patterns, see Martin (1965).

3 This dilemma is vividly represented in the wording of the Economic Opportunity Act of 1964, which requires "maximum feasible participation" of the poor (a tactic to stimulate responsiveness in local
agencies), and at the same time requires the inclusion of political, business, labor and religious leaders; the school board; the employment
service; the public-welfare department; private social agencies; and
neighborhood settlement houses.

4 While Marris and Rein cover some of the events analyzed in
this chapter, they proceed from a very different perspective. Underlying their account is a view of reform as being quite separate from
interests and interest politics—especially from local politics. Accordingly, they treat reform ideals as independent forces, reformers as
essentially disinterested, and the advent of reform as a rare flowering
of public idealism. It is my contention in this chapter that reformers in this case were definitely interested and that their ideals reflected
and complemented their interests—in short, that reform itself must
be understood as one of the themes in the play of interest politics.

5 Many of the historical observations in this chapter draw on evidence collected in an intensive study of Mobilization for Youth covering the period from 1957, when the project was first conceived, until
the fall of 1963, one year after the action program was put into
operation. All quotations not otherwise identified are taken directly
from written memoranda, correspondence, or interviews with participants.

6 By stressing the need for research in delinquency, the National
Institute for Mental Health emphasized in its 1959 report to Congress
just how little was known in the field. Indeed, the report was so
convincing on these grounds that a skeptical reader might wonder
what basis remained for the arguments recommending reforms in treatment methods that the report went on to make.

7 Quoted from one of the earliest Mobilization documents prepared under the auspices of the Henry Street Settlement.

8 This is by no means unusual. NIMH relied on reputable professionals as consultants for its grant decisions. It also sought to make
its grants to reputable professionals. The result was that the funder
and the funded were in many cases associated, or even identical.

9 This account is based on the reports of several people who

were present at the deliberations of the NIMH ad hoc review committee.

[10] For a more detailed discussion of this use of ideas in smoothing the way for political action, see Piven (1968b).

[11] Direct intervention in the ghetto was not the federal government's only strategy for dealing with its political troubles in the cities, although it came to be the most important (see Cloward and Piven, 1967; Piven and Cloward, 1967).

[12] In 1963 Congresswoman Edith Green (D-Ore.) took it upon herself to denounce these claims as extravagant, demanding more modest and practical endeavors, much to the discomfiture of administration officials.

[13] The planning document that described the battery of Mobilization programs, and the structural arrangements to implement them, ran to over 600 pages; even so it was often far from detailed (see Mobilization for Youth, 1961).

[14] During the early sixties another "public problem," that of poverty—especially urban poverty—was rapidly gaining prominence, a shift encouraged by the administration's gradual expansion of its strategy for the inner cities. The opportunity theory of the Mobilization planners lent itself nicely to the shift. Delinquency was presumably associated with inequities in opportunities in the poor community. The language describing programs to reduce delinquency included such phrases as "total community development," which anticipated the language of subsequent federal programs initiated to fight the War on Poverty. It was with the greatest of ease that, in a statement of goals adopted by the Mobilization board in June 1963 (a year after the project had entered its action phase), the first priority was changed to reducing poverty "in order to prevent and control delinquency." In 1964 poverty funds became available and Mobilization became a full-fledged poverty program.

[15] Some time after the project was in operation, another strategy for stimulating institutional change began to be stressed in delinquency prevention as well as in other federal programs, a strategy that is familiar to the reader as "maximum feasible participation of the poor." For a discussion of this later strategy, see Piven (1966; 1970).

[16] Outside agencies sometimes were coadministrators of particular programs and sometimes were contracting agents who actually took over responsibility for a program.

[17] Moynihan might have gone on to point out that each of the goals he describes was in itself rather overwhelming and, in any case, only loosely related to the programs actually launched in the local communities.

## REFERENCES

Anderson, Martin.
  1964  *The Federal Bulldozer*. Cambridge, Mass.: M.I.T. Press.
Beck, Bertram M.
  1965  "Innovations in Combatting Juvenile Delinquency." *Children*
       12 (March–April):69–74.
Children's Bureau.
  1960  *Report to the Congress on Juvenile Delinquency*. [Prepared
       jointly by the National Institute of Mental Health, National
       Institute of Health, Public Health Service, and Children's
       Bureau.] Washington, D.C.: Children's Bureau, Department
       of Health, Education and Welfare (January).
Cloward, Richard A., and Lloyd E. Ohlin.
  1960  *Delinquency and Opportunity: A Theory of Delinquent
       Gangs*. New York: Free Press of Glencoe.
Cloward, Richard A., and Frances Fox Piven.
  1967  "Corporate Imperialism for the Poor." The *Nation* 205(Octo-
       ber 16):365–367.
Gans, Herbert.
  1965  "The Failure of Urban Renewal." *Commentary* 39 (April):
       29–37.
Hartman, Chester.
  1964  "The Housing of Relocated Families." *Journal of the Amer-
       ican Institute of Planners* 30 (November):266–286.
Marris, Peter, and Martin Rein.
  1967  *Dilemmas of Social Reform: Poverty and Community Action
       in the United States*. London: Routledge and Kegan Paul.
Martin, Roscoe C.
  1965  *The Cities and the Federal System*. New York: Atherton
       Press.
Mobilization for Youth.
  1961  *Proposal for the Prevention and Control of Delinquency by
       Expanding Opportunities*. New York: Mobilization for
       Youth, Inc.
Moynihan, Daniel P.
  1966  "What Is 'Community Action'?" *Public Interest* (Fall): 3–8.
Piven, Frances Fox.
  1966  "Participation of Residents in Neighborhood Community-
       Action Programs." *Social Work* 2(January):73–80.
  1967a "Professionalism as a Political Skill: The Case of a Poverty
       Program." Pp. 37–50 in *Personnel in Anti-Poverty Programs:*

*Implications for Social Work Education.* New York: Council on Social Work Education.

1967b "The Demonstration: A Federal Strategy for Local Change," in George Brager and Francis Purcell (eds.), *Community Action Against Poverty.* New Haven, Conn.: College and University Press Services.

1968a "Advocacy as a Strategy of Political Management." *Perspecta, the Yale Architectural Review* 12 (Fall):37–38.

1968b "Dilemmas in Social Planning: A Case Inquiry." *Social Service Review* 42(June):197–206.

1970 "The Great Society as Political Strategy." *Columbia Forum* 13(Summer): 17–22.

Piven, Frances Fox, and Richard A. Cloward.

1967 "Black Control of the Cities: Heading It Off with Metropolitan Government." Part I. *New Republic* 157(September 30):19–21; Part II. *New Republic* 157(October 7):15–19.

President's Committee on Juvenile Delinquency and Youth Crime.

1962 Report to the President [May 31]. Washington, D.C.: Office of the President of the United States (mimeographed).

# The Urban Crisis: Who Got What, and Why?

FRANCES FOX PIVEN

For quite a while, complaints about the urban fiscal crisis have been droning on, becoming as familiar as complaints about big government, or big bureaucracy, or high taxes—and almost as boring as well. Now suddenly the crisis seems indeed to be upon us: School closings are threatened, library services are curtailed, subway trains go unrepaired, welfare grants are cut, all because big-city costs have escalated to the point where local governments can no longer foot the bill. Yet for all the talk, and all the complaints, there has been no convincing explanation of just how it happened that, quite suddenly in the 1960s, the whole municipal housekeeping system seemed to become virtually unmanageable. This is especially odd because, not long ago, the study of city politics and city services was a favorite among American political scientists, and one subject they had gone far to illuminate. Now, with everything knocked askew, they seem to have very little to say that could stand as political analysis.

To be sure, there is a widely accepted explanation. The big cities are said to be in trouble because of the "needs" of blacks for services—a view given authority by the professionals who man the service agencies and echoed by the politicians who depend upon these agencies. Service "needs," the argument goes, have been increasing at a much faster rate than local revenues. The alleged reason is demographic: The large number of impover-

Originally published in *1984 Revisited: Prospects for American Politics*, Robert Paul Wolff, editor, New York, Alfred A. Knopf, Inc., 1973. Reprinted with the permission of the editor and the publisher.

ished black southern migrants to the cities presumably requires far greater investments in services, including more elaborate educational programs, more frequent garbage collection, more intensive policing, if the city is to be maintained at accustomed levels of civil decency and order. Thus, city agencies have been forced to expand and elaborate their activities. However, the necessary expansion is presumably constricted for lack of local revenues, particularly since the better-off taxpaying residents and businesses have been leaving the city (hastened on their way by the black migration).[1] To this standard explanation of the crisis, there is also a standard remedy: namely, to increase municipal revenues, whether by enlarging federal and state aid to the cities or by redrawing jurisdictional boundaries to recapture suburban taxpayers.[2]

It is true, of course, that black children who receive little in the way of skills or motivation at home may require more effort from the schools; that densely packed slums require more garbage collection; that disorganized neighborhoods require more policing. For instance, the New York City Fire Department reports a 300 percent increase in fires the last twenty years. But fires and similar calamities that threaten a wide public are one thing; welfare, education and health services, which account for by far the largest portion of big-city budgets, quite another. And while by any objective measure the new residents of the city have greater needs for such services, there are several reasons to doubt that the urban crisis is the simple result of rising needs and declining revenues.

For one thing, the trend in service budgets suggests otherwise. Blacks began to pour into the cities in very large numbers after World War II, but costs did not rise precipitously until the mid-1960s.[3] *In other words, the needs of the black poor were not recognized for two decades.* For another, any scrutiny of agency budgets shows that, except for public welfare, *the expansion of services to the poor, as such, does not account for a very large proportion of increased expenditures.* It was other groups, *mainly organized provider groups,* who reaped the lion's share of the swollen budgets. The notion that services are being strained to respond to the needs of the new urban poor, in short, takes little account either of when the strains occurred or of the groups who actually benefited from increased expenditures.

# THE GREAT SOCIETY

These two facts should lead us to look beyond the "rising
needs–declining revenues" theory for an explanation of urban
troubles. And once we do, perhaps some political common sense
can emerge. School administrators and sanitation commissioners
may describe their agencies as ruled by professional standards and
as shaped by disinterested commitments to the public good, and
thus define rising costs as a direct and proper response to the
needs of people. But schools and sanitation departments are,
after all, agencies of local government, substructures of the local
political apparatus, and are managed in response to local political forces. The mere fact that people are poor or that the poor
need special services has never led government to respond. Service
agencies are political agencies, administered to deal with political
problems, not service problems.

Now this view is not especially novel. Indeed, if there is any
aspect of the American political system that was persuasively
analyzed in the past, it was the political uses of municipal
services in promoting allegiance and muting conflict. Public
jobs, contracts and services were dispensed by city bosses to
maintain loyal cadres and loyal followers among the heterogeneous groups of the city. Somehow political analysts have for-
gotten this in their accounts of the contemporary urban crisis,
testimony perhaps to the extent to which the doublethink of
professional bureaucrats has befogged the common sense of us
all. That is, we are confused by changes in the style of urban-
service politics, failing to see that although the style has changed,
the function has not. In the era of the big-city machine, municipal authorities managed to maintain a degree of consensus and
allegiance among diverse groups by distributing public goods in
the form of private favors. Today public goods are distributed
through the service bureaucracies. With that change, the process
of dispensing public goods has become more formalized, the
struggles between groups more public, and the language of city
politics more professional. As I will try to explain a little later,
these changes were in some ways crucial in the development of
what we call the urban crisis. My main point for now, however,
is that while we may refer to the schools or the sanitation department as if they are politically neutral, these agencies yield up a
whole variety of benefits, and it is by distributing, redistributing
and adapting these payoffs of the city agencies that urban political

leaders manage to keep peace and build allegiances among the diverse groups in the ctiy. In other words, the jobs, contracts, perquisites, as well as the actual services of the municipal house-keeping agencies, are just as much the substance of urban politics as they ever were.

All of which is to say that when there is a severe disturbance in the administration and financing of municipal services, the underlying cause is likely to be a fundamental disturbance in political relations. To account for the service "crisis" we should look at the changing relationship between political forces—at rising group conflict and weakening allegiances—and the way in which these disturbances set off an avalanche of new demands. To cope with these strains, political leaders expanded and pro-liferated the benefits of the city agencies. What I shall argue, in sum, is that the urban crisis is not a crisis of rising needs but a crisis of rising demands.

Any number of circumstances may disturb existing political relationships, with the result that political leaders are less capable of restraining the demands of various groups. Severe economic dislocations may activate groups that previously asked little of government, as in the 1930s. Or groups may rise in the economic structure, acquiring political force and pressing new demands as a result. Or large-scale migrations may alter the balance between groups. Any of these situations may generate sharp antagonism among groups, and as some new groups acquire a measure of influence, they may undermine established political relationships. In the period of uncertainty that ensues, discontent is likely to spread, political alignments may shift, and allegiances to a politi-cal leadership may become insecure. In the context of this gen-eral unrest, political leaders, unsure of their footing, are far more likely to respond to the specific demands of specific groups for enlarged benefits or new "rights." Periods of political insta-bility, in other words, nurture new claims and claimants. This is what happened in the cities in the 1960s, and it happened at a time when the urban political system was uniquely ill equipped to curb the spiral of rising demands that resulted.

## THE POLITICAL DISTURBANCES THAT
## LED TO RISING DEMANDS

If the service needs of the black poor do not account for the
troubles in the cities, the political impact of the black migration
probably does. Massive shifts of population are almost always
disturbing to a political system, for new relations have to be
formed between a political leadership and constituent groups.
The migration of large numbers of blacks from the rural South
to a few core cities during and after World War II, leading many
middle-class white constituents to leave for the suburbs, posed
just this challenge to the existing political organization of the
cities. But for a long time local governments resisted responding
to the newcomers with the services, symbols and benefits that
might have won the allegiance of these newcomers, just as the
allegiance of other groups had previously been won.

The task of political integration was made difficult by at least
four circumstances. One was the very magnitude of the influx.
Between 1940 and 1960, nearly 4 million blacks left the land
and, for the most part, settled in big northern cities. Consequently, by 1960 at least one in five residents of our fifty largest
cities was a black, and in the biggest cities the proportions were
much greater. It is no exaggeration to say that the cities were
inundated by sheer numbers.

Second, these large numbers were mainly lower-class blacks,
whose presence aroused ferocious race and class hatreds, especially
among the white ethnics who lived in neighborhoods bordering
the ghettos and who felt their homes and schools endangered.
As ghetto numbers enlarged, race and class polarities worsened,
and political leaders, still firmly tied to the traditional inhabitants of the cities, were in no position to give concessions to the
black poor.

Not only was race pitted against race, class against class, but
the changing style of urban politics made concessions to conflicting groups a very treacherous matter. Just because the jobs,
services and contracts that fueled the urban political organization
were no longer dispensed covertly, in the form of private favors,
but rather as matters of public policy, each concession was des-
tined to become a subject of open political conflict. As a result,

mayors found it very difficult to finesse their traditional constituents: New public housing for blacks, for example, could not
be concealed, and every project threatened to arouse a storm of
controversy. Despite their growing numbers and their obvious
needs, therefore, blacks got very little in the way of municipal
benefits throughout the 1940s and 1950s. Chicago, where the
machine style was still entrenched, gave a little more; the Cook
County AFDC rolls, for example, rose by eighty percent in the
1950s, and blacks were given some political jobs. But in most
cities the local service agencies resisted the newcomers. In New
York City and Los Angeles, for example, the AFDC rolls remained virtually unchanged in the 1950s. In many places public
housing was brought to a halt; urban renewal generally became
the instrument of black removal; and half the major southern
cities (which also received large numbers of black migrants from
rural areas) actually managed to reduce their welfare rolls, often
by as much as half.[4]

Finally, when blacks entered the cities they were confronted by
a relatively new development in city politics: namely, the existence of large associations of public employees, whether teachers,
policemen, sanitation men or the like. The provider groups not
only had a very large stake in the design and operation of public
programs—for there is hardly any aspect of public policy that
does not impinge on matters of working conditions, job security
or fringe benefits—but they had become numerous enough, organized enough and independent enough to wield substantial
influence in matters affecting their interests.

The development of large, well-organized and independent
provider groups has been going on for many years, probably beginning with the emergence of the civil-service merit system at
the turn of the century (a development usually credited to the
efforts of reformers who sought to improve the quality of municipal services, to eliminate graft and to dislodge machine leaders).[5]
But although the civil service originated in the struggle between
party leaders and reformers, it launched municipal employees as
an independent force. As city services expanded, the enlarging
numbers of public employees began to form associations. Often
these originated as benevolent societies, such as New York City's
Patrolmen's Benevolent Association, which formed in the 1890s.
Protected by the merit system, these associations gradually gained

some influence in their own right, and they exerted that influence at both the municipal and the state level to shape legislation and to monitor personnel policies so as to protect and advance their occupational interests.

The result was that, over time, many groups of public employees managed to win substantial control over numerous matters affecting their jobs and their agencies: entrance requirements, tenure guarantees, working conditions, job prerogatives, promotion criteria, retirement benefits. Except where wages were concerned, other groups in the cities rarely became sufficiently aroused to block efforts by public employees to advance their interests. But all of this also meant that when blacks arrived in the cities, local political leaders did not control the jobs—and, in cases where job prerogatives had been precisely specified by regulation, did not even control the services—that might have been given as concessions to the black newcomers.

Under the best of circumstances, of course, the task of integrating a new and uprooted rural population into local political structures would have taken time and would have been difficult. But for all of the reasons given, local government was showing little taste for the task. As a result, a large population that had been set loose from southern feudal institutions was not absorbed into the regulating political institutions (or economic institutions, for they were also resisted there) of the city. Eventually that dislocated population became volatile, both in the streets and at the polls. By 1960 that volatility forced the federal government to take an unprecedented role in urban politics.[6]

Urban blacks, who had been loyal Democrats for almost three decades, had begun to defect even as their numbers grew, signaling the failure of the municipal political machinery. New ways to reach and reward the urban black voter were needed. Accordingly, administration analysts began to explore strategies to cement the allegiance of the urban black vote to the national party. What emerged, not all at once but over a number of years, was a series of federal service programs directed to the ghetto. The first appropriations were small, as with the Juvenile Delinquency and Youth Offenses Control Act of 1961, but each program enlarged upon the other, up until the model-cities legislation of 1966. Some of the new programs—in manpower development, in education, in health—were relatively straightforward. All they did was give new funds to local agencies to be used to provide jobs or services for the poor. Thus, funds appropriated under Title I of the Elementary and Secondary Education Act of 1965 were earmarked for educational facilities for poor children; the medicaid program enacted in 1965 reimbursed health agencies and physicians for treating the poor; and manpower agencies were funded specifically to provide jobs or job training for the poor.

Other of the new federal programs were neither so simple nor so straightforward, and these were the ones that became the hallmark of the Great Society. The federal memoranda describing them were studded with terms like "inner city," "institutional change" and "maximum feasible participation." But if this language was often confusing, the programs themselves ought not to have been. The "inner city," after all, was a euphemism for the ghetto, and activities funded under such titles as delinquency prevention, mental health, antipoverty or model cities turned out, in the streets of the cities, to look very much alike. What they looked like was nothing less than the old political machine.

Federal funds were used to create new storefront-style agencies in the ghettos, staffed with professionals who helped local people find jobs, obtain welfare or deal with school officials. Neighborhood leaders were also hired, named community workers, neighborhood aides or whatever, but in fact close kin to the old ward heelers, for they drew larger numbers of people into the new programs, spreading the federal spoils.

But federal spoils were not enough, for there were not many of them. If blacks were to be wrapped into the political organization of the cities, the traditional agencies of local government, which controlled the bulk of federal, state and local appropriations, had to be reoriented. Municipal agencies had to be made to respond to blacks.

Various tactics to produce such reform were tried, at first under the guise of experiments in "institutional change," but the experiments got little cooperation from local bureaucrats. Therefore, as turbulence spread in the northern ghettos, the federal officials began to try another way to promote institutional change—"maximum feasible participation of residents of the areas and members of the groups served." Under that slogan the

Great Society programs gave money to ghetto organizations, which then used the money to harass city agencies. Community workers were hired to badger housing inspectors and to pry loose welfare payments. Lawyers on the federal payroll took municipal agencies to court on behalf of ghetto clients. Later the new programs helped organize the ghetto poor to picket the welfare department or to boycott the school system.

In these various ways, then, the federal government intervened in local politics and forced local government to do what it had earlier failed to do. Federal dollars and federal authority were used to resuscitate the functions of the political machine, on the one hand *by spurring local service agencies to respond to the black newcomers,* and on the other *by spurring blacks to make demands upon city services.*

As it turned out, blacks made their largest tangible gains from this process through the public-welfare system. Total national welfare costs rose from about $4 billion in 1960 to nearly $15 billion in 1970. Big cities that received the largest numbers of black and Spanish-speaking migrants and that were most shaken by the political reverberations of that migration also experienced the largest welfare-budget rises. In New York, Los Angeles and Baltimore, for example, the AFDC rolls quadrupled, and costs rose even faster. In some cities, moreover, welfare costs were absorbing an ever-larger share of the local budget, a bigger piece of the public pie. In New York City, for example, welfare costs absorbed about twelve percent of the city's budget in the 1950s; but by 1970 the share going to welfare had grown to about twenty-five percent (of a much larger budget), mainly because the proportion of the city's population on Aid to Families of Dependent Children increased from 2.6 percent in 1960 to 11.0 percent in 1970.[7] In other words, the blacks who triggered the disturbances received their biggest payoffs from welfare,[8] mainly because other groups were not competing within the welfare system for a share of relief benefits.[9]

But if blacks got welfare, that was just about all they got. Less obvious than the emergence of black demands—but much more important in accounting for increasing service costs—was the reaction of organized whites to these political developments, particularly the groups who had direct material stakes in the running of the local services. If the new upthrust of black claims threatened and jostled many groups in the city, none were so alert or so shrill as those who had traditionally gotten the main benefits of the municipal services. These were the people who depended, directly or indirectly, on the city treasury for their livelihood: They worked in the municipal agencies, in agencies that were publicly funded (e.g., voluntary hospitals), in professional services that were publicly reimbursed (e.g., doctors) or in businesses that depended on city contracts (e.g., contractors and construction workers). Partly they were incited by black claims that seemed to threaten their traditional preserves. Partly they were no longer held in check by stable relationships with political leaders, for these relations had weakened or become uncertain or even turned to enmity: Indeed, in some cases, the leaders themselves had been toppled, shaken loose by the conflict and instability of the times. In effect, the groups who worked for or profited from city government had become unleashed, at the same time that newcomers were snapping at their heels.

The result was that the provider groups reacted with a rush of new demands. And these groups had considerable muscle to back up their claims. Not only were they unusually numerous and well organized, but they were allied to broader constituencies by their class and ethnic ties and by their union affiliations. Moreover, their demands for increased benefits, whether higher salaries or lower work load or greater autonomy, were always couched in terms of protecting the professional standards of the city services, a posture that helped win them broad public support. As a result, even when the organized providers backed up their demands by closing the schools, or stopping the subways, or letting the garbage pile up, many people were ready to blame the inconveniences on political officials.

Local political leaders, their ties to their constituencies undermined by population shifts and spreading discontent, were in a poor position to resist or temper these escalating demands, especially the demands of groups with the power to halt the services on which a broader constituency depended. Instead, to maintain their position they tried to expand and elaborate the benefits—the payrolls, the contracts, the perquisites and the services—of the municipal agencies.

Nor, as had been true in the era of the machine, was it easy to use these concessions to restore stable relationships. Where once political leaders had been able to anticipate or allay the claims of various groups, dealing with them one by one, now each concession was public, precipitating rival claims from other groups, each demand ricocheting against the other in an upward spiral. Not only did public concessions excite rivalry, but political officials lost the ability to hold groups in check in another way as well; unlike their machine predecessors, they could attach few conditions to the concessions they made. Each job offered, each wage increase conceded, each job prerogative granted was now ensconced in civil-service regulations or union contracts and, thus firmly secured, could not be withdrawn. Political leaders had lost any leverage in their dealings; each concession simply became the launching pad for higher demands. Instead of regular exchange relationships, open conflict and uncertainty became the rule. The result was a virtual run upon the city treasury by a host of organized groups in the city, each competing with the other for a larger share of municipal benefits. Benefits multiplied and budgets soared—and so did the discontent of various groups with the schools, or police, or housing, or welfare, or health. To illustrate, we need to examine the fiscal impact of mounting political claims in greater detail.

## RISING DEMANDS AND THE FISCAL CRISIS

Education is a good example, for it is the single largest service run by localities, accounting for forty percent of the outlays of state and local government in 1968, up from thirty percent in 1948.[10] The huge expenditures involved in running the schools are also potential benefits—jobs for teachers, contracts for maintenance and construction, and educational services for children— all things to be gained by different groups in the local community. Accordingly, the educational system became a leading target of black demands,[11] at first mainly in the form of the struggle for integrated schools. Later, worn down by local resistance to integration and guided by the Great Society programs that provided staff, meeting rooms, mimeograph machines, and lawyers to ghetto groups,[12] the difficult demands for integration were transformed into demands for "citizen participation," which meant a share of the jobs, contracts and status positions that the school system yields up.[13]

Blacks made some gains. Boards of education began hiring more black teachers, and some cities instituted schemes for "community control" that ensconced local black leaders in the lower echelons of the school hierarchy.[14] But the organized producer groups, whose salaries account for an estimated eighty percent of rising school costs,[15] made far larger gains. Incited by black claims that seemed to challenge their traditional preserves, and emboldened by a weak and conciliatory city government, the groups who depend on school budgets began rapidly to enlarge and entrench their stakes. Most evident in the scramble were teaching and supervisory personnel, who were numerous and well organized and became ever more strident—so much so that the opening of each school year is now signaled by news of teacher strikes in cities throughout the country. And threatened city officials strained to respond by expanding the salaries, jobs, programs and privileges they had to offer. One result was that average salaries in New York City, Chicago, Los Angeles, Philadelphia, Washington, D.C., and San Francisco topped the $10,000 mark by 1969, *in most instances having doubled* in the decade. Nationally, teachers' salaries have risen about eight percent each year since 1965.[16] Not only did the teachers win rapid increases in salaries but, often prompted by new black demands, they exploited contract negotiations and intensive lobbying to win new guarantees of job security, increased pensions and "improvements" in educational policy that have had the effect of increasing their own ranks—all of which drove up school budgets, especially in the big cities where blacks were concentrated.[17] In Baltimore, where the black population has reached forty-seven percent, the school budget increased from $57 million in 1961 to $184 million in 1971; in New Orleans from $28.5 million to $73.9 million in 1971; in Boston school costs rose from $35.4 million in 1961 to $95.7 million in 1971.[18] Total national educational costs, which in 1957 amounted to $12 billion, topped $40 billion by 1968,[19] and the U.S. Office of Education expects costs to continue to rise, by

at least thirty-seven percent by 1975. In this process, blacks may
have triggered the flood of new demands on the schools, but
organized whites turned out to be the main beneficiaries.

What happened in education happened in other services as
well. Costs rose precipitously across the board as mayors tried to
extend the benefits of the service agencies to quiet the discordant
and clamoring groups in the city. One way was to expand the
number of jobs, often by creating new agencies, so that there was
more to go around. Hence, in New York City the municipal
payroll expanded by over 145,000 jobs in the 1960s, and the rate
of increase doubled after Mayor John V. Lindsay took office in
1965.[20] By 1971, 381,000 people were on the municipal payroll.
Some 34,000 of these new employees were black and Puerto
Rican "paraprofessionals," according to the city's personnel
director. Others were Lindsay supporters, put on the payroll as
part of his effort to build a new political organization out of
the turmoil.[21] Most of the rest were new teachers, policemen and
social workers, some hired to compensate for reduced work loads
won by existing employees (teachers won reduced class sizes,
patrolmen the right to work in pairs), others hired to staff an
actual expansion that had taken place in some services to appease claimant groups who were demanding more welfare, safer
streets or better snow removal.[22] As a result, total state and local
governmental employment in the city rose from 8.2 percent of
the total labor force in 1960 to 14 percent in 1970. A similar
trend of expanded public employment took place in other big
cities. In Detroit state and local employment rose from 9 percent
of the labor force in 1960 to 12.2 percent in 1970; in Philadelphia
from 6.9 percent to 9.8 percent; in Los Angeles from 9.8 percent
to 12.0 percent; in San Francisco from 12.2 percent in 1960 to
15.2 percent in 1970.[23]

Another way to try to deal with the clamor was to concede
larger and larger salaries and more liberal pensions to existing
employees who were pressing new demands, and pressing hard,
with transit, or garbage, or police strikes (or sick-outs or slowdowns) that paralyzed whole cities.[24] In Detroit, garbage collectors allowed refuse to accumulate in the streets when the city
offered them only a six-percent wage increase after the police
won an eleven-percent increase.[25] In Cincinnati, municipal
laborers and garbage collectors threatened a "massive civil-dis-

obedience campaign" when they were offered less than the $945 annual raise won by policemen and firemen.[26] In Philadelphia, garbage collectors engaged in a slowdown when a policeman was appointed to head their department.[27] A San Francisco strike by 7500 city workers shut down the schools and the transit system and disrupted several other services simultaneously.[28] An unprecedented wildcat strike by New York City's policemen, already the highest-paid police force in the world, would have cost the city an estimated $56,936 a year for every policeman (and $56,214 for every fireman) if demands for salaries, pensions, fringe benefits and reduced work time had been conceded.[29] If these demands were perhaps a bit theatrical, the pay raises for city employees in New York City did average twelve percent each year in 1967, 1968 and 1969. Meanwhile, the U.S. Bureau of Labor Statistics reported that the earnings of health professionals in the city rose by eighty percent in the decade, at least double the increase in factory wages. In other cities across the country similar groups were making similar gains; municipal salaries rose by seven to ten percent in both 1968 and 1969, or about twice as fast as the Consumer Price Index.[30]

The pattern of crazily rising municipal budgets is the direct result of these diverse and pyramiding claims on city services, claims triggered by political instability.[31] Accordingly, budget trends followed political trends. New York City, for example, received about 1.25 million blacks and Puerto Ricans in the years between 1950 and 1965, while about 1.5 million whites left the city. The political reverberations of these shifts weakened the Democratic party organization and resulted in the Lindsay victory on a fusion ticket in 1965. But the Lindsay government was extremely unstable, without ties to established constituents, virtually without a political organization and extremely vulnerable to the demands of the different groups, including the ghetto groups whose support it was trying to cultivate. New York also had very strong and staunch provider groups, as everyone knows from the transit, garbage, teacher and police strikes, each of which in turn threatened municipal calamity. The subsequent escalation of demands by blacks and Puerto Ricans on the one hand, and municipal provider groups on the other, produced the much-publicized turmoil and conflict that wracked the city.

To deal with these troubles, city officials made concessions, with the result that the municipal budget almost quadrupled in the last decade. And as the turmoil rose, so did city costs: An annual budget rise of 6 percent in the 1950s and 8.5 percent in the early 1960s became an annual rise of 15 percent after 1965.[32] New York now spends half again as much per capita as other cities over a million (excluding educational costs), twice as much per capita as cities between 500,000 and a million, and three times as much as the other 288 cities.[33]

A few cities where the existing political organization was firmly entrenched and machine-style politics still strong were spared. Chicago is the notable example, and Chicago's political organization shows in lower welfare costs, in per-pupil expenditures that are half that of New York City, in garbage-collection costs of $22 a ton compared to $49 in New York City. Mayor Daley never lost his grip. With the white wards firmly in tow, he made modest concessions to blacks earlier and without fear of setting off a chain reaction of demands by other groups. And so he never gave as much, either to blacks or to organized whites. But most other large cities show a pattern of escalating discontent and escalating service budgets more like New York City than Chicago.[34] By 1970 the total costs of local government had risen about 350 percent over 1950.

The cities are unable to raise revenues commensurate with these expenditures; and they are unable to resist the claims that underlie rising expenditures. And that is what the fiscal crisis is all about. Cities exist only by state decree, and depend entirely on the state governments for their taxing powers.[35] Concretely this has meant that the states have taken for themselves the preferred taxes[36] leaving the localities to depend primarily on the property tax (which accounts for seventy percent of revenues raised by local governments),[37] supplemented by a local sales tax in many places, user charges (e.g., sewer and water fees) and, in some places, a local income tax.[38] The big cities have had little choice but to drive up these local taxes to which they are limited, but at serious costs.[39] New York City, for example, taxes property at rates twice the national average, yielding a property-tax roll three times as large as any other city. New York City also has an income tax, which is rising rapidly. Newark, plagued by racial conflict, ranks second in the nation in its rate of property tax.[40]

The exploitation of any of these taxes is fraught with dilemmas for localities. By raising either property or sale taxes excessively, they risk driving out the business and industry on which their tax rolls eventually depend, and risk also the political ire of their constituents. For instance, it was estimated that a one-percent increase in the New York City sales tax had the effect of driving six percent of all clothing and household-furnishing sales out beyond the city line, along with thousands of jobs.[41] A New York property-tax rate of four percent of true value on new improvements is thought by many to have acted as a brake on most new construction, excepting the very high-yielding office buildings and luxury apartments. Boston's six percent of true-value property tax brought private construction to a halt until the law was changed so that new improvements were taxed only half as heavily as existing buildings.[42] Increases in either sales- or property-tax rates thus entail the serious danger of diminishing revenues by eroding the tax base. To make matters worse, with the beginning of recession in 1969, revenues from sales and income taxes began to fall off, while the interest the cities had to pay for borrowing rose, at a time when local governments were going more and more into hock.[43]

## FISCAL CONSTRAINTS AND POLITICAL TURMOIL

In the face of fiscal constraints, demands on city halls do not simply stop. Indeed, a number of frustrated claimants seem ready for rebellion. When pension concessions to some employees in New York City were thwarted by the state legislature, the enraged municipal unions closed the bridges to the city and closed the sewage plants, while the president of Local 237 intoned that "Governor Rockefeller needs to be reminded that the teamsters are made of sterner stuff than the people of Czechoslovakia and Austria who caved in so easily to Hitler three decades ago."[44] If most groups were less dramatic in pressing their demands, it is probably because they were more quickly conciliated than these workers, many of whom were black and Puerto Rican. The political instability, which escalating demands both signify and exacerbate, rocked one city government after another. Indeed, many big-city mayors simply quit the job, something that does not happen very often in politics.

The reason they give is money—money to appease the anarchic demands of urban groups. Joseph Barr, former mayor of Pittsburgh and a past president of the United States Conference of Mayors, explained that "the main problem of any mayor of any city of any size is money . . . we are just choked by the taxes. The middle classes are fleeing to the suburbs and the tax base is going down and down . . . if the mayors don't get relief from the legislatures, God help them! . . . Any mayor who is not frustrated is not thinking." Arthur Naftalin, former mayor of Minneapolis and also a past president of the United States Conference of Mayors, said that the "most difficult and most important problem [is that the city] can't reach the resources. The states have kept the cities on a leash, tying them to the property tax—which is regressive. Old people and low-income people live in the city, and they catch the burden increasingly." Thomas C. Tarrington, mayor of Denver 1963–1968, when he resigned in midterm, said when he left:

> I hope to heaven the cities are not ungovernable . . . [but] with perhaps few if any exceptions, the financial and organizational structures of most large cities are hardly up to the needs of 1969 or 1970. Our cities were structured financially when we were a rural nation and our structures of government are such that the mayors lack not only the financial resources but the authority to do the job.

Ivan Allen, Jr., mayor of Atlanta since 1962: "At my age I question whether I would have been physically able to continue for another four years in the face of the constant pressure, the innumerable crises, and the confrontations that have occurred in the cities." A. D. Sillingson, mayor of Omaha from 1965: "I've gone through three and a half tough years in this racial business, and I could just stand so much." And the country's first black mayor, Carl B. Stokes of Cleveland, interviewed before he was reelected by the slimmest of margins in 1969, announced that the biggest challenge facing someone in his position was "obtaining the necessary money with which to meet the necessary needs of a big city."[45] Mr. Stokes declined to run again in 1971, leaving Cleveland politics fragmented

among eleven different candidates. The list of prominent mayors who threw in the sponge includes such celebrated urban
reformers as Jerome P. Cavanaugh of Detroit and Richard C.
Lee of New Haven. Nearly half the United States Conference
of Mayors Executive Committee and Advisory Council have
retired or announced their intentions of retiring after their
present term, an "unprecedented" number according to a conference spokesman.

Whether the candidates were new aspirants moving in to fill
the vacuum or older hands sticking it out, by 1969 big-city elections throughout the country reflected the instability of the
times. Mayor Lindsay was reelected, but with only forty-two
percent of the vote. The same year two Democrats ran against
each other in Detroit. In Pittsburgh Peter F. Flaherty, an insurgent Democrat, won only to promptly repudiate the ward
chairman who turned out the vote for him; in Youngstown, a
solidly Democratic city, a Republican was elected; in Philadelphia, where registration is heavily Democratic, the Democratic party was unable to block a Republican sweep headed
by District Attorney Arlen Specter, putting him in line for a
try at the mayor's office. Of 156 Connecticut towns and cities
that held elections in 1969, forty-six municipalities switched
parties. And an assembly of eighty-five representatives of federal, state and local governments, labor and religious leaders,
editors and educators, meeting at Arden House in 1969, pronounced:

> America is in the midst of an urban crisis demonstrating an
> inadequacy and incompetency of basic policies, programs and
> institutions and presenting a crisis of confidence. These fail-
> ures affect every public service—education, housing, welfare,
> health, and hospitals, transportation, pollution control, the
> administration of criminal justice, and a host of others—
> producing daily deterioration in the quality of life. Although
> most visible in the large cities, that deterioration spreads to
> suburbia, exurbia, and beyond. Frustration rises as govern-
> ment fails to respond.[46]

This pronouncement came not from a radical caucus but from
a gathering of the most prestigious representatives of American
institutions.

Those who for the time survived the turmoil were even shriller in sounding the alarm. Mayor Joseph Alioto of San Francisco said simply: "The sky's falling in on the cities; it really is. We've had six cops killed in San Francisco since I took office. We need jobs and money for the poor and haven't money for either. . . . We can't go on like this. Even the capitalistic system's not going to survive the way we're going." Kenneth Gibson, the black mayor of Newark: "Wherever the cities are going, Newark's going to get there first. . . . If we had a bubonic plague in Newark everybody would try to help, but we really have a worse plague and nobody notices." Mayor Wesley Uhlman of Seattle said he was so busy putting out fires he had no time to think about anything else. Moon Candrieu, the mayor of New Orleans: "We've taxed everything that moves and everything that stands still, and if anything moves again, we tax that too. . . . The cities are going down the pipe and if we're going to save them we'd better do it now; three years from now will be too late." "Boston," said Mayor Kevin White, "is a tinderbox. . . . The fact is, it's an armed camp. One out of every five people in Boston is on welfare. Look, we raise 70 percent of our money with the property tax, but half our property is untaxable and 20 percent of our people are bankrupt. Could you run a business that way?" And Mayor Lindsay of New York proclaimed: "The cities of America are in a battle for survival. . . . Frankly, even with help in Washington, I'm not sure we can pull out of the urban crisis in time."[47] (Not long afterwards, Governor Rockefeller suggested that perhaps New York City's government, at least, ought not to survive, that it might be a good idea to abolish the present city structure and begin all over.)[48]

The mayors speak of the twin troubles of scarce revenues and racial confrontation. And it is no accident that the troubles occur together and are most severe in the biggest cities. It was the biggest cities that experienced the most serious disturbance of traditional political relations as a result of the influx of blacks and the outflux of many whites. In this context, demands by black newcomers triggered a rush of new demands by whites, especially the large and well-organized provider groups that flourished in the big cities. The weakened and vulnerable mayors responded; they gave more and more of the jobs, salaries, contracts and services that had always worked to win and hold the allegiance of diverse groups. The eventual inability of the cities to garner the vastly increased revenues needed to fuel this process helped bring the urban political process to a point of crisis. The fiscal crisis is indeed real—not because of mounting "needs" for services but because of mounting demands for the benefits associated with the municipal bureaucracies. To block the responses of the bureaucracies to these demands for lack of revenues is to block a process of political accommodation in the largest population centers of the nation. The defection of the mayors was another sign of how deep the disturbances were, not in health agencies or welfare agencies, but in the urban political structure.

## FEDERALISM AS A CONSTRAINING INFLUENCE

If mayors cannot resist the demands of contending groups in the cities, there are signs that the state and federal governments can, and will. The fiscal interrelations that undergird the federal system and leave the cities dependent on state and federal grants for an increasing portion of their funds are also a mechanism by which state and federal politics come to intervene in and control city politics. This is happening most clearly and directly through changes in state expenditures for the cities.

With their own taxing powers constricted from the outset, the mayors had little recourse but to turn to the states for enlarged grants-in-aid, trying to pass upward the political pressures they felt, usually summoning the press and the urban pressure groups for help. Since governors and legislators were not entirely immune to pressures from the city constituencies, the urban states increased their aid to the big cities.[49] Metropolises like New York City and Los Angeles now get roughly a quarter of their revenues from the state.

Accordingly, state budgets also escalated, and state taxes rose.[50] All in all, at least twenty-one states imposed new taxes or increased old taxes in 1968, and thirty-seven states in 1969, usually as a result of protracted struggle.[51] North Carolina enacted the largest program of new or increased taxes in its history; Illinois and Maine introduced an income tax, bringing to thirty-eight the number of states imposing some form of income tax; South Carolina passed its first major tax increase in a decade. Even Ohio moved to change its tradition of low-tax and low-service policies that had forced thirteen school districts in the state to close. Overall, state and local taxes rose from five percent of the Gross National Product in 1946 to more than eight percent of the GNP in 1969. Americans paid an average of $380 in state and local taxes in the fiscal year 1968, $42 more per person than the previous year, and more than double the fiscal year 1967. The rate tended to be highest in urban states: In New York the per-person tax burden was $576; in California, $540; in Massachusetts, $453. The low was in Arkansas, with a tax rate of $221.[52]

But raising taxes in Albany or Sacramento to pay for politics in New York City or Los Angeles is no simple matter, for the state capitals are not nearly as vulnerable as city halls to urban pressure groups, but are very vulnerable indeed to the suburbs and small towns that are antagonized by both higher taxes and city troubles. Besides, the mass of urban voters also resent taxes, especially when taxes are used to pay off the organized interests in the service systems, without yielding visibly better services.[53] Accordingly, even while taxes are raised, state grants to the cities are cut anyway. Thus, the New York State legislature reduced grant-in-aid formulas in welfare and medicaid (programs that go mainly to the central cities and mainly to blacks in those cities) in 1969[54] and again in 1971 (1970 was an election year and so the governor proposed increased aid to the cities without tax increases). Each time, the cuts were effected in all-night marathon sessions of the legislature, replete with dramatic denouncements by Democratic legislators from the cities and cries of betrayal from the mayors. Despite the cuts, anticipated state spending still rose by $878 million in 1969, the highest for any single year excepting the previous fiscal year in which the rise had been $890 million. By 1970, when the proposed budget had reached $8.45 billion, requiring $1.1 billion in new taxes, the outcry was so terrific that the governor reversed his proposals and led the legislature in a budget-slashing session, with welfare and medicaid programs the main targets.

When Governor Ronald Reagan, a self-proclaimed fiscal conservative, nevertheless submitted a record-breaking $6.37-billion budget for the 1969–1970 fiscal year, he met a storm of political protest that threatened a legislative impasse, leaving California without a budget. The next year Reagan proposed to solve the state's "fiscal crisis" by cutting welfare and medicaid expenditures by $800 million; even so, he submitted another record budget of $6.7 billion. When the long legislative battle that ensued was over, the governor signed an unbalanced budget of $7.3 billion, with substantial cuts in welfare and medicaid nevertheless.

Pennsylvania's former Republican Governor Raymond P. Shafer, in his short two years in office, managed to win the opposition of all but twenty-three percent of Pennsylvania voters as he and the legislature fought about how to raise $500 million in new revenues. At the beginning of his term in 1967 the governor was forced to raise state sales taxes to six percent, despite his campaign pledge of no new taxes, and early in 1969, with the budget $200 million short, he proposed that state's first income tax. When Shafer left office the income tax was enacted by his successor, Democratic Governor Milton Shapp, only to be voided by the Pennsylvania Supreme Court in 1971. A modified income-tax law was finally passed, but by that time the state legislature was also making spending reductions, including a fifty-percent cut in state education appropriations for ghetto districts.[55]

When Connecticut's 1969 biannual state budget proposal required a $700-million tax increase despite cuts in the welfare budget, the Democratic-controlled General Assembly rebelled, forcing a hectic special session of the state legislature to hammer out a new budget and tax program. In the tumultuous weeks that followed, a compromise package presumably agreed upon by the Democratic governor and the Democratic majority in both houses was repeatedly thrown into doubt. When the session was over, Connecticut had passed the largest tax program in its history, had borrowed $32.5 million, and Governor John N. Dempsey had announced he would not seek reelection.

Two years later Republican Governor Thomas J. Meskill engaged the legislature in battle again over another record budget that the governor proposed to pay for with a seven-percent sales tax—the highest in the country. Not only the legislature, but the insurance industries, the mayor of Hartford and 5000 marchers took part in the protest that ensued, leading to a compromise tax package that replaced the sales-tax increase with a new state income tax, together with more borrowing and new welfare cuts as well. A few short months later, after new public protests, the income tax was repealed, the sales-tax increase was restored, and more spending cuts were made, mainly in state grants to municipalities and in welfare appropriations.

The New Jersey legislature, at a special session called by Democratic Governor Richard Hughes in 1969 to plead for added revenues for urban areas, rejected a new tax on banks and lending institutions—this despite the urging of the governor, who called the cities of the state "sick" and its largest city, Newark, "sick unto death," and despite the clamor of New Jersey's mayors. The legislature eventually agreed to redirect some existing urban-aid funds to pay for increased police and fire salaries—a measure made particularly urgent after Newark's firemen went on strike, forcing the city to make emergency salary arrangements. When Republican Governor William T. Cahill took office later that year he signed a measure raising the New Jersey sales tax to five percent, claiming he faced a "major state fiscal crisis" of a $300-million deficit.

Other state governments are locked in similar fiscal and political battles. Michigan began the 1972 fiscal year without authorization to spend money after the legislature had been virtually paralyzed by a six-month struggle over the $2-billion budget, which the governor had proposed to finance with a thirty-eight percent increase in the state income tax. Wisconsin cut welfare and urban-aid expenditures over Governor Ody J. Fish's protest and, having enacted a new and broadened sales tax, precipitated a march on the capital by Milwaukee poor. Not long afterward, Governor Fish resigned, imperiling the Wisconsin Republican party. In Rhode Island, Democratic Governor Frank E. Licht promised no new taxes in his re-election campaign in 1970 and two months later recommended an income tax, amidst loud voter protest. When Texas, having passed the largest tax bill in its history in 1969, faced a deficit of $400 million in 1971, Governor Preston E. Smith vetoed the entire second year of a two-year budget, which totaled $7.1 billion.

In brief, pressures from the big cities were channeled upward to the state capitals, with some response. At least in the big urbanized states, governors and legislatures moved toward bailing out the cities, with the result that state expenditures and state taxes skyrocketed. But the reaction is setting in; the taxpayers' revolt is being felt in state legislatures across the country. And as raucous legislative battles continue, a trend is emerging: The states are turning out to be a restraining influence on city politics, and especially on ghetto politics.

While, in the main, grants-in-aid were not actually reduced, they were not increased enough to cover rising city costs either, and the toll is being taken. Some municipalities began to cut payroll and services. By 1971 vacancies were going unfilled in New York City, Baltimore, Denver and Kansas City. San Diego and Cleveland reduced rubbish collection; Dallas cut capital improvements; Kansas City let its elm trees die.[56] Detroit started closing park toilets. And some city employees were actually being dismissed in Los Angeles, Cleveland, Detroit, Kansas City, Cincinnati, Indianapolis, Pittsburgh and New York City. "This is the first time since the Depression that I have participated in this kind of cutback of education," said Cincinnati's superintendent of schools.[57] "You run as far as you can, but when you run out of gas you've got to stop," said Baltimore's Mayor Thomas J. D'Alesandro.

But the biggest cuts imposed by the states were in the programs from which blacks had gained the most as a result of their emergence as a force in the cities. Special state appropriations for health and education in ghetto districts were being cut; nine states cut back their medicaid programs;[58] and most important, at least nineteen states reduced welfare benefits by mid-1971, according to a *New York Times* survey. Moreover, new state measures to root out "welfare fraud," or to reinstitute residence restrictions, or to force recipients into work programs threatened far more drastic erosion of black gains in the near future.

There are signs that the federal government has also become a restraining influence on city politics. In the early 1960s the national Democratic administration had used its grants to the cities to intervene in city politics, encouraging ghetto groups to demand more from city halls and forcing recalcitrant mayors to be more responsive to the enlarging and volatile ghettos, whose allegiance had become critical to the national Democratic party. But a Republican administration was not nearly so oriented to the big cities, least of all to the ghettos of the big cities. Accordingly, the directions of the Great Society programs that the Nixon administration had inherited were shifted; bit by bit the new federal poverty agencies were scattered among the old-line federal bureaucracies, and the local agencies that had been set up in the ghettos were given to understand that confrontation tactics had to be halted. By now the Great Society looks much like traditional grant-in-aid programs; the federal fuel for ghetto agitation has been cut off. And new administration proposals for revenue sharing would give state and local governments firm control of the use of federal grants, unhampered by the "maximum feasible participation" provisions that helped to stir ghetto demands in the 1960s.

There are other signs as well. The wage freeze stopped, at least temporarily, the escalation of municipal salaries, and this despite the outcry of teachers across the country. Finally, and perhaps most portentous for blacks, the administration's proposal for "welfare reform" would give the federal government a much larger role in welfare policy, lifting the struggle for who gets what outside of the arena of city politics where blacks had developed some power and had gotten some welfare.

Nor is it likely, were the Democrats to regain the presidency and thus regain the initiative in federal legislation, that the pattern of federal restraint would be entirely reversed. The conditions that made the ghettos a political force for a brief space of time seem to have changed. For one thing, there is not much action, either in the streets or in the voting booths. The protests and marches and riots have subsided, at least partly because the most aggressive people in the black population were absorbed; it was they who got the jobs and honorary positions yielded to blacks during the turmoil. These concessions, together with the Great Society programs that helped produce them, seem to have done their work, not only in restoring a degree of order to the streets but in restoring ghetto voters to Democratic columns.

In any case, it was not ghetto insurgency of itself that gave blacks some political force in the 1960s. Rather it was that the insurgents were concentrated in the big cities, and the big cities played a very large role in Democratic politics. That also is changing; the cities are losing ground to the suburbs, even in Democratic calculations, and trouble in the cities is not likely to carry the same weight with Democratic presidents that it once did.

To be sure, a Democratic administration might be readier than a Republican one to refuel local services, to fund a grand new cornucopia of social programs. The pressures are mounting, and they come from several sources. One is the cities themselves, for to say that the cities are no longer as important as they once were is not to say Democratic leaders will want the cities to go under. Moreover, the inflated costs of the city are spreading to the suburbs and beyond, and these communities are also pressing for federal aid. Finally, there is the force of the organized producers themselves, who have become very significant indeed in national politics; the education lobby and the health lobby already wield substantial influence in Washington, and they are growing rapidly. But while these pressures suggest that new federal funds will be forthcoming, the rise of the suburbs and the parallel rise of the professional lobbies indicate that it is these groups who are likely to be the main beneficiaries.

The future expansion of the federal role in local services has another, perhaps more profound, significance. It means that the decline of the local political unit in the American political structure, already far advanced, will continue. No matter how much talk we may hear about a "new American revolution," through which the federal government will return revenues and power to the people, enlarged federal grants mean enlarged federal power, for grants are a means of influencing local political developments, not only by benefiting some groups and not others but through federally imposed conditions that come with the new moneys. These conditions, by curbing the discretion of local political leaders, also erode the power of local pressure groups. As localities lose their political autonomy, the forces that remain viable will be those capable of exerting national political influence. Some may view this change as an advance, for in the past local communities have been notoriously oligarchical. But for blacks it is not an advance; it is in the local politics of the big cities that they have gained what influence they have.

The general truths to be drawn from this tale of the cities seem clear enough and familiar enough, for what happened in the 1960s has happened before in history. The lower classes made the trouble, and other groups made the gains. In the United States in the 1960s, it was urban blacks who made the trouble, and it was the organized producer groups in the cities who made the largest gains. Those of the working and middle classes who were not among the organized producers got little enough themselves, and they were made to pay with their tax moneys for gains granted to others. Their resentments grew. Now, to appease them, the small gains that blacks did make in the course of the disturbances are being whittled away.

There is, I think, an even more important truth, though one perhaps not so quickly recognized. These were the events of a political struggle, of groups pitted against each other and against officialdom. But every stage of that struggle was shaped and limited by the structures in which these groups were enmeshed. A local service apparatus, which at the outset benefited some and not others, set the stage for group struggle. Service structures that offered only certain kinds of benefits determined the agenda of group struggle. And a fiscal structure that limited the contest mainly to benefits paid for by state and local taxes largely succeeded in keeping the struggle confined within the lower and middle strata of American society. Schoolteachers turned against the ghetto, taxpayers against both, but no one turned against the concentrations of individual and corporate wealth in America. Local government, in short, is important, less for the issues it decides than for the issues it keeps submerged. Of the issues submerged by the events of the urban crisis, not the least is the more equitable distribution of wealth in America.

## NOTES

[1] This view of the urban problem was given official status by the "Riot Commission." According to the commission:

[The] fourfold dilemma of the American city [is:] Fewer tax dollars come in, as large numbers of middle-income tax payers move out of central cities and property values and business decline; More tax dollars are required, to provide essential public services and facilities, and to meet the needs of expanding lower-income groups; Each tax dollar buys less, because of increasing costs. Citizen dissatisfaction with municipal services grows as needs, expectations and standards of living increase throughout the community [*Report of the National Advisory Commission on Civil Disorders* (New York: Bantam, 1968), p. 389].

Similarly, Alan K. Campbell and Donna E. Shalala write: "Most of the substantive problems flow, at least in part, from . . . the fact that the central cities have been left with segments of the population most in need of expensive services, and the redistribution of economic activities has reduced the relative ability of these areas to support such services" ["Problems Unsolved, Solutions Untried: The Urban Crisis," in *The States and the Urban Crisis* (Englewood Cliffs, N.J.: Prentice-Hall, 1970), p. 7]. The conventional wisdom is again echoed by the U.S. Advisory Commission on Intergovernmental Relations:

The large central cities are in the throes of a deepening fiscal crisis. On the one hand, they are confronted with the need to satisfy rapidly growing expenditure requirements triggered by the rising number of "high cost" citizens. On the other hand, their tax resources are growing at a decreasing rate (and in some cases actually declining), a reflection of the *exodus of middle and high income families and business firms from the central city to suburbia* [italics in original] [*Fiscal Balance in the American Federal System: Metropolitan Fiscal Disparities* (Washington, D.C.: Government Printing Office, 1967). Vol. *II*, p. 5].

Politicians share this view. "In the last 10 years, 200,000 middle-class whites have moved out of St. Louis," said Mayor A. J. Cervantes, "and 100,000 blacks, many of them poor, have moved in. It costs us *eight times as much* to provide city services to the poor as to the middle-class" [italics in original] [the *New York Times,* May 22, 1970].

[2] As a matter of fact, city revenues have not declined at all, but have risen astronomically, although not as astronomically as costs. Presumably, if the city had been able to hold or attract better-off residents and businesses, revenues would have risen even faster, and the fiscal aspect of the urban crisis would not have developed.

[3] It should be made clear at the outset that the costs of government generally rose steadily in the years after World War II. This is the subject of James O'Connor's analysis in "The Fiscal Crisis of the State," *Socialist Revolution.* 1, 1 (January/February 1970), 12–54; 1, 2 (March/April 1970), 34–94. But while all government budgets expanded, state and local costs rose much faster, and costs in the central cities rose the most rapidly of all, especially after 1965. Thus, according to the Citizens' Budget Commission, New York City's budget increased almost eight times as fast in the five fiscal years between 1964 and 1969 as during the postwar years 1949 to 1954. From an average annual increase of 5.5 percent in 1954, budget costs jumped to 9.1 percent in 1964 and to 14.2 percent in 1969 (the *New York Times,* January 11, 1960). It is with this exceptional rise that this article is concerned.

[4] For a discussion of the uses of welfare in resisting black migrants, see Frances Fox Piven and Richard A. Cloward, *Regulating the Poor: The Functions of Public Welfare* (New York: Pantheon, 1971), Chapters 7 and 8.

[5] At least some of the employees in all cities with more than 500,000 inhabitants are now under civil service; in about half of these cities, virtually all employees have such protections.

[6] See Piven and Cloward, *op. cit.,* Chapters 9 and 10, on the impact of the black migration on the Democratic administration of the 1960s.

[7] *Changing Patterns of Prices, Pay, Workers, and Work on the New York Scene,* U.S. Department of Labor, Bureau of Labor Statistics (New York: Middle Atlantic Regional Office, May 1971), Regional Reports No. 20, p. 36.

[8] The dole, needless to say, is a very different sort of concession from the higher salaries, pensions and on-the-job prerogatives won by other groups. For one thing, the dole means continued poverty and low status. For another, it is easier to take away, for recipients remain relatively weak and unorganized.

[9] That poor minorities made large gains through the welfare "crisis" and other groups did not is important to understanding the furious opposition that soaring welfare budgets arouse. Organized welfare-agency workers were competing for the welfare dollar, of course, but were not nearly so successful as the workers in other services, for they were not in a position to take much advantage of political turmoil. They were not nearly so numerous or well organized as teachers, policemen or firemen, and they could not use the threat of withholding services to exact concessions nearly so effectively. Unlike schoolteachers or garbage men, their services were of importance only to the very poor.

[10] See *State and Local Finances: Significant Features 1967–1970,*

U.S. Advisory Commission on Intergovernmental Relations (Washington, D.C.: Government Printing Office, 1969), Figure 6, p. 39.

11 Conflict and competition over the schools have been further heightened because the proportion of blacks in the schools has increased even more rapidly than the proportion of blacks in the population, owing to the youthfulness of blacks and the flight of whites to private schools. In Washington, blacks constituted fifty-four percent of the local population in 1965, but ninety percent of the school children; in St. Louis blacks were twenty-seven percent of the population, but sixty-three percent of the school population; in Chicago, they were twenty-three percent of the general population, but fifty-three percent of the school population; in New York City, where blacks and Puerto Ricans make up about twenty-seven percent of the population, fifty-two percent of the children in the schools were black or Puerto Rican. Of the twenty-eight target cities in the nation, seventeen had black majorities in the school system by 1965. See *Racial Isolation in the Public School,* U.S. Commission on Civil Rights (Washington, D.C.: Government Printing Office, February 20, 1967), Table II–2.

12 The federal government was also providing direct funds to improve the education of the "disadvantaged" under Title I of the Elementary and Secondary Education Act of 1965. However, although in four years following the passage of the act, $4.3 billion was appropriated for Title I, it was widely charged that these funds were misused and diverted from the poor by many local school boards.

13 A series of training guides to such efforts, prepared with federal funds by a local poverty program known as United Bronx Parents, included a kit on "How to Evaluate Your School" and a series of leaflets on such matters as "The Expense Budget—Where Does All the Money Go?" "The Construction Budget—When the Community Controls Construction We Will Have the Schools We Need," as well as an all-purpose handbook on parents' rights vis-à-vis the schools. Not surprisingly, Albert Shanker, president of the teachers union in New York City, charged there was "an organized effort to bring about rule in the schools by violence," involving the use of flying squads of disrupters who went from school to school and who, he said, had been trained with government (i.e., poverty program) funds (the *New York Times,* November 16, 1970, p. 2).

14 See Urban America, Inc., and the Urban Coalition, *One Year Later: An Assessment of the Nation's Response to the Crisis Described by the National Advisory Commission on Civil Disorders* (New York: Praeger, 1969), pp. 34–35. See also Naomi Levine with Richard Cohen, *Oceanhill-Brownsville: A Case History of Schools in Crisis* (New York: Popular Library, 1969), pp. 127–128.

15 This estimate was reported by Fred Hechinger, the *New York Times,* August 29, 1971.

16 Averaging $9200 in 1970–1971, according to the National Education Association.

17 State averages reflect the political troubles in big cities. Thus, in an urban state like New York, $1251 was spent per pupil in 1969–1970, and New Jersey, California, Connecticut and Massachusetts were not far behind. This represented an increase of about eighty percent in per-pupil expenditures since 1965–1966.

18 Educational costs have also risen sharply outside the central cities, particularly in the adjacent suburban school districts. These rises are a direct reverberation of troubles in the cities. Suburban school boards must remain competitive with the rising salary levels of educational personnel in the central cities, particularly considering the high priority placed on education by the middle-class suburbs. For example, between 1958 and 1959, enrollment in the Westchester, New York, schools increased by 1.5 percent, and the operating budget by 12 percent. In Fairfield, Connecticut, enrollment increased by 5.2 percent, the budget by 13.2 percent. In Suffolk County, New York, enrollment increased by 6.6 percent, the budget by 11.6 percent. In Monmouth, New Jersey, enrollment increased by 4.4 percent, the budget by 19 percent. Moreover, there are also increasing numbers of blacks in some of the older suburbs, with the result that these towns are experiencing political disturbances very similar to those of the big cities.

19 *State and Local Finances, op. cit.,* p. 39.

20 *Changing Patterns of Prices, Pay Workers, and Work, op. cit.,* pp. 7–8.

21 Some 25,000 of the new jobs were noncompetitive (the *New York Times,* May 28, 1971). Not surprisingly, the governor suggested that the mayor economize by cutting these, instead of always talking about cutting the number of policemen and firemen.

22 Welfare is the main example of an actual expansion of services, for the number of welfare employees increased largely as a reflection of increasing case loads. But so were new policemen hired to appease a broad constituency concerned about rising crime, sanitation men to answer demands for cleaner streets, and so forth.

23 *Changing Patterns of Prices, Pay, Workers, and Work, op. cit.,* p. 9. Moreover, big payrolls were a big city phenomenon. A study showed that, in three states studied in detail, the ratio of public employment per 100 population varied sharply by city size, more so in New Jersey and Ohio, less markedly in Texas. See *Urban and Rural America: Policies for Future Growth,* U.S. Advisory Commission on

Intergovernmental Relations (Washington, D.C.: Government Printing Office, April 1968), pp. 47–49.

24 According to Harold Rubin:

Time lost by state and local government employees due to work stoppages climbed from 7,510 man-days in 1958 to 2,535,000 mandays in 1968, according to the U.S. Bureau of Labor Statistics. Such strikes have not been limited to those performing "nonessential duties." For example, during the first half of 1970 there have been strikes by prison guards (New Jersey), sanitation men (Cincinnati, Ohio; Phoenix, Arizona; Atlanta, Georgia; Seattle, Washington; and Charlotte, North Carolina), teachers (Youngstown, Ohio; Minneapolis, Minnesota; Butte, Montana; Tulsa, Oklahoma; Boston, Massachusetts; Newark and Jersey City, New Jersey; and Los Angeles, California, to list only some of the larger school systems involved), bus drivers (Cleveland, Ohio; Tacoma, Washington; and San Diego, California), hospital employees (State of New Jersey; Detroit, Michigan), policemen (Newport, Kentucky; Livonia, Michigan; and Winthrop, Massachusetts), and firemen (Newark, Ohio, and Racine, Wisconsin) ["Labor Relations in State and Local Governments," in Robert A. Connery and William V. Farr (eds.), *Unionization of Municipal Employees* (New York: Columbia University, The Academy of Political Science, 1971), pp. 20–21.]

25 The *New York Times*, June 13, 1971.

26 The *New York Times*, January 31, 1970.

27 The *New York Times*, February 26, 1970.

28 The *New York Times*, March 17, 1970.

29 The *New York Times*, March 15, 1971. These estimates were given to the press by the city's budget director.

30 Rising wages and pension benefits among municipal employees are frequently attributed to unionization, which has indeed spread in the 1960s, rather than to changes in city politics. Membership in the American Federation of State, County, and Municipal employees increased from 180,000 to 425,000 in one decade; The American Federation of Teachers enlarged its ranks from 60,000 members in 1961 to 175,000 in 1969. But to point to unionization as a cause simply diverts the argument, since the spread and militancy of unionism among city employees in the 1960s must itself be explained. In any case, a Brookings Institution study of nineteen local governments showed no conclusive differences between unionized and nonunionized wages; both had risen substantially. See David Stanley, "The Effect of Unions on Local Governments," Connery and Farr (eds.), *op. cit.*, p. 47.

31 Norton Long and others have argued that the city's economic problems are largely the result of efforts by city employees to keep up

with pay scales in the private sector, despite the absence of productivity increases in public-service jobs comparable to those that justify wage increases in the private sector ("The City as Reservation," *The Public Interest*, No. 25 [Fall 1971]). This argument, however, presumes that city pay scales lag behind private scales and that city workers are merely straining to catch up. Quite the opposite has come to be true in some big cities. A 1970 study by the Middle Atlantic Bureau of Labor Statistics of pay rates in the New York metropolitan area found city pay rates to be much higher than private-industry rates. For example, carpenters, electricians and plumbers who worked for the city earned fully sixty percent more than those in private industry; painters and automobile mechanics earned thirty-six percent more; even messengers, typists, switchboard operators and janitors were substantially better off when they worked for the city. Moreover, *city workers also received far better holiday, vacation, health insurance and pension benefits.* It should also be noted that all but the last grouping were also much better paid in the city than in the suburbs. And so were patrolmen, firemen, sanitation man and social workers substantially better paid in the city than in the suburbs. A similar conclusion was reached by Bennett Harrison, who compared mean weekly earnings in the public and private sector of twelve metropolitan areas, using 1966 data. His calculations reveal a sharp disparity between public and private earnings in the central cities (although in 1966 some categories of suburban earnings were higher than the central city). See his *Public Employment and Urban Poverty* (Washington, D.C.: The Urban Institute, 1971), p. 30.

[32] Put another way the average annual increase in New York City's expense budget during the last five years was $582 million, or eight times as high as the $71-million annual average increase from fiscal 1949 to fiscal 1954.

[33] "Report on Financing Our Urban Needs," *Our Nation's Cities* (Washington, D.C.: Government Printing Office, March 1969), p. 21.

[34] According to *Fiscal Balance in the American Federal System:*

National aggregates for 1957 and 1962 and more restricted data for 1964–65 indicate that local government in the metropolitan areas spends more and taxes more per person than in the remainder of the country . . . there is a striking contrast in non-educational expenditures—which include all the public welfare, health, hospital, public safety and other public services essential to the well-being of citizens. These general government costs are two-thirds higher in the metropolitan areas than they are in the rest of the country [*op. cit.,* Vol. II, p. 59].

Specifically, per-capita expenditures during 1964–1965 averaged $301.20 in the thirty-seven largest metropolitan areas, compared to $218.31 in small or nonmetropolitan areas (*ibid.*, Table 16, p. 60). As for the central cities themselves, "central cities contained 18.6 percent of the population (in 1964–65), but accounted for almost 25 percent of all local expenditure." In per-capita terms, local government expenditure in the large central cities "was 21 percent higher than in their outside regions, and almost two-thirds above that for the rest of the nation" (*ibid.*, p. 62). Moreover, when educational costs are omitted (suburban communities spend a great deal on education), the thirty-seven largest central cities "had an outlay of $232 per capita in 1965—$100 greater than their suburban counterparts" (*ibid.*, p. 6). By 1966–1967, the disparity had become more dramatic in many cities. Per-capita general expenditures, *including* education costs, was $475 in Washington, D.C., compared to $224 in the Washington suburban ring; $324 in Baltimore, compared to $210 in the suburban ring; $441 in Newark, compared to $271 in the suburban ring; $335 in Boston, compared to $224 in the suburban ring; $267 in St. Louis, and $187 in the suburbs (*State and Local Finances, op. cit.*, p. 70). Similarly, a study of fifty-five local governments in the San Francisco–Oakland metropolitan area showed that both the property-tax rate and the level of per-capita expenditures were higher in the central city. In dormitory suburbs, per-capita expenditures were only fifty-eight percent of those in the central city. See Julius Margolis, "Municipal Fiscal Structure in a Metropolitan Region," *Journal of Political Economy*, 65 (June 1957), p. 232.

[35] The New York State Constitution, for example, specifies that:

It shall be the duty of the Legislature, subject to the provisions of this Constitution, to restrict the power of taxation, assessment, borrowing money, contracting indebtedness, and loaning the credit of countries, cities, towns and villages, so as to prevent abuses in taxation and assessments and in contracting of indebtedness by them. Nothing in this article shall be construed to prevent the Legislature from further restricting the powers herein specified (Article VIII, Section 12).

Traditionally the states have granted powers of taxation to the localities only very reluctantly.

[36] Not only do states limit the taxing powers of localities, but they have the authority to mandate local expenditures (e.g., salary increases for police and firemen) with or without adjusting local taxing powers to pay for them. They also have the authority to vote tax exemptions at local expense for favored groups. State legislatures are given to doing exactly that, exacerbating the financial plight of local governments.

[37] This was $27 billion out of $40 billion that localities raised in revenues from their own sources in 1967–1968 (*State and Local Finances, op. cit.*, Table 8, p. 31). It should be noted that property taxes are

declining relative to other sources of local revenue. At the turn of the
century about eighty percent of state and local budgets were financed
by the property tax. Today the states hardly rely on it at all. Nevertheless, local governments still finance about half their budgets with
property taxes.

[38] The first city income tax was levied in Philadelphia, in 1939,
when the city was on the verge of bankruptcy. The use of the income
tax by big cities spread in the 1960s, with Akron and Detroit adopting
it in 1962, Kansas City in 1964, Baltimore and New York City in 1966
and Cleveland in 1967. See *City Income Taxes* (New York: Tax Foundation, Inc., 1967), Research Publication No. 12, pp. 7–9. City income
taxes must, of course, also be approved by the state, an approval that
is not always forthcoming.

[39] By 1964–1965, per-capita local taxes in the central cities of the
thirty-seven largest metropolitan areas had risen to $200 per capita. In
Washington, D.C., taxes were $291 per capita; in New York City $279;
and in Newark $273. Overall, central-city residents were paying seven
percent of their income in local taxes and in the biggest cities ten
percent (*Fiscal Balance in the American Federal System, op. cit.*, Vol.
II, pp. 75–79).

[40] By 1968 official statistics for the nation as a whole showed local
property taxes totaling $27.8 billion. The annual rise since then is
estimated at between $1 and $3 billion.

[41] *Our Nation's Cities, op. cit.*, p. 24.

[42] *Our Nation's Cities, op. cit.*, pp. 36–37. To understand the full
impact of property taxes, one must remember that these are taxes on
capital value, and not on income yielded. Thus, a three percent-of-
true-value tax on improvements can easily tax away seventy-five percent of the net income that a new building would otherwise earn—a
loss, economists generally agree, that tends to be passed on to consumers. See, for example, Dick Netzer, *Economics of the Property Tax*
(Washington, D.C.: The Brookings Institute, 1966), pp. 40–62.

[43] Local tax collections increased by 500 percent between World
War II and 1967, but costs have risen ten percent faster, and the bigger
the city, the tighter the squeeze. If the process were to continue, and
today's growth rate of city spending vs. city revenues to continue, a
recent study commissioned by the National League of Cities estimates
a gap of $262 billion by 1980 (*Our Nation's Cities, op. cit.*, p. 22).
Measured another way, state and local indebtedness combined rose by
400 percent since 1948, while the federal debt rose by only twenty-six
percent (*U.S. Fiscal Balance in the American Federal System, op. cit.*,
Vol. I, p. 55). In the thirty-six large central cities alone, the cumulative tax gap could reach $25 to $30 billion by 1975 (*ibid.*, Vol. II, p.

91). A special Commission on the Cities in the Seventies, established by the National Urban Coalition, concluded that by 1980 most cities will be "totally bankrupt" (the *New York Times,* September 24, 1971).

[44] The statement went on to say "that which is good enough for white cops and firemen is good enough for black and Puerto Rican employees of New York City" (the *New York Times,* June 8, 1971). According to city officials, the annual cost of pension benefits, which had been $215 million in 1960, was projected to reach $1.3 billion in the next ten years (the *New York Times,* June 9, 1971).

[45] The *Christian Science Monitor,* September 4, 1969.

[46] The *States and the Urban Crisis,* Report of the Thirty-Sixth American Assembly (Harriman, N.Y.: Arden House, October 30– November 2, 1969). The Report went on, not surprisingly, to recommend increased state and federal aid for the cities.

[47] James Reston, "The President and the Mayors," the *New York Times,* March 24, 1971. In another column on April 21, 1971, Reston summarized the reports of the big-city mayors as: "First, they felt the crisis of the cities was the major threat to the security of the nation— more serious than Vietnam or anything else. Second, they felt that the bankruptcy and anarchy were underestimated. . . . They sound like communiques from a battlefield. . . . They have got beyond all the questions of race or party and are looking for power and leadership to deal with the urban problem."

[48] The governor said he had in mind a new structure like the London County Council. City political leaders, for their part, had been proposing to abolish city-state relations by declaring New York City a separate state.

[49] By 1966–1967, per-capita intergovernmental aid was substantially higher for the central cities than suburban localities (contrary to popular impression). Per-capita aid to Washington, D.C., was $181, compared to $81 in the outlying suburbs; $174 to Baltimore, and $101 to the suburbs; $179 to Boston, and $74 to the suburbs; $220 to New York City, and $163 to the suburbs; $144 to Newark, and $53 to the suburbs; $70 to Philadelphia, and $61 to the suburbs; $88 to Chicago, and $55 to the suburbs; $126 to Detroit, and $115 to the suburbs (*State and Local Finances, op. cit.,* Table 29, p. 69).

[50] Arthur Levitt, controller of the state of New York, recently released figures showing that state spending had increased from $1.3 billion in 1956 to $3.9 billion in 1964, to approximately $8 billion in 1968. In the four years ending in 1968, state spending rose by an annual average of $875 million, or 18.7 percent. In 1968 the spending increase was $1.4 billion, or 22.1 percent over the previous year (the *New York Times,* April 2, 1969–July 7, 1969). During this same five-year period,

state revenues from taxes and federal aid increased from $3.7 billion
to $7.2 billion. In other words, spending exceeded revenues, and by
greater margins in each of the successive years. The total deficit for
the five-year period amounted to $2.5 billion, which, of course, had to
be borrowed. A large part of this rise in New York State's budget reflects
aid to localities, which increased from $622 million in fiscal 1955 to
$1.04 billion in fiscal 1960, to $1.67 billion in 1965, and $3.23 billion
in fiscal year 1969. State spending for aid to education has doubled in
the last six years, and the state share of welfare and medicaid costs
doubled in only four years.

[51] By 1971 the estimated difference between revenues and outlays
were in excess of $500 million in New York, California and Texas.
Florida was short $120 million; New Jersey $100 million; Connecticut
$200 million (the *New York Times,* January 3, 1971). A handful of
rural states, however, were considering tax cuts.

[52] Data provided by the Commerce Clearing House, as reported
in the *New York Times,* September 27, 1970.

[53] A Gallup poll in 1969 showed that forty-nine percent would not
vote for more money to pay for schools if additional taxes were sought,
against forty-five percent who would (the *New York Times,* August 17,
1969). Another key fact in understanding the populist character of the
tax revolt is that state and local taxes consist mainly in sales and
property taxes and various user charges, all of which tend to be relatively regressive. Even the state income tax, when it is used, is usually
imposed as a fixed percentage of income (unlike the graduated federal
income tax, which takes more from those who have more, at least in
principle). In any case, fully two-thirds of state revenues were raised
from sales and gross receipt taxes. [*State and Government Finances in
1967,* U.S. Bureau of the Census (Washington, D.C.: Government Printing Office, 1968), Table I, p. 7]. Consequently, the new taxes have had
a severe impact on the working and middle classes, who are paying a
larger and larger percentage of personal income to state and local
government. In New York, state and local taxes now absorb over thirteen percent of personal income; in California, over twelve percent; in
Illinois and Ohio over eight percent. As a result of rising state and
local taxes (and price inflation), per-capita disposable personal income
fell considerably between 1965 and 1969. See Paul M. Schwab, "Two
Measures of Purchasing Power Contrasted," *Monthly Labor Review*
(April 1971). By contrast, federal taxes declined as a percent of Gross
National Product between 1948–1968, during which period state and
local taxes rose from about five percent to eight percent of GNP
(*State and Local Finances, op. cit.,* Figure 5, p. 29). The "tax revolt" in
the states should be no surprise.

[54] Most of the 1969 welfare cuts were restored within a short time, but the 1971 cuts were not.

[55] The *New York Times*, February 16, 1971; June 9, 17, 19, 25, 1971; and July 2, 1971.

[56] The *New York Times*, August 30, 1970; November 27, 1970; and May 25, 1971.

[57] Nationally, the annual rise in teacher salaries slumped to only 5.5 percent, after rising by about 8 percent each year for several years.

[58] Usually by limiting eligibility, or limiting the types of services covered, or requiring co-payments by patients. See *Health Law Newsletter* (Los Angeles: National Legal Program on Health Problems of the Poor, June 1971), p. 2.

RICHARD A. CLOWARD is a sociologist and social worker on the faculty of Columbia University.

FRANCES FOX PIVEN is a political scientist and urban planner at Boston University, and is currently on a Guggenheim Fellowship. Together they have written extensively on urban politics and social movements. Their articles in *The Nation* are widely credited with stimulating the formation of the National Welfare Rights Organization (NWRO), a grass-roots protest movement of welfare recipients. They are now completing another book in which they analyze the role played by activists in recent movements of the poor, tentatively entitled *Poor People's Movements and Why They Failed.*

Their book on the welfare system, *Regulating the Poor*, also available in Vintage Books won the C. Wright Mills Award of the Society for Study of Social Problems in 1971. Professor Cloward's book, written with Lloyd E. Owen, on the origins of gang delinquency won the Dennis Carroll Award of the International Society of Criminology in 1965.